HEALTH AND POPULATION

Volume 6

The Therapeutic Nightmare
The battle over the world's most controversial sleeping pill

Full list of titles in the set
HEALTH AND POPULATION

The Therapeutic Nightmare
The battle over the world's most controversial sleeping pill

John Abraham and Julie Shepherd

earthscan
from Routledge

First published in 1999

This edition first published in 2009 by Earthscan

Earthscan

2 Park Square, Milton Park, Abingdon, Oxon OX14 4RN

711 Third Avenue, New York, NY 10017

Earthscan is an imprint of the Taylor & Francis Group, an informa business

Simultaneously published in the USA and Canada by Earthscan

ISBN 978-1-85383-650-3 (Volume 6)
ISBN 978-1-84971-030-5 (Health and Population set)
ISBN 978-1-84407-930-8 (Earthscan Library Collection)

For a full list of publications please contact:

A catalogue record for this book is available from the British Library

Library of Congress Cataloging-in-Publication Data has been applied for

Publisher's note
The publisher has made every effort to ensure the quality of this reprint, but points out that some imperfections in the original copies may be apparent.

The
Therapeutic
Nightmare

HEALTH AND THE ENVIRONMENT SERIES
Edited by Erik Millstone

The
Therapeutic
Nightmare

The battle over the world's most controversial sleeping pill

JOHN ABRAHAM & JULIE SHEPPARD

EARTHSCAN
Earthscan Publications Ltd, London

First published in the UK in 1999 by
Earthscan Publications Ltd

Copyright © John Abraham and Julie Sheppard, 1999

A catalogue record for this book is available from the British Library

ISBN: 1 85383 650 8 paperback
       1 85383 552 8 hardback

Typesetting by PCS Mapping & DTP, Newcastle upon Tyne

Cover design by Declan Buckley

For a full list of publications please contact:
Earthscan Publications Ltd
120 Pentonville Road
London, N1 9JN, UK
Tel: +44 (0)171 278 0433
Fax: +44 (0)171 278 1142
Email: earthinfo@earthscan.co.uk
http://www.earthscan.co.uk

Earthscan is an editorially independent subsidiary of Kogan Page Ltd and publishes in association with WWF-UK and the International Institute for Environment and Development

This book is printed on elemental chlorine free paper

Contents

Acronyms and Abbreviations

ABPI	Association of the British Pharmaceutical Industry
ADR	adverse drug reaction
AMA	American Medical Association
APA	American Psychiatric Association
BBC	British Broadcasting Corporation (UK)
BGA	Bundesgesundheitsamt (German drug regulatory agency)
BMA	British Medical Association
CDER	Centre for Drug Evaluation and Research (FDA)
CNS	central nervous system
CPMP	Committee for Proprietary Medicinal Products (EEC/EU)
CRF	case report form (for individual patients/subjects)
CRM	Committee on the Review of Medicines (UK)
CSD	Committee on the Safety of Drugs (UK)
CSM	Committee on Safety of Medicines (UK)
CTC	clinical trial certificate
DES	Division of Epidemiology and Surveillance (FDA)
DMOH	Dutch Ministry of Health
DoH	Department of Health (UK)
DPDP	Division of Psychopharmacological Drug Products (FDA)
ECJ	European Court of Justice
EEC	European Economic Community
EMIC	Evaluation of Medications for Insomnia in Canada
ESRC	British Economic and Social Research Council
EU	European Union
FDA	Food and Drug Administration (US)
FoIA	Freedom of Information Act (US)
FR	*Federal Register* (US)
GAO	General Accounting Office (US)
HRG	Health Research Group (PC)
IND	Investigational New Drug
INDA	Investigational New Drug Application
IoM	Institute of Medicine (US NAS)
JCP	Joint Committee on Prescribing (UK)
MCA	Medicines Control Agency (UK)
mg	milligramme
NAS	National Academy of Sciences (US)
NDA	New Drug Application

NDTI	National Disease and Therapeutic Index
NHS	National Health Service (UK)
NIH	National Institutes of Health (US)
NIMH	National Institutes of Mental Health (US)
ODE	Office of Drug Evaluation (FDA)
OES	Office of Epidemiology and Statistics (FDA)
P321	Protocol 321
PC	Public Citizen (US)
PCHRG	Public Citizen's Health Research Group (US)
PDAC	Psychopharmacological Drugs Advisory Committee (US)
PL	product licence (UK)
PMS	post-marketing surveillance
R&D	research and development
SBA	summary basis of approval (US FDA)
SEAR	Subcommittee on Efficacy and Adverse Reactions (CSM)
SRS	spontaneous reporting system (FDA)
UK	United Kingdom
US	United States of America
WHO	World Health Organization

List of Tables

WARNING

Psychotropic drugs, including prescription tranquillizers and sleeping pills can produce withdrawal symptoms, which are emotionally and physically distressing, sometimes life-threatening. Use of these drugs should be discontinued only with professional guidance. This book is no substitute for individualized medical or psychological care.

Introduction

This book is about one of the most controversial drugs ever marketed. Banned in the UK, the sleeping pill, Halcion, remains available on prescription in North America, most of Europe and many other countries. It was manufactured in the 1970s and marketed from the late 1970s to the 1990s by the pharmaceutical company Upjohn which entered into a US$7 billion merger with Pharmacia in 1995.[1]

Halcion has been taken by millions of patients around the world and has been of enormous commercial value. Yet according to the safety standards of the British regulatory agency, the Medicines Control Agency (MCA), those patients have been exposed to an unsafe medication. While Upjohn and others claim the drug is safe and effective, the Public Citizen Health Research Group, an American consumer interest organization, is campaigning for its withdrawal from the US market because of unacceptable risks.

Over the years, Halcion has been associated with amnesia, hallucinations, aggression and even homicide in some patients. The drug has not only caused trouble for patients. Upjohn scientists have been dragged through the courts and embarrassed on television over Halcion. Senior members of the medical profession have 'rubbished' each others work in battling over the safety and effectiveness of the drug. The British Broadcasting Corporation (BBC) found themselves defending a libel charge by Upjohn about a Panorama programme. The BBC's nightmare was that they lost the libel case, costing them around £1.5 million – one of the largest libel costs in the BBC's history. Some government officials, who are supposed to regulate drug safety, have also referred to Halcion as 'a bit of a nightmare'.[2] One of our sources told us that the US drug regulatory authority, the Food and Drug Administration (FDA), has been 'torn apart' over the Halcion controversy.

In this book we penetrate deeply into the science and politics of the dispute over Halcion's safety and effectiveness, especially in the UK and the US. Are unacceptable risks being taken with patients' lives? Why was this drug marketed initially at four to eight times the dose that was recognized as safe in the UK? Why is it now banned as unsafe in the UK, but still on the market in the US? By getting at the truth about these and other questions pertinent to the Halcion controversy, we reveal flaws in drug testing and raise serious questions about the adequacy of the current systems for drug development and control. We believe that there are important lessons to be learned from it for consumers, the medical profession, regulators and industry alike, not to mention policy analysts and social scientists.

In Chapter 1 we explain the therapeutic and commercial background of tranquillizers and sleeping pills, including what is known about the risks and benefits they pose for consumers. Chapter 2 describes the political context in which efforts to control the safety and effectiveness of medicines have developed. This is essential to an understanding of how regulators behaved towards Halcion. Chapters 3–6 then tell the disturbing story of how patients have been exposed to unnecessary risks from Halcion because of inadequacies in the systems of drug testing and control. In Chapter 7 we make concrete proposals for reforming the system in the interests of public health.

This book is written to be accessible to a general audience. In particular, we wish to impress upon readers that there are choices to be made about how medicines ought to be controlled. In part, the quality of medicines' control will depend upon the extent to which the public participates in making those choices. Hence, specialist 'jargon' and inaccessible technicalities are kept to a minimum. Nevertheless, our research for this book is a social scientific investigation and readers interested in the details of our methodological framework can find them in an appendix at the end of the book.

Acknowledgements

Our research for this book began in 1993. We are very grateful to the British Economic and Social Research Council (ESRC) for funding our research from 1994 to 1996. Thanks are also due to all those who agreed to be interviewed and/or gave us their time to provide valuable documents and references. We are particularly grateful to Tim Reed, Michael Mosher, Erik Millstone, Mike Lewis, Frances MacDermott and staff at the Food and Drug Administration, the Medicines Control Agency and Public Citizen Health Research Group for their assistance and cooperation.

1

The Nature of Tranquillizing Drugs

Introduction

Drugs that have effects on mental function are known as psychotropic. There are many types of psychotropic drugs including antidepressants, antipsychotics ('major' tranquillizers) used in the management of psychosis, and 'minor' tranquillizers intended primarily for use in managing anxiety and insomnia. Tranquillizers have a long history dating back to the medicinal use of opium by Hippocrates in Ancient Greece. In the 19th century, opium and alcohol were used separately and in combination to treat 'nervous restlessness' and 'sleeplessness'. A more refined and more potent form of opium, called morphine after the Greek god of sleep, Morpheus, was isolated in 1805 and by the middle of the 19th century was used by doctors in place of opium. Other tranquillizers with a significant impact in that century – and which came to replace opium – are the bromides which were used as sedatives, and chloral hydrate which was used as a hypnotic (ie to treat insomnia) and as an anaesthetic.[1]

The early 20th century saw the development of a much more technically sophisticated pharmaceutical industry. This was reflected in the development of tranquillizers. In 1903 the first barbiturate, known as Veronal (barbitone), was manufactured. By mid century about 2500 kinds of barbiturates had been synthesized, of which about 50 were marketed for clinical use as sedatives or to induce sleep. During the 1930s the barbiturates came to replace the bromides and chloral hydrate because doctors believed that they were safer.[2] By the 1960s the modern minor tranquillizers, known as benzodiazepines, were being introduced. It is the benzodiazepine family of tranquillizers, of which Halcion (triazolam) is a member, that we are mostly concerned with in this book. Other well-known benzodiazepines are Valium (diazepam), Librium (chlordiazepoxide), Mogadon (nitrazepam), Ativan (lorazepam), Dalmane (flurazepam), Xanax (alprazolam) and Restoril (temazepam).

The benzodiazepines are central nervous system depressants. In this sense their clinical effects are similar to alcohol or barbiturates. Medically, the benzodiazepines are often defined as 'sedative-hypnotics' because they produce relaxation (sedation) at lower doses and sleep (hypnosis) at higher doses. At even higher doses, benzodiazepines can induce unconsciousness, which can make them useful as anaesthetics.[3] Some benzodiazepines, such as Halcion, Dalmane, Mogadon and Restoril, which have been developed to treat insomnia, are known as hypnotics (ie sleeping pills). Others, such as Ativan and Valium, are called anxiolytics because they are used primarily to reduce anxiety. It is believed that drugs such as the benzodiazepines affect the body by acting on 'receptors' in the nerve endings which are sensitive to (or 'receive') the chemical compounds (or 'signals') called neurotransmitters which facilitate communication between the nerves of the body and the brain. Because of its resemblance to a neurotransmitter, a drug may interact with (or 'bind' to) the receptors and cause the nerves to respond as though they were being activated by the 'sending' nerves and their neurotransmitters. The benzodiazepines bind to particular receptors, and it is believed that the more effective a benzodiazepine is in relieving anxiety or inducing sleep, the more strongly it binds to those particular receptors. However, it is important to appreciate that the relationship between human behaviour and the biochemical processes in the brain – the so-called 'mind-brain problem' – remains highly controversial and we make no attempt to solve it in this book.

The demand for a quiet life

Modern societies have made great strides in raising the health of their populations. In particular, public health measures, antibiotics and vaccines have all made a contribution to reducing the prevalence of infectious diseases. On the other hand, the increasing complexities and fragmentation of modernity, combined with our growing expectations about quality of life, have made us vulnerable to psychic distress and disorders. Some people are more vulnerable than others; but, as Professor George Brown and his colleague Tirril Harris have shown, this is by no means limited to the biological make up of the brain. They found that women in Britain were much more vulnerable to depression if they lacked a close relationship/lover, had lost their mother in early childhood, had more than two children living at home and/or were unemployed.[4] Moreover, research on healthy, young and educated British civil servants in 1983 found that about one third reported impaired concentration, fatigue and anxiety.[5]

It is difficult to know how many people are suffering mental distress in our communities because of the imprecise nature of diagnosis. In 1979 Morton Kramer showed that a patient admitted to mental hospital in Britain with a particular set of symptoms would be ten times more likely to be diagnosed as a manic depressive than someone with identical symptoms in the US.[6] Another good example of this is the treatment of depression with tranquillizers. It might be expected that depression would be treated with antidepressants rather than tranquillizers, which are themselves depressants of the central nervous system. However, there is evidence of widespread use of tranquillizers for the treatment of depression. In a series of studies of hundreds of depressed women in the UK in the late 1970s and early 1980s, it was found that they were more likely to be prescribed a minor tranquillizer than an antidepressant when they sought medical help.[7]

While the American Psychiatric Association (APA) and the World Health Organization (WHO) have done much to improve diagnostics in this field since the late 1970s, it remains an inexact science.[8] In 1993, a Dutch survey of general practice found that doctors were much more likely to prescribe tranquillizers for women than for men, even when neither their symptoms nor the diagnosis warranted such drug treatment. Doctors frequently diagnosed women with symptoms such as headache and general fatigue as suffering from anxiety, stress or insomnia, and thus as candidates for benzodiazepines.[9]

According to Inglis, it was estimated that in 1981, in the Western industrialized countries, about a third of all patients in hospitals had been admitted for psychiatric treatment, although currently in the US the figure is closer to 6 per cent.[10] Moreover, a large number of non-hospitalized patients are treated by general practitioners for milder psychotic, neurotic or stress-related symptoms such as anxiety, depression, irritability, sleep disturbance, impaired concentration and fatigue. According to Professor Anthony Clare, in one year, 'an average British general practitioner will deal with around 200 minor emotional illnesses, at least 12 patients will present with severe depression, and approximately 55 of his/her patients will be suffering from chronic mental illness and will be living in the community'.[11] In 1990 in the US, the National Institute of Mental Health declared that anxiety afflicted 8 per cent of the population, including three million people suffering from panic disorders or recurrent attacks of anxiety and 11 million suffering from phobias, obsessions, compulsions and/or chronic levels of apprehension.[12] It was estimated in 1997 that there was a 10 per cent prevalence of chronic insomnia in the American adult population, with an associated annual cost of US\$90–107 billion.[13]

Apart from patients' demands for tranquillizers, it has been cynically suggested that these drugs had a greater effect on the psychiatrists and psychiatric nurses working in hospitals than on the patients because, at last, these health professionals could relax and treat their inmates as patients rather than as prisoners.[14] Others have commented that outside the hospital context, doctors are 'hooked on medicalizing' social and psychological problems and diagnosing them as if they can be treated with drugs. These commentators tend to reject entirely the treatment of anxiety and sleep disturbance with tranquillizers.[15]

Yet some patients certainly benefitted from more community-based mental health care, which was made possible partly by the use of psychotropic drugs. Moreover, long-term users of psychotropic drugs have found them useful for travelling, shopping, mixing with people, running the home, work, family problems, marriage, financial matters and housing problems.[16] Here again research has revealed the significance of social differences in the vulnerability to long-term desire for medication in our communities. Long-term users of tranquillizers are more likely to be divorced and not to have children living at home; they are more likely to be women; and if they are living with partners or children, they are more likely to find those relationships unsupportive.[17]

For a few profits more

On the whole, the pharmaceutical industry may be said to be research-based and highly profitable. It is the large research-based companies which dominate the market. For example, in terms of sales, the top 25 companies out of about 10,000 in the world are all research-based. This relatively small number of huge companies accounts for about 45 per cent of the market. With the growing tendency towards mergers between large companies, this concentration of market influence is on the increase. Moreover, average pre-tax profits in the industry are about 17 per cent, though profits on sales can be as high as 29 per cent in the most commercially successful companies.[18]

Dominance by large companies is partly due to the extensive costs, equipment, materials and organization required in new drug research and development (R&D). These, too, have been increasing steadily over the years. In the UK in 1963, a typical new drug would take three years and cost UK£3 million to develop and bring to the market; by the late 1980s it took seven to ten years and cost UK£50 million. Similar trends can be found in the US and other Western countries. Globally, it is estimated that the pharmaceutical industry spends about US$15 billion on R&D.[19] For example, in 1994, GlaxoWellcome spent UK£1197 million on R&D, more than any other company – with Roche a close third spending UK£1160.[20]

Yet the huge number of barbiturates that saturated the market in the 1950s illustrates the mismatch between the modern pharmaceutical industry's research activities and therapeutic need. Many of the barbiturates were 'me-too' drugs, which were very similar to existing compounds and offered little or no therapeutic advantage over what was already on the market. Such drugs are sufficiently inventive to obtain patents even though they may be superfluous to medical need because patents are awarded on the basis of chemical uniqueness. A patent protects a new chemical entity's use by competitors for many years, providing its manufacturer with an exclusive market whether or not it turns out to be an especially safe or effective medicine. Bearing this in mind, it is not so surprising to find estimates that one fifth of the barbiturates marketed would have been sufficient to meet therapeutic needs.[21]

More generally, numerous studies in the 1980s have found that the number of therapeutically significant new drug products in Western industrialized countries is only about 4 to 10 per cent of the drugs introduced within those markets.[22] While therapeutic breakthroughs for common illnesses or diseases are bound to be profitable, they are also rare and usually require very considerable time and expenditure on R&D. Thus, the industry's motivation for the development of me-too drugs is that they are relatively safe financial ventures involving a modest amount of time and research, and that they enable the industry to maintain high levels of profits while engaging in the high-risk activity of searching for genuinely innovative medicines. As a former medical director of Squibb pharmaceutical company put it:

> The incidence of disease cannot be manipulated and so increased sales volumes must depend at least in part on the use of drugs unrelated to their real utility or need.[23]

Research-based as the industry certainly is, it is also important to appreciate that its expenditure on R&D is only about 10 per cent of sales and 60 per cent of net profits. This compares with an expenditure on product promotion and other marketing techniques of between 15 and 20 per cent of sales.[24] In other words, on average, the industry spends twice as much on promotion and marketing as it does on R&D. Thus, there is certainly scope for more R&D into genuine therapeutic advances and for less promotion of me-toos.

The highly competitive nature of the pharmaceutical sector fuels aggressive marketing. Two important structural aspects of the industry explain why companies place such importance on promotional activities. Firstly, while most Western countries grant patents for 15 to 20 years, it may take eight to 12 years to get a drug marketed, especially in the US. Once the patent expires, competing companies can begin marketing that drug without having invested in its R&D. Consequently, manufacturers run a race against time in order to recover their R&D costs before the patent expires. One way to achieve this is to reach the largest market possible as rapidly as possible, which means extensive promotion. And secondly, because there are so many me-too products, various new drugs will not find their place on the doctor's prescription pad purely on the basis of their exceptional safety or effectiveness. Vigorous promotion, which emphasizes any conceivable, and sometimes inconceivable, advantages of such products is needed to make up the therapeutic shortfall, and to gain a market advantage over competitors.

The manufacturers of tranquillizers have not been shy about promoting their products to doctors for a wide and loosely defined range of psychic distress. In 1969 McNeil advertised the barbiturate Butisol (sodium butabarbital) as a 'daytime sedative for everyday situational stress' in the *Journal of the American Medical Association* and Roche ran an advertisement in the *British Medical Journal* which read:

> WHATEVER THE DIAGNOSIS in the face of ill-health there is anxiety and where there is anxiety either as a complicating factor or as a cause of illness itself there is a place for LIBRIUM.[25]

Such promotion encouraged doctors to prescribe tranquillizers extensively and patients to demand them from doctors, thus creating markets. An obvious medical danger is that doctors may 'overprescribe' and 'overdiagnose' – that is, they may prescribe tranquillizers for patients who do not need them and/or prescribe too many too often for patients who may sometimes be in need of them. As Professor Malcolm Lader, a psychopharmacologist at the Institute of Psychiatry in London, commented:

> ... the indications for these drugs are being insidiously widened and the boundary between normality and illness increasingly blurred.[26]

In Britain by the mid 1970s, only one tranquillizer prescription in eight was for a recognized psychiatric disorder.[27] Research in France, Spain and the UK indicates that doctors have continued to overprescribe tranquillizers into the

1990s. For example, in a three month period in 1991, over two-thirds of general practitioners and hospital consultants in one UK health authority prescribed psychotropic drugs to children of 17 years or younger.[28] Research also implies that both new and long-term tranquillizer use can frequently occur in response to physical rather than psychological disorder.[29]

According to patients themselves, they have been prescribed tranquillizers for problems as diverse as bereavement, nursing a sick relative, socialising, lack of confidence, business problems, jury service, violent husbands, divorce, menopause, rugby injuries, shyness, infertility, cystitis, abortion, asthma, retirement and many others.[30] Benzodiazepines are prescribed for about 10 per cent of the population in Europe and the US. Of these about one third are long-term users. There is evidence that the excessive use of these drugs continues as a result of repeat prescriptions, which accounted for 89 per cent of benzodiazepine use in some medicines policy research.[31] Such repeat prescriptions are usually given by an assistant on the patient's request, without re-evaluation by the doctor.

The commercial implications of tranquillizer prescription and use are phenomenal. In 1983 worldwide sales of anxiolytics exceeded US$1 billion, while those of sleeping pills were more than US$250 million. By the 1990s, these figures had doubled.[32] The global market for psychotropic drugs is estimated to be about US$7 billion of which the tranquillizers' market (including the hypnotics) makes up about US$3 billion. The market for psychotropic drugs in the US alone is worth about US$5.5 billion, representing nearly a fifth of all American prescriptions.[33] It has been estimated that about US$800 million is spent annually on benzodiazepines in the US.[34] By the mid 1970s, 200 million tranquillizers, antidepressants and sedatives were being prescribed annually in the US, notably a lower rate per person than in the UK, where the number of prescriptions for benzodiazepines rose steadily from 20 million in 1972 to 31 million in 1979.[35] Worldwide some 100 million people are thought to have been taking tranquillizers each day during the peak of their sales in the late 1970s. During this period, one in five of all prescriptions issued under the British National Health Service (NHS) were for minor tranquillizers of which 70 per cent were for Librium or Valium.[36] Ten years later, between 15 and 25 million prescriptions, for over a million patients, were issued for benzodiazepines in the UK, while there were at least 60 million, and maybe as many as 100 million, such prescriptions per year in the US.[37]

Beyond barbiturates

Barbiturates continued to be widely used well into the 1960s. In 1964 medical commentaries suggested that in Britain every tenth night of sleep was drug induced, mainly by barbiturates.[38] However, there are several drawbacks with these drugs. Barbiturates are effective only within a narrow dose-range. This means that it is relatively easy for patients to overdose, which may be therapeutically undesirable or even life threatening. For example, in the treatment of anxiety a slight overdose with barbiturates could induce sleepiness or intoxication that would interfere with a patient's daily life. Barbiturates also tended to produce 'tolerance' and 'dependence' (sometimes called addiction). Tolerance is a physical and/or behavioural adaptation to a drug in which larger amounts are required to produce the original effects or, over time, a fixed amount produces decreasing effects. Tolerance may urge the patient to take more of the drug in order to try to restore its original effects. This is a problem: if increasingly higher doses are taken by a patient, there is a greater chance of suffering from dangerous side effects stemming from overdose or dependence. If dependence occurs, then it usually means that the body has adapted to the presence of the drug (often after long-term use) so that its absence produces withdrawal symptoms. In the case of barbiturates, common withdrawal symptoms are tremors, hallucinations and even convulsions.

It took about ten years before medical experts and doctors recognized the serious safety problems associated with the barbiturates' narrow range of effective dose. Today this seems an extraordinarily slow detection rate, but it is relatively quick by the tragic standards of barbiturate risk assessment. By 1913, Veronal made it into the list of top ten drugs implicated in fatal accidents and suicide.[39] From the 1920s to the 1960s, the risks of barbiturates due to potential overdose were acknowledged and debated by the medical profession, usually in terms of drug abuse by patients. Yet, as Charles Medawar recounts, it took a staggering 50 years before the profession and drugs manufacturers recognized and accepted the problem of dependence with barbiturates:

> Doctors believed until the 1950s that true drugs of addiction would cause physical symptoms on withdrawal – whereas psychic symptoms signalled personal inadequacy rather than the direct effect of a drug... Doctors believed there was no 'true' addiction to the barbiturates, so even if they had come across major withdrawal symptoms, they would have been inclined to seek other explanations for them.[40]

In particular, doctors spoke of their patients as having 'addictive personalities'. Moreover, the withdrawal symptoms of barbiturates could be similar to the underlying psychic distress for which they were first prescribed; therefore, when withdrawal symptoms appeared after a patient stopped taking the barbiturate, doctors might well have interpreted them as a return of the patient's illness and prescribed more barbiturates, thus masking dependence. By the late 1950s the addictive qualities of barbiturates were widely acknowledged, though even in the late 1960s some expert medical scientists believed that addiction was rare. Nevertheless, barbiturates fell from favour as better alternatives became available: namely, the benzodiazepines.

In 1955 Dr Leo Sternbach, a chemist working for Hoffman La Roche, synthesized chlordiazepoxide – what was later to become Librium, the first benzodiazepine. However, at the time, this chemical was ignored by the company because of interests in other projects. Rather fortuitously, a renewed interest was shown in the compound two years later when it was sent for pharmacological screening by the company's scientists. These scientists were surprised to find that it had an impressive capacity to prevent convulsions and induce calmness and muscle relaxation in laboratory animals, including wild monkeys. Trials on humans seemed to produce similar effects and by 1960 Librium had been introduced on to the market in the UK and the US, primarily as an anxiolytic – that is, a drug to reduce anxiety. Just a few years later, Roche had launched a second anxiolytic benzodiazepine: Valium. These two drugs were enormous commercial successes. For many years, returns on capital for Librium and Valium were over 100 per cent – vastly more profitable than the average for the pharmaceutical industry.[41] In 1970 the sales of Librium and Valium alone accounted for about 70 per cent of Roche's turnover.[42]

In 1965, Roche introduced yet another benzodiazepine; this time a hypnotic (sleeping pill) called Mogadon which was promoted to treat insomnia. By the early 1970s, Mogadon had become the most prescribed hypnotic in the UK. The barbiturates, which had been commonly prescribed for insomnia, were displaced by Mogadon and other benzodiazepines in the 1970s because medical reports confirmed that the latter were relatively safe in overdose, whereas the barbiturates were implicated in suicides and fatal poisonings. A patient who tried to commit suicide by consuming a high dose of sleeping pills, or who became confused after taking some sleeping medication and so accidentally took more, was in much less danger if the drug was a benzodiazepine than if it was a barbiturate. The benzodiazepines were also thought to be safer than barbiturates in interacting with other drugs.[43]

Another reason why benzodiazepines displaced barbiturates is that they were believed be much less likely to cause dependence. Certainly there was much less evidence of dependence with benzodiazepines than with barbiturates, but then the barbiturates had been around for over half a century while the benzodiazepines were just taking off. In the UK, the medical profession and the government's health department ran campaigns in the 1970s aimed at reducing the use and prescription of barbiturates, frequently by substituting benzodiazepines for them.[44] Indeed, benzodiazepines were often used to treat patients with barbiturate withdrawal symptoms. For all the differences between barbiturates and benzodiazepines, this showed their fundamental similarity. It is precisely because benzodiazepines have many effects in common with barbiturates that a patient undergoing withdrawal symptoms from barbiturates will receive relief from withdrawal and respond as if receiving barbiturates when taking benzodiazepines instead.

Too much of a 'good thing': benzodiazepine accumulation and dependence

As the largely successful campaigns to convert patients from barbiturates came to a close in 1977, benzodiazepine consumption in the UK peaked at 30 million prescriptions per year.[45] Over the years some 25 different types of benzodiazepines have been marketed. By the mid 1970s four other benzodiazepines, including Ativan, had joined Librium, Valium and Mogadon on the UK market, but some of the limitations of this family of drugs were beginning to emerge. Research into sleep and medication on both sides of the Atlantic implied that hypnotic benzodiazepines, such as Mogadon, lost their sleep-inducing effect in a matter of weeks, if not days, of continual use. In 1979 the Institute of Medicine (IoM) of the US National Academy of Sciences (NAS) noted that hypnotics seemed to lose their sleep-promoting properties within three to 14 days of continual use.[46] Moreover, by 1980, the governmental authorities responsible for drug safety had reached the conclusion that benzodiazepines, when used for anxiety, probably lost their effectiveness after four months of continuous use.[47]

Despite this apparent problem of tolerance, doctors prescribed, and patients wanted to take, hypnotics for much longer than several days or weeks. Epidemiological research indicates that the rise in the prescription of benzodiazepines in the 1970s was due mainly to an increase over time in long-term use, which went hand in hand with substantial increases in the extent to which these drugs were prescribed on an 'unseen repeat' basis.[48] This suggested that there could be a problem of dependence with these drugs – a conjecture fuelled by the hypothesis that hypnotic sedatives used to induce sleep might themselves produce a worse form of sleeplessness (called 'rebound insomnia') upon withdrawal of medication.[49] Indeed, some commentators have estimated that between 15 and 44 per cent of long-term users of benzodiazepines become dependent upon them.[50] To compound the problem, 'rebound insomnia' could easily be mistaken by doctors and patients for the original problem of sleeplessness. This was made more likely by the fact that, during the 1970s, the manufacturers of the benzodiazepines disputed the implication that these drugs caused dependence, believing instead that the difficulties experienced by the patient on withdrawal of medication resulted from a return of the underlying illness. Similar issues regarding 'rebound anxiety' came to the fore with the anxiolytic benzodiazepines.[51]

Further problems with the benzodiazepines emerged in the late 1970s, most notably the accumulation of Mogadon and Dalmane in elderly patients. This was particularly significant because long-term users of benzodiazepines were predominantly middle-aged and elderly women, who are more likely to be at risk from drug accumulation than, say, young men due to a combination of lower body weight and decreased efficiency of kidneys and liver.[52] Both these hypnotics had relatively long 'half-lives'– that is, it takes longer for them to be eliminated from the body than other benzodiazepines. Initially this was thought to be an advantage because it meant that they worked in the body as sleeping pills for longer – a particularly important point for the manufacturers with regard to the long-term efficacy of hypnotics. However, because elderly people generally take longer to eliminate drugs, they were particularly prone to toxic accumulation, which could lead to their confusion, disorientation and lack of coordination. This could, in turn, lead to falls: the sixth leading cause of death in the elderly.[53] Research shows that about one in 20 elderly people who fall suffer a hip fracture, and that long half-life benzodiazepine use by elderly patients is associated with increased risk of hip fractures.[54,55] Consequently, since the late 1970s, there was an increasing tendency to develop and prescribe benzodiazepines with shorter half-lives.

As the years went by, benzodiazepines became associated with more adverse effects on patients. For example, in a number of patients, some of these drugs seemed to produce amnesia and 'paradoxical reactions',[*] such as aggression, agitation, anxiety, confusion and disorientation.[56]

All this made the issue of dependence of even greater importance. In the early 1980s about 2 per cent of the population in the UK and the US were *long-term* users of benzodiazepines – that is, they had been taking the drugs for more than one year.[57] One of the major reasons for using these substances on a long-term basis had been chronic insomnia.[58] Despite problems of tolerance and concomitant loss of efficacy, about 750,000 people in the UK had been taking benzodiazepines at normal therapeutic doses for years.[59] This implied that many thousands of patients might be at risk of dependence. It has been estimated that after six months of continuous treatment with benzodiazepines at clinical doses, about 5 to 10 per cent of patients exhibit a withdrawal syndrome after discontinuation of treatment.[60]

In 1984, medical researchers reported that benzodiazepine withdrawal therapy was associated with a syndrome of perceptual distortions, agoraphobia and depression in some patients. They concluded that such withdrawal is 'very clearly a severe illness'.[61] Patients persisted in using sleeping pills because they experienced poor sleep when they stopped the medication and therefore felt compelled to continue taking them. Indeed, insomnia has been reported to be among the most frequent withdrawal symptoms after dependence has developed from the use of benzodiazepines at therapeutic doses for months or years.[62]

By the mid 1980s, such dependence on benzodiazepines was widely recognized, not least by patients – 12,000 of whom joined a legal action in the UK claiming compensation for dependence against the manufacturers of these drugs.[63] In the US in 1989, the Federal Drug Abuse Warning Network cited about 2000 emergency room admissions per year resulting from use of benzodiazepines in New York State alone. After mounting an investigation into the problem, the New York State Health Department concluded that benzodiazepines can cause dependence even at therapeutic doses and established rules to monitor prescribing.[64]

Conclusion

In Western societies there is a relatively high prevalence of psychic distress and there is a huge commercial market for tranquillizers. Supposedly, two major advantages of benzodiazepines over barbiturates are a wider margin of safety and effective dose and a low likelihood of dependence. However, benzodiazepines have been found to create their own problems of dependence and withdrawal symptoms, such as rebound insomnia.

In discussing the nature of tranquillizing drugs so far we have mentioned their commercial and therapeutic significance as well as their drawbacks. The pharmaceutical industry, prescribing doctors and, of course, patients are central to understanding these issues. However, we have not yet considered

---

[*] By 'paradoxical reactions', medical scientists mean reactions opposite from those that would be expected with a medication, especially in the patient involved.

one set of key actors, namely governments. The role of government is crucial because it defines the framework within which the testing, licensing and marketing of new drugs are regulated. More specifically, it is governments who are supposed to be responsible for regulating the pharmaceutical industry in such a way that consumers and patients receive a safe and effective supply of medicines. Therefore, before examining the Halcion case in depth, we need to turn our attention to this vital issue of regulation and how it is that patients have come to be exposed to the wide-ranging risks of powerful drugs.

2

The Political Control of Medicines

Introduction

When we visit the doctor and receive a prescription, we are inclined to think of that as the defining moment in our medical treatment. However, a long process of drug development is hidden behind our face-to-face contact with doctors. Often doctors themselves have only a very limited knowledge about the characteristics of the medicines they prescribe. They are dependent upon the information contained on the product's label. But this information is only a fraction of the data collected in order to assess the safety and effectiveness of prescription drugs.

The people who have most knowledge about new drugs are the pharmaceutical manufacturers and their consultants in the medical profession who have tested the drugs, and the government regulators who are supposed to check the validity and reliability of those tests. Many of the most important developments concerning the safety of a drug may have occurred long before we are prescribed it by our doctor. Thus, the extent of intervention and vigilance by government regulators in checking drug testing is key in determining the kind of medicines which are available to doctors in the first place.

Where governments are involved, broad political controversies often come into play. Medicines regulation is no exception. Those who oppose 'big government', in general, seek to minimize regulation of the pharmaceutical industry because they believe that government intervention undermines the enterprise and competitiveness of industrial firms. In recent times they have found powerful allies in the Thatcher and Major Conservative governments in the UK, in the Reagan and Bush administrations in the US, and in the Republican Congress led by Newt Gingrich. By contrast, those who believe that the public interest is best served by regulating the conduct of industry have been more likely to find political allies in British Labour governments and congressional committees led by the Democrats in the US.

Governments as drug safety watchdogs

It is an astonishing fact that pharmaceutical companies were not required to test the safety of their drug products in the UK until 1968 and in the US until 1938. Beforehand, British and American governments neglected to provide consumers with any protection at all regarding the safety of medication. Novices to the field of medicinal policy are often stunned to discover that to this day Western governments permit pharmaceutical companies with commercial interests in the success of their products to conduct and/or direct all the safety testing of those products.

In his startling *Treatise on Adulterations* of 1820, Frederick Accum concluded that nine-tenths of the most potent drugs and chemical preparations used in pharmacy were sold in Britain in an adulterated state.[1] Yet it was not until the Pharmacy Act of 1868 and the 1875 Sale of Food and Drugs Act that the British government legislated on the quality of pharmaceuticals.[2,3] About another half century passed before the British state took some responsibility for overseeing the quality of medical drugs by establishing the Ministry of Health in 1919.[4] In the US, significant pressure to eliminate drug adulteration did not emerge until the last quarter of the 19th century. From 1879 to 1905 at least 190 bills relating to federal control of food and drugs were proposed to Congress, though none were passed.[5] In 1906, the Pure Food and Drugs Act became the first piece of legislation to regulate the quality of medicines in the US.[6]

The introduction of the potent prescription drugs, such as salfa-drugs in the 1930s and penicillin in the 1940s, signalled the beginning of a transformation in the kinds of medicines produced by the pharmaceutical industry.[7] As the industry grew in size and sophistication, the US regulatory authorities responded in kind with the establishment of the federal Food and Drug Administration (FDA) in 1927. During the early 1930s the commissioner of the FDA, Rexford Tugwell, sought to tighten up regulations on drug adulteration and advertising; but he failed due to a lethargic public and widespread opposition and influence from the pharmaceutical industry, which frustrated his legislative proposals in Congress. However, attitudes in the US changed in 1937 when a drug called Elixir Sulfanilamide killed 107 people. Although sulfanilamide was a widely used medicine, a company had marketed it in liquid form using diethylene glycol, but neglected either to test the resulting compound for toxicity in animals or to name the solvent on the label. Most of the deadly compound had, in fact, been prescribed by doctors. The incident brought into sharp focus the fact that the existing legislation did not require the testing of drugs for safety, though it seems to have been ignored in the UK. In the wake of this incident, Congress passed into law the 1938 Food, Drug and Cosmetic Act, which required manufacturers to test any new drug for safety and to report the results to the FDA. The FDA was also authorized to remove from the market any drug it could prove to be unsafe.[8]

Throughout the 1930s and 1940s a series of therapeutic breakthroughs stimulated drug development. Since these required prescription by doctors, industrial promotion of drugs to the medical profession intensified, and the large high-technology firms used patents to command high monopoly prices for their drugs.[9] This was of particular concern to the British government after the establishment of the National Health Service (NHS) in 1948 because the government now had to foot the bill for medical care across the whole population. By 1951 the number of prescriptions under the NHS had more than trebled to 220 million.[10]

In response, British governments became preoccupied with the excessive prices of drugs prescribed under the NHS with knock-on effects for the regulation of drug standards. As early as 1951 the Ministry of Health claimed in an unpublished review of British medicines control:

> ... *a major cause of the proprietary drug bill is the prescription of duplicate or doubtful medicines following skilful propaganda from the drug firms to the doctors in the service, and in some cases following advertising to the public which in turn results in pressure on the doctor by the patient.*[11]

Similar concerns were voiced in the US in the late 1950s, as senator Estes Kefauver berated the pharmaceutical industry in congressional hearings for excessive prices and profits. It was estimated that, in 1958, an average of 24 per cent of the gross income of America's 22 largest pharmaceutical manufacturers went on advertising and promotion.[12] Most witnesses from the industry testified before the Kefauver committee that high profits were required to offset the amount of research needed to obtain a marketable product, especially since only a small number of such endeavours were successful. However, this view was not universal among industrialists.[13] For example, when Kefauver asked Dale Console, a former medical director at the pharmaceutical firm Squibb, whether much of the industry's research led to marketing of useless drugs, he replied:

> *I think more than half are in this category. And I should point out that with many of these products it is clear while they are on the drawing board that they promise no utility. They promise sales.*[14]

Meanwhile in the UK, the Ministry of Health found that there was 'inadequate drug-testing to safeguard the consumer whether it be the public generally or the NHS patient in particular'. The ministry drew the following stark conclusions:

> *(i) there is no effective control over the manufacture and sale of duplicate or dubious proprietary preparations; (ii) there is no effective control over the advertising of proprietary medicines; (iii) the existing provisions for the testing of drugs are inadequate.*[15]

While legislation in the late 19th century had created some consumer protection regarding adulteration-free *quality*, in the UK the industry was left to regulate itself regarding the *safety* and *efficacy* of its new drug products. In the US, the 1938 Food, Drug and Cosmetic Act had enabled the FDA to regulate drug quality and *safety* but *not efficacy*. These deficiencies in medicinal regulation were challenged for the first time in the late 1950s by the Hinchliffe parliamentary committee in the UK, and by Kefauver's congressional committee in the US. Hinchliffe recommended that all new drugs in the UK should be subjected to clinical trials conducted by medical scientists who were 'independent' of the manufacturers, and that the government should set up a clinical trials committee to 'organize clinical trials of new drugs'.[16] Similarly, Kefauver pressed for legislation requiring US drug manufacturers to demonstrate that their products were effective as well as safe.[17] It was the public spectacle of the thalidomide disaster in 1961 which brought urgency to these abstract governmental debates.

The many hundreds of deformed babies caused by thalidomide illustrated the tremendous potential for harm that modern drugs possessed. Soon after, the *Pharmaceutical Journal*, not renowned for radical criticism of the British drug regulatory system, carried an editorial stating:

> *It is hard to imagine a more difficult choice than that which faces a manufacturer who has to decide whether or not to withdraw a profitable drug from the market on the basis of the evidence that, on the one hand, the drug may be dangerous to a small number of patients and, on the other, have valuable properties. So difficult must the choice be that it is questionable whether the manufacturer should be the one to make it.*[18]

Governments got the message. The British government set in motion a process through which it would become legally responsible for medicines safety in the UK. The thalidomide tragedy also galvanized greater support for Kefauver's efforts in Congress, even though American women had been spared the horrors of the drug because it was never approved by the FDA. Consequently, in 1962, the US Congress passed the Kefauver–Harris Drug Amendments (to the 1938 Food, Drug and Cosmetic Law) which authorized the FDA to require pharmaceutical manufacturers to provide 'substantial evidence' of products' effectiveness.

The Food and Drug Administration: American regulation gets serious

The 1962 amendments permanently altered the role and scope of the FDA in relation to approving new drugs in the US. Besides changing the standards for approving new drugs, they transformed the FDA into an active participant in the approval process. The new laws required affirmative FDA approval before marketing could begin. These amendments, together with the 1938 Food, Drug and Cosmetic Act, are the basis for the existing political control of medicines in the US.

Prior to 1962, the FDA had delegated authority to doctors to choose the best drugs for patients in line with their clinical judgements. The 1962 amendments explicitly recognize that doctors do not always have the information or resources to assess the effectiveness of drugs. Hence, the FDA provides direction to physicians by restricting the choice of drugs and advising on their use via approved labelling. To some extent doctors are dependent upon what the FDA and its experts decide is safe and effective for them to prescribe, although once a drug receives marketing approval by the FDA, there is no legal requirement for doctors to prescribe it solely for the uses approved.[19] The 'substantial evidence' which is required to demonstrate effectiveness is defined as consisting of 'adequate and well-controlled investigations by experts qualified by scientific training and experience to evaluate the effectiveness of the drug involved'.[20]

The FDA's review process for new drugs involves a number of distinct stages. After initial laboratory tests, the manufacturer conducts short-term tests with the drug on animals to explore potential toxic effects, and to examine how it is absorbed, metabolized and excreted (eliminated) by the body at different doses. Long-term animal studies to test for the carcinogenicity (cancer-inducing potential) of the drug may also begin at this stage. If the manufacturer believes that this testing reveals no serious health risks associated with the drug, then it submits an Investigational New Drug Application (INDA) to the FDA in order to obtain approval for clinical testing in humans. If the FDA approves the INDA, then the manufacturer may proceed to clinical testing but is required to notify the regulatory agency of adverse reactions via regular progress reports on the drug's safety. The manufacturer coordinates these clinical tests, rather than the FDA. Long-term animal testing, such as carcinogenicity testing, may proceed in tandem with clinical trials.

Clinical testing is typically carried out in three phases involving progressively larger numbers of people. During phase I the new drug is tested on a small group of healthy volunteers for a fairly short period of time in order to explore potential adverse effects in humans. Phase II usually involves giving the drug to several hundred patients for a relatively short period of time in order to assess the effectiveness of the drug in treating the specific disease or condition from which they suffer. Any information about the patients' adverse experiences with the drug should also be recorded at this stage. In phase III many more patients are involved and for much longer. Several thousand patients may be involved for as long as a year or more in phase III clinical trials, whose purpose is to demonstrate that the drug is both safe and effective for a specific indication (use). If the manufacturer believes that, taking all the animal and clinical testing together, safety and efficacy have been demonstrated, then it will normally submit a New Drug Application (NDA) to the FDA in order to obtain marketing approval. The regulatory agency then reviews the NDA but, contrary to popular belief, does not do any of its own independent drug-testing concerning NDAs. All drug-testing for NDAs is conducted by the pharmaceutical industry.

When the NDA arrives at the FDA it is assigned to a review team led by an FDA physician known as a medical officer who evaluates the design of the clinical trials and the data they have generated. The medical officer is assisted by chemists who analyse the drug's composition and quality; pharmacologists who assess the animal tests; statisticians who check the significance of data; experts in biopharmaceutics who review how the drug is distributed and used in the body; and, in some cases, FDA investigators who inspect the manufacturing facilities of the pharmaceutical firm to ensure that good manufacturing quality is being maintained. Having reviewed the initial NDA, the FDA may approve, non-approve or keep the application, pending the submission of further data.

If the FDA gives marketing approval at this stage, then that approval is attached to a specific labelling on how the drug should be used. A drug product is both the compound and its label. The label details the conditions under which the drug should and should not be taken (indications and contra-indications), the appropriate dosage, possible adverse effects and specific precautions and warnings. Marketing approval implies approval to market the drug under the specifications of its label. Indeed, the manufacturer is required to submit a draft label, which is then reviewed by the FDA as part of the NDA process. From the 1970s to the mid 1990s the FDA published a summary basis of approval (SBA) for each drug product which gained marketing approval, but this practice was abandoned in 1996 when the quality of some of the agency's SBAs was challenged in the courts.

Once the drug is marketed the manufacturer is required to submit to the FDA periodic reports on adverse reactions and other significant aspects of the drug's experience. Additional risks may be identified through this post-marketing surveillance (PMS), which is intended to detect previously unsuspected adverse drug reactions (ADRs). As a result of these reports, the agency may identify additional risks associated with the drug which require a change to labelling or perhaps more drastic regulatory action, possibly including the withdrawal of the drug from the market. Modifications to the labelling may reflect either negligible post-approval risks or a serious medical problem which requires changes to the warnings, contra-indications, precautions and/or adverse reactions listed.

The FDA is the largest drug regulatory agency in the world with some 1500 staff working on medicines. The umbrella organizational unit within the agency concerned with evaluating new drug products is the Centre for Drug Evaluation and Research (CDER). The work of the CDER is divided between six divisional offices, namely, the Office of Epidemiology and Statistics (OES), the Office of Compliance, two Offices of Drug Evaluation (ODE), the Office of Drug Standards and the Office of Generic Drugs. The bulk of the work relating to the review and approval of new drugs is carried out by the two ODE offices, each of which contains several reviewing divisions with responsibility for different therapeutic classes of drugs. For example, the division responsible for reviewing benzodiazepines, such as Halcion, is the Division of Psychopharmacological Drug Products (DPDP).

Most of the decisions concerning a particular drug are expedited by the reviewing division. The reviewing division can seek assistance from other divisions, say in the OES, regarding analysis of data on post-marketing ADRs. Despite offering such services, the OES cannot take regulatory action, which is the preserve of the reviewing division. In addition, the CDER may seek the opinions of expert scientists outside the employment of the FDA by consulting its advisory committees, such as the Psychopharmacological Drugs Advisory Committee (PDAC). However, the FDA is not legally required to call on the advice of its expert science advisory committees regarding any regulatory matter, and when it does, it is not required to accept or act upon it.

Since 1966 all regulatory agencies in the US, except those concerned with national security, have been required to operate under the legislative framework of the American Freedom of Information Act (FoIA). Thus, it is now recognized among US regulators, at least de jure if not always de facto, that medicines' control is best served by extensive public access to regulatory decision-making. Under the provisions of the 1966 FoIA, the FDA is required to publish all regulations and proposals for regulations in the *Federal Register* (FR) and to make publicly available final opinions, including concurring and dissenting views and statements of policy and interpretation which have been adopted by the agency but not published in the FR.[21] The consequence of the US FoIA is that the public can access and scrutinize reviews of, and internal discussions about, individual drug products conducted by FDA scientists, although those documents become available only after the agency has made its decision whether to approve marketing. Furthermore, most expert science advisory committees to the FDA hold their hearings in public, even when they meet prior to the FDA's regulatory decision.

The British Department of Health: secrets and shoestrings

In response to thalidomide, the Conservative government of the day took modest action; it appointed a Committee on the Safety of Drugs (CSD) which began operations on 1 January 1964. Its members were expert medical scientists outside industry who would advise the Department of Health on the safety of new drugs. To assist it in this task, the committee established a voluntary system by which doctors could voluntarily report suspected adverse reactions to medicines on the market. This was intended to act as an 'early warning system' designed to detect a potential drug disaster in the hope of offsetting it. It became known as the 'yellow card' system because doctors were asked to complete a yellow form reporting the suspected ADR and to send it to the CSD, who would treat the information with the utmost confidence.

Within its terms of reference, the CSD was to invite reports on toxicity tests from the manufacturer, consider whether the drug should be put to clinical trial, obtain reports of such trials, and take into account the safety, efficacy and adverse effects of the drug.[22] However, the CSD had no legal powers; it was a voluntary operation with few resources. Thus, the CSD relied on the industry's cooperation. In order to get that cooperation, the CSD pledged that information submitted to it by manufacturers about new drugs would be treated as confidential.[23] Consequently, a veil of secrecy dropped over British medicines' regulation from its inception. The 'light-touch' regulation also meant that the CSD implicitly placed substantial trust in the good intentions of the industry. As Dr Cahal, the CSD's medical assessor, explained:

One is often asked how the committee manages to comply with its terms of reference with so small staff. The answer is 'decentralization', which means, since there is nowhere else to which we can decentralize, decentralization to industry.[24]

Moreover, regulatory review was deliberately rapid, averaging three months for new drugs and one month for novel reformulations (see Table 2.1). On average less than 5 per cent of applications were refused by the CSD. Later, a former member of the CSD explained how its dependence upon industry had influenced the committee's attitude towards regulation:

Looking back I see only one major error in our performance. We were so aware of the enormous cooperation that we received from the drug industry that the main committee made every effort it could to see that submissions from firms were handled as rapidly as possible – as a result... the adverse reactions subcommittee and ... the work of that subcommittee suffered.[25]

Table 2.1 *Regulatory review of drug-product licence applications by the Committee on the Safety of Drugs*

Year	Submissions	Accepted	Refusals	Requested more data	Still under consideration	Withdrawn
1965	1041	807	19	49	47	119
1966	1004	771	24	39	84	86

Source: Committee on the Safety of Drugs, 1966, 1967, *Annual Reports 1965 & 1966*, Her Majesty's Stationery Office, London

When Labour came to power, they established the 1968 Medicines Act, which is the basis for the existing medicines regulations in the UK. Under this act the Department of Health, headed by the minister of health, is the Licensing Authority for new drugs. Final decisions about whether to permit a new drug a licence for clinical trials or to allow it to be marketed rest with the Licensing Authority. A Medicines Commission of experts was also established to oversee the operation of the act and to advise on the membership of expert scientific committees. The most important expert science advisory committee regarding human medicines in the UK is the Committee on Safety of Medicines (CSM), which advises the Licensing Authority on specific aspects of the quality, safety and efficacy of new drugs seeking marketing approval. The CSM may be regarded as the successor to the CSD, which was abolished in 1971, though the yellow card system remains.

The licensing system was operated on behalf of the Licensing Authority by the medicines division of the Department of Health until 1989 when the division changed its name to the Medicines Control Agency (MCA). Like the FDA in the US, the British regulatory authorities do not actually carry out safety or efficacy testing of new drugs, but merely review and assess the results of testing conducted and submitted by industry. The MCA is staffed by a relatively small full-time scientific secretariat, whose licensing division reviews data on new drugs submitted by manufacturers, such as pre-clinical animal tests, clinical trials with healthy volunteers and clinical trials with patients. There are only about 500 professional and other staff in the British government involved in regulating medicines. If the manufacturer's application is to license a new drug, then – unlike their American counterparts at the FDA – the MCA must refer the application to the expert advisory body: the CSM. In cases where the MCA has a mind to refuse, suspend or revoke a licence, it must also seek the advice of the CSM. While the MCA is not legally obliged to agree with, or act upon, that advice, it is extremely rare for it to reject it.

After a pharmaceutical company has submitted its data on the pre-clinical and clinical testing of a new drug, the MCA produces an assessment report on the submission which is forwarded to the CSM for expert advice. If the CSM recommends approval, then the drug will almost certainly be granted marketing approval under the conditions of its label, known in the UK as the 'data sheet'. The data sheet is supposed to furnish prescribing doctors with fundamental information about the new drug and provide the scientific basis for any promotional or advertising claims made by the manufacturer.

This licensing process occurs behind an extensive cloak of secrecy. British medicines regulation is one of the most secretive in the Western industrialized world, and regulation of the pharmaceutical sector is more secretive than in any other part of UK industry, except for the military-industrial complex. The 1911 Official Secrets Act makes it illegal for civil servants, including any member of the MCA, to divulge any government business without authorization. Hence, any information about medicines regulation received by expert advisors from the MCA cannot be passed on to the public without risk of prosecution. Moreover, the 1968 Medicines Act cemented the secrecy of the CSD. Section 118 of the Medicines Act requires the MCA to treat all information pertaining to product licence application with complete secrecy and imposes secrecy on all the expert advisors who sit on the CSM and the Medicines Commission. Furthermore, this double blanket of secrecy operates not merely during the licensing procedure but for at least 30 years following.

Once on the market, the MCA's pharmacovigilance division and the CSM continue to monitor the safety of the drug in use by collecting data on adverse reactions. The three main sources of such data are the yellow card system, reports from pharmaceutical companies, who have a statutory duty to report all ADRs, and post-marketing surveillance studies, which may be conducted by pharmaceutical companies or other medical researchers. If the drug is found to be hazardous, then the regulatory action taken by the MCA may vary according to the risk involved, the nature of the illness and the effectiveness of the drug in treating the illness. In many cases the MCA may decide that additional warnings about adverse effects and/or recommendations on how to prevent or reduce their likelihood are required, sometimes involving a reduction in dosage or a warning against use (contra-indication) in certain groups of patients. However, if the hazard is judged to be very serious, then the Licensing Authority may wish to severely restrict the use of the drug or even withdraw it from the market completely.

While many discussions about a drug's safety are conducted via informal negotiations between the MCA, the CSM and the manufacturer, there is also a formal appeals system through which companies can challenge regulatory decisions which either refuse to license a new drug, or suspend/revoke an existing licence for a drug already on the market. The appeals procedure does not directly involve the Licensing Authority itself, though the authority retains ultimate power and responsibility regarding regulatory action at all stages. In the first instance, the manufacturer is granted a formal hearing with the CSM. This gives the company the opportunity to persuade the committee to change its mind. If the CSM maintains its negative recommendation and the MCA accepts it, then the manufacturer can appeal to the Medicines Commission. If the Medicines Commission upholds the appeal, but the MCA decides to act against the advice of the commission, then the manufacturer may appeal to a special panel of 'persons appointed' by the secretary of state for health. While the appeal hearings before the CSM and the commission must be held in secret, the hearing before the special panel can be in public or in private according to the preference of the manufacturer. If the special panel upholds the appeal, the MCA may still choose to retain its original decision. There is no further opportunity to appeal under the Medicines Act, though the manufacturer can pursue the case into the British High Court and even beyond, if desired.

Who is government's best friend: industry or consumers?

Although the British government had been advised that the CSD should be 'entirely independent of industry', members of the committee were permitted to, and did, retain consultancies with pharmaceutical companies.[26] In 1970, however, the UK Department of Health invited the Association of the British Pharmaceutical Industry (ABPI) to consider a change of policy whereby individuals holding consultancies in the industry would not be appointed to the CSD or its subcommittees. The ABPI refused to support such a change and it was never made.[27] Indeed, all the major elements of regulatory organizations concerned with drug safety and efficacy have exhibited a close relationship with the pharmaceutical industry via direct representation, consultancies or prior and/or subsequent employment.[28] For example, John Griffin, who was medical director of a pharmaceutical company before joining the Department of Health's medicines division in 1971, the CSM's secretariat, resigned from his position as head of the medicines division in 1984 in order to take up the directorship of the ABPI. Within a week he had gone from being the UK's top regulator of the pharmaceutical industry to becoming the head of that industry. On joining the ABPI, Griffin revealed that the extent of the exchange of personnel between industry and the medicines division – the so-called 'revolving door' phenomenon – went well beyond his own case:

> *All my deputies [at the medicines division], principal medical officers, have been in industry. All the superintendent pharmacists that I had working for me, all came from industry. It is equally clear that within the last 12 months I am not the only*

member of the medical staff of the division to move back into industry.[29]

Given the longevity of Griffin's important position at the medicines division, his views about this are significant and worth quoting at some length:

> *It is abundantly clear to me that the medicines division could not function if it did not recruit the expertise that it requires from the industry. I have always opposed the development of any attitude which I could only classify as adversarial, and I have resisted any attempts by either the industry, the permanent staff of the medicines division, or the committees to adopt an adversarial role. The role of the regulators is, in fact, to achieve the release on to the market of those products which have had peer review, which has shown them as satisfactory for the indications for which they were going to be marketed.*[30]

Evidently the cooperative relationship of trust between industry and regulators established by the CSD had been fostered and maintained over the years, and the extensive industry–regulator 'revolving door' has had significant consequences.

Due to the cloak of secrecy which has typically surrounded British medicines control, more systematic information about the industrial interests of the expert scientific advisors to the British regulatory authorities only became available for the first time in 1989. Table 2.2 shows that a significant number of these advisors on the three key scientific committees, the CSM, the Medicines Commission and the Committee on the Review of Medicines (CRM), have consultancies with pharmaceutical companies.*

Table 2.2 *Industrial interests of expert scientific advisors on medicines regulation in 1989 and 1991*

	Personal interests[a]	Non-personal interests[b]	Neither
Medicines Commission (n = 24 [23][c])	17 [11]	7 [3]	5 [9]
CSM (n = 21 [20])	14 [11]	15 [2]	4 [7]
CRM (n = 17 [16])	7 [5]	10 [1]	6 [10]

Source: Delamothe, T, 1989, 'Drug watchdogs and the drug industry', *British Medical Journal*, vol 299, p 476. Scrip, 1991, 'UK licensing officials' interests in pharma firms', *Scrip: World Pharmaceutical News*, 1 March, pp 8–9
a   Defined as consultancies, fee paid work and shareholding.
b   Defined as payments that benefit department for which member is responsible but are not received by member personally.
c[ ] = figures for 1991.

---

* The Committee on the Review of Medicines (CRM), which was set up in 1975 to make a fresh assessment of the therapeutic value of products put on the market before the 1968 Medicines Act, has now completed its work and has been disbanded.

In particular, in 1989, only a fifth of these expert advisors had neither personal nor non-personal interests in the industry. In 1996 the figure remained as low as a quarter.[31] Of the 23 members of the CSM with industrial interests in 1996, three had interests in at least 20 companies, seven had interests in at least ten companies and 20 members had interests in at least five companies.[32]

The American system of drug regulation also has had its problems with conflicts of interests among regulators and expert advisory committees, although they tend to have been discussed publicly. The issue was first subjected to thorough public scrutiny in 1976 when the Democratic Congressional Committee on Government Operations held hearings on the FDA's use of advisory committees. The commissioner of the FDA argued that the regulatory agencies and industry regularly make use of the same expert advisors because of the limited pool of scientific experts available.[33] Undoubtedly, there is some merit in this argument: a 1990 survey by the American Federation for Clinical Research found that 34 per cent of its members received research grants from industry, averaging US$30,000 per year.[34] Moreover, the policing of conflicts of interest is very difficult because their influence may be unacknowledged. As one FDA commissioner noted:

The conclusions drawn by an advisory committee can come from many things other than what is actually reported in the transcript... at least where men are concerned, often the most important discussion occurs in the men's john, or it occurs over lunch, or it occurs in the automobile to and from the meetings, or it occurs in the bar at the hotel before the next morning's sessions. None of these really ever appear on the verbatim transcript yet they influence the final decision and the bases on which final decisions were made.[35]

Nevertheless, the FDA managed to establish some principles to limit conflicts of interests on expert advisory committees. For example, an expert should be excluded if he/she: is a past or present investigator on the drug's application; holds research grants from the manufacturer; or is an investigator on a competitor's product. These three conditions can be readily identified and appropriate action taken. However, the other main FDA guideline is much more subjective. It states that an expert should also be excluded if there 'is an appearance of conflicts of interests, or possible embarrassment to the employee or FDA'.[36] Despite the agency's efforts, the Democratic leader of the congressional committee criticized the FDA for overusing advisory committees 'as window dressing to gain physician support for its decisions and to dilute its responsibility for effective regulation of the drug industry'.[37] This is particularly worrying because FDA advisory committees are convened on an ad hoc basis by the agency officials, who might continue to do so when it is politically expedient.

The FDA received further criticisms regarding conflicts of interests of its own officials following an investigation by the US government's General Accounting Office (GAO). Consumers would justifiably find this troubling because agency officials may have considerable influence on drug regulation. In 1976, the GAO reported that about 10 per cent of FDA employees had apparent conflicts of interest. It was also found that about 10 per of the senior staff recruited by the FDA came directly from pharmaceutical firms, while about 10 per cent of those who left the FDA immediately took up positions within the industry. These results worried consumer organizations in the US who feared that the FDA's relationship with industry was too close, although the industry–regulator 'revolving door' seems substantially less pronounced in the US than in the UK.

During the 1970s the pharmaceutical industry maintained its strategic influence over the UK Department of Health and its advisory committees through close consultation about regulations on data requirements for clinical trial certificates (CTCs) and product licences (PLs).[38] Nevertheless, the mid 1970s saw British medicines regulation at its most stringent towards industry. In February 1974, a Labour government was returned to power with a manifesto containing proposals to take over sections of the industry. Moreover, in 1975 the CRM was established to comply with a European Economic Community (EEC) directive, which required all medicines to be reviewed and assessed according to the current licensing standards. In effect, this meant that 4000 prescription drugs which had been put on the market before the 1968 Medicines Act could be removed retrospectively from the market. Regulatory review of the industry's applications regarding new drugs also became more demanding. In 1977 just over one third of CTC applications were granted without requesting further information, compared with 74 per cent in 1971.[39] Evidently, this provided greater consumer protection because, during this period, there were fewer bogus new therapies reaching the British market.[40]

The industry complained about this new regulatory stringency, claiming that the average time before clinical testing in the UK was four times that required in several other major Western countries.[41] According to industrial representatives, companies were starting to shift investment in clinical trials to locations outside of the UK.[42] In 1979 the Conservatives were elected with a commitment to reduce state intervention in the economy. The new government was extremely receptive to industry's complaints and by March 1981 it had persuaded the medicines division of the Department of Health to greatly reduce the data submissions required from industry in order to obtain a CTC.[43] In effect, this reduced the regulatory authority's inclination to check pre-clinical data and reinforced the British regulators' overly cosy relationship with the industry.

The 1980s were dominated by a Conservative government determined to reduce public expenditure and regulation of private industry. Throughout the early and mid 1980s, the industry continued to complain about the delays in the licensing process to a Conservative government which was ready to reform radically the civil service, especially those aspects responsible for regulation, such as the medicines division. The government instigated a review of medicines control, which proposed several organizational changes aimed at increasing the 'efficiency' of British medicines regulation. In particular, the Conservative government welcomed the pharmaceutical industry's suggestion that firms could pay the cost of medicines approval if that were to result in a more 'efficient service'.[44] Previously the medicines division had been funded

65 per cent by licensing application fees from the pharmaceutical industry and 35 per cent by the government via taxes.[45] Following the review, in 1989 the medicines division became the Medicines Control Agency (MCA), almost entirely funded by industry fees. The MCA is run as a business, selling its regulatory services to the industry and promoting itself as the fastest licensing authority in the world for new drugs.[46]

The switch to the business-like MCA does not seem to have improved public accessibility to the regulatory process since there is a UK£250 admission fee to its annual meetings which are ostensibly held to 'hear and take account of the views of those whom it provides services'.[47] Since the fee almost ensures that only company representatives will be able to attend, we can conclude that the regulatory authority regards industry, rather than consumers, as its primary constituency of service. Moreover, in 1993, the Medicines Information Bill, which proposed to make British medicinal control more transparent by providing consumers with rights of access to information about regulatory decisions, failed to get through parliament because it was not supported by the Department of Health. If the Medicines Information Bill had been passed in full, then British consumers would have been able to make their regulators as accountable as the FDA has been since the late 1960s.

We are not suggesting that the FDA has been immune from deregulatory influences in American politics. For example, in the early 1970s under the Nixon administration the 'industry-friendly' Charles Edwards was appointed as commissioner of the FDA. During this period FDA management instigated its policy of 'neutralizing' medical scientists within the organization who were 'adversarial' towards industry. This was revealed in 1974 when a Democratic congressional committee heard remarkable testimonies from nine scientific officers at the FDA's Bureau of Drugs and two physicians who had previously worked in the agency. All were, or had been, responsible for reviewing some part of the data submitted by drug companies to obtain marketing approval for new products. These medical scientists claimed that when they recommended approval of a drug, their analyses were rarely challenged but their recommendations for non-approval were unjustifiably overruled. Many of them testified that when they insisted on recommending non-approval they experienced harassment within the agency and were sometimes removed from reviewing the particular drug in question.[48]

Congress set up a special panel to investigate allegations of 'undue industry influence', 'improper transfers, details or removals', 'improper use of advisory committees' and 'improper use of medical officer recommendations'.[49] In 1977 the panel reached stunning conclusions about America's most important agency charged with protecting the public from unsafe and ineffective drugs. It took the view that, although the FDA had not been 'dominated' by the pharmaceutical industry, 'inappropriate contacts with drug companies occurred'. Furthermore, according to the panel, since 1970 the FDA's management established and sought to implement a deliberate policy of 'making the agency less adversarial towards and more cooperative with drug manufacturers, and to neutralize reviewing medical officers who followed a different philosophy' such as those who gave testimony to Congress.[50] As to the method of 'neutralization', the panel revealed:

> *The programme to neutralize the more adversarial reviewers
> was carried out by various devices, including a systematic
> pattern of involuntary transfers to positions which the incum-
> bents did not want, and in a few cases removal from the review
> of particular drugs. FDA management generally concealed the
> truth about the reasons for the transfers from the persons
> affected.*[51]

During the Reagan and Bush Republican administrations of the 1980s, the US
saw determined efforts from the White House to reduce regulatory intervention. The justification was that 'big government' was bad for industry and
competitiveness. Consequently, the FDA was continually under pressure to limit
its regulatory activities and to avoid hampering industrial competitiveness. In
particular, the FDA was asked to accelerate its new drug approval rates, often
with fewer resources than before. Thus, it became of increasing political importance for FDA regulators to show that they could approve new drugs faster than
their counterparts in other countries, and to search for ways of so doing.

In this context, the FDA made a number of regulatory decisions which
deeply worried public interest groups concerned about public health and drew
critical attention from a Congress controlled by the Democrats. Indeed, during
the 1980s, Democratic congressional committees investigated the FDA's
approval of specific drug products on no less than five occasions.[52] Each and
every one of those drugs had to be withdrawn from the market because of
major risks to public health. Despite the election of a Democratic administration in the US, and of a Labour government in the UK in the 1990s, the legacy
of this pro-industry perspective remains in both countries, especially in the US
where Congress has come under the control of the Republicans since 1994.

Conclusion

Throughout the history of medicines, industry has, in effect, controlled the
safety of drugs. Consumers who sought medication to treat their illnesses were
expected to entrust their health to drug manufacturers. In the UK and the US,
it is only in the last few decades that the collective resources of government
have been utilized to conduct some checks on drug safety and effectiveness.
Even now, throughout most of Europe, the details of those safety checks
remain hidden from public view in order to protect the commercial interests
of pharmaceutical companies. And in the US, it is only since the late 1960s that
citizens have had any rights of access to information about the FDA's safety
assessments of new drugs.

Nevertheless, in Britain and America, there has been relentless pressure
on drug regulators to satisfy the interests of the industry. This has led to
conflicts of interests within the regulatory process and concerns that the
responsibility to protect public health has been eroded and captured by an
industrial agenda. It is in this political context that the battle over the safety of
Halcion has taken place.

3

The Rise of Halcion: Getting Approval

Introduction

Halcion, whose generic name is triazolam, was first synthesized by Upjohn as a triazolobenzodiazepine in 1969, code-named U-33,030. By the early 1970s it had been shown to have hypnotic, anticonvulsant and muscle relaxant properties in animals.[1] By 1975 a number of clinical trials, in which Halcion was given to patients for up to a week, had demonstrated that a daily dose of 0.5 milligrammes (mg) to 1.0 mg was initially effective in inducing and maintaining sleep.[2] When the drug was clinically tested in the early 1970s, it became clear not only that it had therapeutic potential as a sleeping pill, but that it also had a very short (metabolic) half-life – a measure of the time taken for the drug (or its metabolites) to be cleared from the body. For example, Halcion has an elimination half-life of about three hours compared with Mogadon's half-life of about 24 hours.[3] This can be significant because sleep maintenance and next-day carry over, sometimes referred to as 'the hangover effect', are related to half-life as well as dosage. A benzodiazepine with a short half-life is likely to produce less adverse daytime effects, such as grogginess, than one with a longer half-life.[4*]

British acceptance of Halcion

As Upjohn sought approval to market the drug in various European countries in the late 1970s, Halcion's short half-life was seen by many as an advantage over the other major sleeping pills on the market which had long half-lives, namely Mogadon and Dalmane. By the late 1970s medical experts had become concerned that the long half-lives of Mogadon and Dalmane were contributing to adverse effects in the elderly who are particularly prone to the risks of toxic drug accumulation because they generally take longer to eliminate drugs from the body. These adverse effects might include daytime confusion, disorienta-

---

* However, it is important to appreciate that this is subject to variation between individuals, and that there are other factors which determine a drug's effects.[5]

tion and/or lack of coordination. Moreover, diminished daytime performance resulting from the hangover effect can pose a serious risk for individuals in occupations requiring high levels of visual-motor coordination. With its short half-life, Halcion is cleared rapidly from the body and it promised to reduce the risk of toxic accumulation, leaving little or no hangover effect the following morning. In this respect, Halcion appeared to offer some therapeutic advance in the treatment of insomnia.

Some early clinical studies in the mid 1970s seemed promising. In a 14-day trial, Dr Thomas Roth and his colleagues at the Department of Psychiatry in Cincinnati University found that a daily dose of 0.25 mg of Halcion significantly improved the time taken to fall asleep (sleep onset) for six adult insomniacs under the age of 26, though the drug did not significantly reduce their number of awakenings (sleep maintenance).[6] In the same year Dr Robert Reeves, the director of Olympia Medical Investigators in Washington, compared the effects of 0.25 mg of Halcion with 15 mg of Dalmane and placebo for 28 days in 41 geriatrics suffering from insomnia. Halcion was found to be significantly better than Dalmane at improving total sleep time, but not at decreasing sleep onset or the number of awakenings. Compared with placebo, Halcion was significantly better on all of these efficacy measures.[7] Also around the same time, Dr John Lipani from Seattle conducted a two-night comparison of 0.125 mg of Halcion with placebo in 42 geriatrics suffering from insomnia. He found that the drug was significantly better than placebo in reducing the time of sleep onset and in increasing total sleep time, but not in reducing the number of awakenings.[8]

On the other hand, in 1976, in the *Journal of Clinical Pharmacology*, Professor Anthony Kales and his colleagues at the Sleep Research Centre in Pennsylvania State University reported some drawbacks with Halcion. They gave 0.5 mg per day of the drug to seven patients with sleep difficulties for two weeks. According to their results, Halcion was effective for up to one week, but lost its effectiveness in the second week. Thus, they concluded:

> *This medication appears to be quite useful in clinical situations where hypnotic medication is indicated for a short period of time. However, the majority of patients treated for insomnia require adjunctive pharmacological therapy for at least an intermediate-term and often long-term period. The loss of effectiveness for triazolam with intermediate-term use suggests that the drug has little utility in these patients.[9]*

Kales's team also found that sleep difficulties increased significantly after the drug was withdrawn ('rebound insomnia'), and that two patients experienced episodes of amnesia while on the drug. For these reasons they argued that:

> *If a drug, such as triazolam, has been demonstrated to be effective for only short-term use, it should be so labelled and promoted, rather than simply stating that the drug is effective and implying that this effectiveness extends across intermediate and long-term use. Also, any worsening of sleep following drug*

*withdrawal, such as that noted with triazolam [Halcion],
should be described in the package insert.*[10]

The results reported by Kales and his colleagues were not welcomed by scientists at Upjohn. On 4 November 1976, Upjohn held a meeting where 'various courses of action were discussed on how to lessen the impact of the Kales publication' which entailed organizing new research and publishing reviews of research to meet Kales's criticisms, writing to the editor of the *Journal of Clinical Pharmacology* 'to refute' his data, and conducting a survey of his influence on prescribing physicians.[11,12] The company's approach to Kales's article seems to be captured by one Upjohn scientist who commented:

> *I have just read the Kales article in the September issue of the*
> Journal of Clinical Pharmacology. *Like everyone else, I am most
> disturbed by it and strongly support the PR&D [Ujohn's pharma-
> ceutical research and development division] effort to marshall
> a defence against it.*[13]

Despite Kales's reservations, Halcion gained marketing approval in Belgium and The Netherlands where it was launched in 1977. Upjohn applied for a UK product licence to market the drug in October 1976 with a recommended daily dose of 0.5 mg. In support of its application the company submitted data from 87 clinical trials, 34 of which lasted for one week or longer. The application was considered by the British regulatory authorities, then known as the medicines division of the Department of Health, and the expert scientific advisory body, the Committee on Safety of Medicines (CSM). On 13 May 1977, the CSM advised Upjohn by letter that the Committee 'had a mind to refuse' the licence application because it was particularly concerned about the therapeutic margin of safety of Halcion and the short duration of the clinical trials used to test it.[14]

   At Upjohn's request a formal hearing before the committee took place on 18 May 1978 at which the company proposed reductions in the recommended daily dose, possibly to a maximum of 0.25 mg, rather than 0.5 mg, in response to the CSM's concern about its narrow margin of safety. On the duration of clinical trials and especially the inadequacy of long-term data, Upjohn asserted that:

> *Triazolam [Halcion] was administered chronically to 60 insom-
> niacs for 91 days. Three hundred patients received 1.0 mg of
> triazolam for periods up to 42 days. In all cases the drug was
> well tolerated and no serious side effects occurred. Side effects
> observed were those usually associated with a CNS [central
> nervous system] depressant.*[15]

This claim was derived from several trials, known as protocols P6049, P6023, P321 and P6047. The 60 insomniacs who took Halcion for 91 days were 37 subjects on P6049 and 23 patients on P6023. The 300 people who received 1.0 mg per day of Halcion for up to 42 days were 17 subjects on P321, while the others were (supposed to be) subjects on either P6047 or P6023. Of these 300 people, *only the 17 subjects on P321 took the drug for more than 15 days*, while 258 of them took Halcion for *one day only*. In summarizing these longer-term data at the hearing before the CSM, Upjohn elaborated:

> *Based upon our experience in 300 patients, it can be concluded that a dose of 1.0 mg of triazolam, twice the highest recommended dose, is a safe and effective dose for inpatients.* Side effects with 1.0 mg dose in this patient population are minimal... *Fourteen subjects received 1.0 mg for a period of 42 days. Triazolam was an effective hypnotic in these subjects and there was no indication of deleterious effects on laboratory tests or vital signs (emphasis added).*[16]

The CSM and the medicines division accepted these reassurances at face value, although they insisted that the maximum daily dose was restricted to 0.25 mg. Consequently, the British Licensing Authority granted Upjohn licences for Halcion at the 0.25 mg and 0.125 mg tablet strengths in September 1978. The starting dose for geriatric patients was to be 0.125 mg 'to decrease the possibility of development of oversedation, dizziness or impaired coordination', though it could be increased to 0.25 mg if necessary.[17] Upjohn's data sheet, which the medicines division approved for Halcion, stated that the drug could be 'administered effectively for short-term and intermittent use in patients with recurring insomnia and poor sleeping habits', and that 'long-term use is not recommended'. However, the precise meanings of 'short term' or 'long term' in terms of the number of weeks were not specified. While the data sheet mentioned amnesia as a rare adverse reaction, it dismissed the concerns of Kales's team by stating that 'the preponderance of data from sleep laboratory studies indicates that there would be no significant withdrawal effects after cessation of treatment'.[18]

The Dutch crisis

As Halcion was launched in Belgium in 1977 with a recommended dose of 0.25 to 1.0 mg, a study, unpublished until 1992, was completed. Belgian researchers had found that 22 out of 44 psychiatric patients receiving high-dose (2.0 mg) Halcion experienced amnesiac events, including anxiety, panic attacks and suicidal inclinations. The reactions stopped when Halcion treatment ceased, but the researchers apparently attached no significance to these results until 15 years later.[19] Meanwhile, in November 1977, Halcion was licensed in The Netherlands at the daily doses of 1.0 mg and 0.5 mg as well as 0.25 mg. The Dutch package insert stated:

> *The dose varies from 0.25 mg to 1.0 mg and should be adjusted to ensure optimum effect. The following may be taken as a guideline:*

- *0.25 mg to 0.5 mg for elderly patients and patients who have not previously used hypnotics or tranquillizers;*
- *0.5 mg to 1.0 mg for hospitalized patients, psychiatric patients, chronic alcoholics and patients who have already used other hypnotics or tranquillizers.*[20]

Within a month Upjohn was selling the drug on the Dutch market. Thus, elderly patients in The Netherlands were receiving up to four times the recommended starting dose in the UK where doctors were cautioned against such high dosage because of the risk of oversedation.

In March 1979 a Dutch psychiatrist, Dr Kees van der Kroef, wrote to the *Lancet* stating that he had noted some 40 side effects in 25 of his patients who were prescribed Halcion over a two-month period. The adverse reactions were serious, including amnesia, paranoia and aggression. They led him to question fundamentally the safety of the drug.[21] In a letter published in the *Lancet* later that year, van der Kroef claimed:

> *During the past nine months I have been confronted in psychiatric practice with a syndrome which is almost certainly induced by the benzodiazepine triazolam ('Halcion'). I have made a close study of 25 patients. Triazolam can produce the following symptoms: severe malaise; depersonalization and derealization; paranoid reactions; acute and chronic anxiety; continuous fear of going insane; depression and deterioration of existing depressions; nightmares; restlessness; inability to concentrate; verbal and physical aggression; severe suicidal tendencies; hallucinations; impulse actions; amnesia; disphagia [difficulty in swallowing] accompanied by nasty taste, painful tongue and mucous membranes, dry mouth, loathing of food, rigid feeling in the throat and emaciation up to two and a half stone; cervical pains; headaches that are often extremely sensitive to sound; pressure on the ears; numb and cold feeling in fingers and toes, extending to distal parts of the extremities; tingling feeling, muscular cramps and paralyses; catatonically impaired motor functioning; reading complaints and blurred vision; dysfunctional speaking and writing; and sweating.*[22]

In May 1979, Upjohn became aware that van der Kroef's findings were soon to be published in full as an article in the *Dutch Medical Journal*. Consequently, on 23 May 1979, Upjohn's Dutch subsidiary made enquiries to the Dutch regulatory authorities, the Ministry of Health (DMOH), about the number of Halcion adverse drug reactions (ADRs) reported to the Dutch regulators at that time. Within a few weeks, the DMOH informed Upjohn that they had received 14 reports of 'psychological symptoms' associated with Halcion.[23] In addition, Upjohn's European medical affairs director visited van der Kroef and asked to see details of his records, but he refused.[24]

In early July 1979 van der Kroef's article was published in the *Dutch Medical Journal*, by which time the DMOH had received 30 ADR reports concerning Halcion. Van der Kroef also appeared on Dutch television, AVRO-TV, describing his findings. Later that month DMOH sent a letter to doctors requesting them to report any data they might have that was relevant to the safety of Halcion. During July, the DMOH saw an enormous increase in the number of doctors' reports of adverse reactions associated with Halcion. On 6 August 1979 the DMOH suspended Halcion from the Dutch market on grounds of safety after Upjohn refused to revise the labelling to include mention of adverse reactions, such as extreme anxiety and fear, suicidal tendencies, aggression and paranoia.[25] By the time the Dutch regulatory authorities had suspended the drug's licence in August 1979, they had already received over 1000 adverse reaction case reports from doctors concerning Halcion, 'exceeding the number of reports on all other drugs [filed in The Netherlands] in that year'.[26]

Upjohn was not alone in arguing that the huge increase in ADR reports about Halcion was a result of the publicity received by the drug rather than because it was less safe than other drugs of its type. Writing in the *Lancet*, Dr Louis Lasagna of the University of Rochester School of Medicine argued that Halcion had been subjected to 'trial by media':

> *Whatever the final verdict on triazolam may be, there is reason to question whether regulatory decisions forced by flamboyant media coverage are in the public interest... Until recently the drug appeared to represent at least a modest advance in therapeutics. Almost overnight, the situation changed. In July 1979, the drug was branded as 'worse than thalidomide' and the cause of 'stark raving madness' in thousands of patients... The published report of van der Kroef discusses only four patients. In contrast, approximately 5400 patients were studied in controlled clinical trials involving triazolam. In controlled trials adverse behavioural effects – such as depression, confusion, disorientation, paraeshesias [abnormal sensations] and excessive stimulation – were seen, but less often than with placebo. Hallucinations were reported in five of 5397 patients on triazolam and two of 1471 on flurazepam.*[27]

On the other hand, even if media coverage motivated doctors to report adverse reactions to Halcion more than to other drugs, the large number of reports about Halcion pointed to the very substantial amount of under-reporting of problems with the drug which had occurred without media attention. Moreover, according to Professor Graham Dukes, then a leading regulator at the DMOH, some of the adverse reactions to Halcion were very unusual. In his analysis of the ADR data for Halcion, he found that in 63 cases the 'entire functioning of the patient had been deranged'. He described several hundred of these ADR cases as 'rock solid' and, in some cases, he found the evidence implicating Halcion to be 'compelling' because of 'positive rechallenge' – that is, when patients stopped taking the drug their adverse symptoms receded, but returned on restarting the medication.[28]

These adverse effects were reported more frequently at the higher doses of 1.0 mg and 0.5 mg than with 0.25 mg. In November 1979, Upjohn Netherlands offered to withdraw the 1.0 mg tablet. However, the DMOH wished to cancel the approval of both the 0.5 mg and 1.0 mg tablets, and to approve the 0.25 mg tablet back on the market only if there was a revised label referring to the adverse events at higher doses. Upjohn refused to accept this proposal; therefore, Halcion remained banned in The Netherlands for some years. By contrast, the British authorities took no regulatory action against Halcion at that time because they supposed that the high level of serious ADRs in The Netherlands was due to the higher doses approved there, which were not licensed in the UK, and due to the adverse publicity following van der Kroef's television appearance. No changes were made to the British data sheet to even inform doctors that the van der Kroef reports had occurred.

The decision by the Dutch regulatory authorities to suspend Halcion in the wake of the van der Kroef data was perceived by Upjohn as very threatening. One senior Upjohn scientist felt that the situation could reach crisis proportions for the future of the drug unless the company took action to prevent it. He was particularly concerned that the situation in The Netherlands might jeopardize the marketing approval of Halcion in the US, which was then still under consideration by the FDA:

> *The UK CSM were giving credence to the van der Kroef data... They do not*, for the moment, *see any problem in the UK data from the monitored release [post-marketing trials]*, but *they do believe van der Kroef. Thus, the Dutch disease spreads... I can see only one plan of action which will stop the otherwise inevitable. The Dutch adverse reaction 'data' must be shown to be false. We must stop further publication by van der Kroef in major journals ... (I think it need not be said that I have no doubts about Halcion and that I feel a strong revulsion about the recent happenings). We must learn everything possible about van der Kroef and be prepared to use the evidence. It should be clear that someone is going to get hurt and this is going to be a long and tough battle (emphases in original).*[29]

On 10 September 1979, a meeting was held at Upjohn to discuss the establishment of a 'Halcion thought leader conference'. The special conference was to be financed by Upjohn and held in Boston later that year. According to an internal Upjohn memo, the objectives of the conference were: to 'provide the scientific basis on which the DMOH could gracefully reverse its suspension of the Halcion product licence'; to 'neutralize the efforts of the DMOH and van der Kroef to spread the "Dutch hysteria" about Halcion to other countries'; to 'provide "scientific reassurance" to regulatory agencies and lay press'; and to 'attract as much lay press publicity to reassure the public and thus relieve pressure on politicians'.[30]

At this time, Upjohn's American headquarters in Kalamazoo, Michigan, asked Dr Frank Ayd, Clinical Professor of Psychiatry at West Virginia, to set up the Boston conference. Ayd had been in contact with Upjohn since 1955. He had performed clinical research for the company and had served as a consultant for Upjohn since 1963 but had not previously worked on Halcion. Ayd felt that he was given a free hand to choose the expert participants at the conference and that no pressure came from Upjohn to reach particular conclusions. Moreover, he took the view that Upjohn had a good reputation, and that the experts at the conference trusted the company to disclose all of the data relevant to an assessment of van der Kroef's claims.[31]

The participants at the Boston conference, which was chaired by Ayd, consisted of hand-picked, internationally renowned medical scientists. These experts were asked to evaluate the significance of the van der Kroef findings based on data supplied to them by Upjohn. The experts had before them a large volume of Upjohn data, but no independent scientific evidence against Halcion, except, of course, van der Kroef's findings.[32] According to Ayd, the Upjohn representative at the conference told the experts that there was no material from research trials carried out by Upjohn indicating that van der Kroef might be right.[33] The experts trusted the veracity of this statement and were consequently sceptical of van der Kroef's results.

The principal outcome of the Boston conference was a letter to the *Lancet*. It was based on information from Upjohn, signed by most of the participants and published in November 1979. It cast doubt on the adverse effects found by van der Kroef and questioned the validity of his conclusions. The letter cited clinical trials comparing Halcion with Dalmane (flurazepam), another hypnotic, and placebo, which according to the signatories indicated that 'the frequency and severity of side effects attributable to triazolam are equal to or less than those attributable to flurazepam', and also noted that the symptoms described by van der Kroef could have been 'due to the size of the triazolam doses authorized in The Netherlands'.[34]

Reporting back on the conference to Upjohn, Dr Robert Purpura, one of the company's medical directors and head of Upjohn's psychopharmacology unit, believed that 'several important suggestions came out of the meeting and either have or will result in actions favourable to Halcion and the Upjohn company'.[35] According to Purpura:

> ... *the one point that was made over and over again, by virtually all the medical panelists was 'the 1.0 mg dose is too high – the 0.5 mg dose may be too high'.*[36]

Purpura's interpretation of this was that the conference's doubts about the appropriateness of the 1.0 mg dose could allow the Dutch regulatory authorities 'a simple, face-saving way of allowing Halcion back on the market in Holland' because 'it allows the DMOH an explanation for the alleged adverse effects (possibly of too high a dose) and allows the Upjohn company a bargaining point (elimination of the 1.0 mg dose).[37] Clearly, then, the Boston conference was convened partly as an attempt by Upjohn to get Halcion back on the Dutch market and to undermine van der Kroef's damaging criticisms of the drug on the international scene, especially in the US where the drug's approval was still under consideration by the FDA. According to Dr William Barry, who was director of Upjohn's drug experience unit from 1979 to 1990, after the van der Kroef reports, the company formed what became known as the 'Halcion defence committee' because Upjohn placed great importance on getting the drug marketed in the US.[38] Furthermore, despite the van der Kroef findings, the British regulatory authorities did not require Upjohn to alter the 1980 or 1981 UK data sheets for Halcion in order to warn doctors about the possibility of abnormal adverse psychological and/or behavioural reactions to the drug.

Mobilizing American approval

Upjohn filed its New Drug Application (NDA) to market Halcion in the US with the FDA in 1976. The company sought to market the drug to American consumers at doses as high as 1.0 mg. As early as January 1977, the FDA's chief medical reviewing officer, Dr Theresa Woo, expressed concern about the drug's adverse effects. Specifically, she found that the clinical trial data indicated that Halcion was associated with five and 15 times as many cases of amnesia as Dalmane and placebo respectively.[39] She also noted that 'after seven nights on 1.0 mg triazolam, insomnia was worse than it was before the drug was administered'.[40] At that time she recommended that 'since the safety of triazolam as a short-term hypnotic has not been adequately demonstrated, this application is not approvable' and that 'amnesia associated with triazolam administration needs to be more thoroughly evaluated'.[41,42]

In March 1977 the FDA convened a meeting of its Psychopharmacological Drugs Advisory Committee (PDAC) to consider the Halcion NDA together with Woo's recommendations. At the meeting Dr Rudzik, Upjohn's medical monitor for Halcion studies, presented evidence of Halcion's efficacy. He suggested that the amnesiac effects of the drug were of limited concern. According to Rudzik, in phase I trials, patients on placebo were just as likely to develop amnesia as patients taking Halcion – seven out of 82 on Halcion and three out of 35 on placebo. Apparently confident of the safety and efficacy of Halcion, he proposed that the recommended daily dose for the drug should vary from 0.25 mg to 1.0 mg, depending upon the patient.[43]

Woo told the PDAC that she accepted the efficacy of Halcion but was concerned about its safety.[44] She had found at least 50 subjects who had reported amnesia to the clinicians during all phases of clinical trials:

> *The other thing I am very concerned about is the chemically induced amnesia... I had to really search carefully 147 volumes of the NDA to collect 50 cases and I am sure this is under-reported and it is not the kind of thing you would find unless you looked for it.*[45]

Nevertheless, the PDAC concluded that amnesia associated with the administration of Halcion did not present problems over and above those experienced with other benzodiazepines. The committee was also impressed with the efficacy of the drug and its lack of 'hangover effect'. Consequently, the PDAC unanimously recommended that Halcion should be approved for marketing in the US, although there were some reservations expressed about the potential toxic effects of marketing it at the high dose of 1.0 mg – as occurred in The Netherlands six months later.[46]

Despite this recommendation Halcion was not approved in the US until October 1982 because FDA scientists deemed Upjohn's original pre-clinical tests in animals to be inadequate, especially tests to measure potential cancer-producing effects (carcinogenicity).[47] However, several years later the company produced a carcinogenicity test acceptable to the agency. Meanwhile, in June 1977 Kales met with the FDA to discuss Halcion at his request. In the 1970s, Kales had been involved in writing the FDA's hypnotic guidelines and was an FDA consultant. He told the FDA he had found that Halcion lost its effectiveness after two weeks of continuous treatment, and that he was concerned about the fact that he had two cases of spontaneously reported amnesia in his study – something he had not seen with other hypnotics. Kales also felt that he had come under a lot of pressure from Upjohn, whom he perceived as impressing upon him that his was the only study that showed these negative results.[48]

Following a review of van der Kroef's findings and other clinical data, Woo concluded that 'we should not be lulled into the myth of benzodiazepine safety'.[49] She rejected the idea that benzodiazepines should be treated as a homogeneous class of drugs and identified Halcion as capable of inducing 'hallucinations and confusion', unlike Dalmane.[50] On the other hand, Dr Paul Leber, Woo's superior at the FDA, took a somewhat different view. He suggested that the problems with Halcion in The Netherlands derived from the drug being approved at too high a daily dose, namely 1.0 mg, and claimed that 'our staff believes that many of the [adverse] events attributed to Halcion are not unique to it at all, but are common to the class of benzodiazepines'.[51] While it was true that adverse psychiatric effects were reported more frequently by patients taking the 1.0 mg dose in The Netherlands, according to Sigelman, one survey showed that 73.7 per cent of the Dutch patients reporting psychiatric disturbances had taken 0.5 mg or less of Halcion.[52]

Published studies with the drug, though sometimes favourable, did not suggest that it was anything approaching a breakthrough in therapy for insomnia. In 1980, Drs Nicolson and Stone at the Royal Air Force Institute of Aviation Medicine in Hampshire reported a one-night study showing that 0.25 and 0.5 mg of Halcion, in six healthy volunteers, significantly increased total sleep time and decreased number of awakenings, but did not significantly reduce sleep onset.[53] In the same year, Dr Ogura and colleagues at the Universities of Tottori in Japan and Rochester in New York found that a single dose of 0.25 or 0.5 mg of Halcion improved sleep onset and total sleep time in 16 healthy adults compared with placebo. Their sleep laboratory measures suggested that Halcion had fewer 'hangover' effects than Dalmane or Mogadon, but the subjective experiences relayed by the patients in the study did not support that suggestion.[54]

A year later, published reports were less positive. In a five-day study, Mexican researchers examined the effects of 0.25 and 0.5 mg of Halcion on eight young adult insomniacs. Neither dose significantly improved sleep onset and only the 0.5 mg dose significantly improved total sleep time, while, oddly, only the lower dose significantly decreased number of awakenings.[55]

Furthermore, after a double-blind trial with 47 geriatrics for seven nights, Dr Day and colleagues at St Helier Hospital in Surrey found that there were no significant differences between 0.125 mg of Halcion and Mogadon in improving sleep onset, total sleep time or quality of sleep.[56] Slightly more positively, in 1982, Dr Mary Carakadon and her collaborators at Stanford University and the New England Medical Centre Hospital found that 0.25 mg of Halcion and 15 mg of Dalmane were significantly better than placebo at improving total sleep time in a five-night study with 13 elderly insomniacs; but Halcion was not significantly better than placebo at improving sleep onset or decreasing number of awakenings, while Dalmane did significantly reduce awakenings. On the other hand, these researchers also found that daytime vigilance was impaired by Dalmane but not by Halcion.[57] In Germany, 0.25 mg of Halcion was not particularly impressive either. Researchers there found that, though it did reduce patients' time to fall asleep, increase the duration of sleep and lessen their number of awakenings, it was no better at doing any of these things than a standard benzodiazepine called brotizolam.[58]

However one reads the published research on Halcion's effectiveness up to 1982, it is clear that Woo had misgivings about the safety of the drug and attempted to mitigate any possible adverse effects by progressively recommending its limited use for shorter periods of time and at lower dosages. For example, in late 1981 she recommended that Halcion should be used only for 'the short-term treatment of insomnia' and concluded that the drug was not effective beyond 21 days.[59,60] By early 1982 she was recommending that Halcion should 'not be administered consecutively beyond 14 days'.[61] In August that year, she argued that the recommended dosage on the Halcion labelling should be 0.25 mg for adults; not 0.5 mg:[62]

> *It is this medical reviewer's opinion that triazolam should be marketed only in 0.125 mg and 0.25 mg dosage forms as it is in the UK. The proposed 0.5 mg tablets should be denied.*[63]

At this time medical scientists within Upjohn were beginning to show signs of frustration. In a memo to a colleague at the company, Purpura warned:

> *If my sources are anywhere near correct, the FDA will never approve Halcion without tremendous pressure. We have the people willing to exert the pressure but we must orchestrate it.*[64]

In the same memo he provided his view of the approach taken by another pharmaceutical company in attempting to obtain approval for Restoril (temazepam) when facing what he perceived to be similar regulatory obstacles:

> *Sandoz amassed an 'overwhelming' number of consultants who testified in favour of approving the drug. They created an environment which virtually demanded approval. This approval, along with the labelling, was rapidly obtained. I*

> *suggested a similar approach a long time ago. Perhaps it is time*
> *for reconsideration.*[65]

Purpura's comments reveal some of the thinking within the company about the relationship between expert consultant scientists and the drug regulatory process in the US. They also tend to support the suggestion that the Boston conference was organized, in part, to help push the drug through the FDA's approval process, though whether it had such an impact is unknown.

Nevertheless, we can be confident that Leber not only disagreed with Woo's viewpoint but also seems either to have been unaware of Woo's objections to the 0.5 mg dose or to have disregarded them, although he was aware that approving that dose was controversial in some quarters *outside* the FDA:

> *... it is possible that some outside groups might allege that the*
> *FDA is somewhat* reckless *[emphasis in original] in allowing a*
> *0.5 mg tablet to reach the marketplace. Psychopharmacology*
> *unit staff, however, are satisfied that this tablet size is safe... I*
> *support this conclusion.*[66]

According to some correspondence between Upjohn officials, Woo viewed the approval of Halcion, which had gone ahead over her objections, as a compromise between Upjohn and the FDA.[67] Dr William Barry, director of Upjohn's drug experience unit, had also been told that Leber made the decision to recommend the approval of Halcion 'contrary to the concerns of Dr Woo'.[68] Furthermore, an FDA inspection report on Halcion suggests that 'at least one FDA reviewer recommended against approval, and after being overruled, this same reviewer argued in favour of limiting the dose to 0.25 mg, but backed off because most of the efficacy data was based on higher doses'.[69] We were unable to obtain an interview with Woo to verify these suggestions. Nevertheless, the official FDA record implies that in October 1982 Woo finally recommended approval for the 0.5 mg dose as follows:

> *The evidence for efficacy was based primarily on the 0.5 mg*
> *dosage; therefore, this strength should also be approved.*[70]

Thus, she recommended the 0.5 mg dose despite her reservations about its safety because at that dose there was sufficient clinical evidence of effectiveness. By contrast, it was doubtful that there was sufficient clinical data regarding the 0.25 mg and 0.125 mg doses to provide the 'substantial evidence of efficacy' required by law under the 1962 amendments to the US Food, Drug and Cosmetic Act.

On 15 November 1982 Halcion was approved in the US at a daily dose of 0.5 mg, except for geriatrics whose doctors were advised to prescribe 0.125 to 0.25 mg – double the recommended dose in the UK. It was to be used for 'short-term' management of insomnia, as in the UK, but effectiveness in studies up to 42 days were also cited under 'indications and usage' in the American label, giving the impression that 'short term' should be equated with six weeks. This impression was reinforced by stating that the incidence of adverse reactions had been derived from clinical trials of 'relatively short duration (ie one to 42 days)'. Regarding the reactions themselves, doctors were warned that:

> *As with some but not all benzodiazepines, anterograde amnesia of varying severity and paradoxical reactions have been reported following therapeutic doses of Halcion.*[71]

Under 'adverse reactions', the label stated:

> *As with all benzodiazepines, paradoxical reactions, such as stimulation, agitation, increased muscle spasticity, sleep disturbances, hallucinations and other adverse behavioural effects, may occur in rare instances and in a random fashion.*[72]

At about this time, the UK Halcion data sheet available to doctors was also changed, though it did not mention hallucinations. In 1983, it stated under 'adverse reactions':

> *As with other benzodiazepines, occasional cases of anterograde amnesia have been reported. Abnormal psychological reactions to most benzodiazepines have been reported. Rare behavioural adverse effects include paradoxical aggressive outbursts, excitement and the uncovering of depression with suicidal tendencies.*[73]

Perhaps the most noticeable aspect of these comments in the drug's labelling on both sides of the Atlantic is that they give the impression that Halcion's adverse effects were indistinguishable from other benzodiazepines. Much less noticeable, but nevertheless important, was the observation in the American label that overdose could occur at 2.0 mg – just four times the recommended dose in the US and only double the dose initially recommended in Belgium and The Netherlands. This was the first public signal of Halcion's low margin of safety, but it was not made explicit and went largely unscrutinized even by the Belgian researchers who had worked with the 2.0 mg dose in 1977.

Halcion is number one

Adverse reactions to Halcion continued to be reported in the early and mid 1980s. In 1982 Ian Oswald, Professor of Psychiatry at Edinburgh University, and his colleague Kevin Morgan published an article in the *British Medical Journal* in which they argued that the drug's short half-life, far from being a benefit, might be a distinct *disadvantage*.[74] In a double-blind study with 21 patients with poor sleep, they found that 0.5 mg per day of Halcion increased the patients' anxiety and was associated with significantly more anxiety than a comparator benzodiazepine with a long half-life. Morgan and Oswald concluded:

Drugs used as hypnotics are the same as those used to diminish anxiety – for example, alcohol, barbiturates and benzodiazepines – and their presence leads to adaptive changes in the central nervous system, as if to counteract the drug. When the drug is stopped the induced changes persist, with resultant insomnia and anxiety. These rebound phenomena are features of the first few weeks after stopping benzodiazepines. The more rapidly the drug is eliminated the earlier the rebound. A measurable rebound in sleep may occur within a single night. We presume that the large dose [0.5 mg] of triazolam each evening was rapidly metabolized and so led to daytime rebound anxiety, in contrast to the more familiar reduction of anxiety by the longer-persisting loprazolam [the comparator benzodiazepine] (emphasis added).[75]

Like the papers by Kales and van der Kroef, this paper also received a hostile reception from Upjohn. Purpura criticized it as being 'sensational, unsubstantiated and unscientific speculation'.[76] Purpura's approach to reports of unusual adverse effects associated with Halcion was to seek explanations that did not implicate the drug, as shown by the following extract from his writing on the subject in a report in July 1982:

We know that Halcion use increases daytime alertness, decreases daytime sleepiness and improves daytime performance. Under certain situations this may lead to a daytime perception of 'restlessness' or 'anxiety' which, given certain premorbid personalities, may lead to bizarre feelings such as a 'racing mind', derealization or even an increased awareness that one's senses may perceive 'hallucinations'. Such a theory may be far-fetched but could possibly explain some of the reports.[77]

The FDA, however, clearly felt that the Morgan and Oswald paper warranted serious attention. As a result of the paper, and despite objections from Upjohn, the agency required reference in the Halcion package insert to 'the appearance of increased signs of daytime anxiety reported by one author in a selected groups of patients'.[78]

In the same year, in response to a parliamentary question, the British government revealed that more ADRs were associated with Halcion per million prescriptions in the UK than with Restoril (temazepam).[79] Indeed, of the 20 benzodiazepines licensed in the UK between 1979 and 1984, the CSM received more ADR reports for Halcion than any other benzodiazepine in each of those years, except for 1983 and 1984 when the drug was associated with the second and fifth most ADR reports respectively.[80]

Nevertheless, Upjohn managed to persuade doctors that Halcion was a useful product. Since 1977, the US National Institutes of Health (NIH) have held 'Consensus Development Conferences' to improve the lines of communication from the health research community to the practising physician and the public. In November 1983 there was a NIH Consensus Development Conference on drugs and insomnia. The conference discussed the advantages and disadvantages of short-term/transient therapy versus long-term therapy for treatment of insomnia. In this context, the comparative risks and benefits of Halcion and Dalmane were also debated. Despite the criticisms made of Halcion at this conference, within Upjohn the proceedings appear to have been interpreted as a victorious battleground for the company and the drug, as indicated by Purpura's report on his trip to the NIH:

> *Halcion, Dr Dement and the appropriateness of drug therapy in transient/short-term insomnia were clearly the winners. Dr Dement did a truly outstanding job in carrying the conference... The open hostility of the meeting, initiated by Kales, was both surprising and refreshing. Kales started by and continued to attack Halcion, then began attacking the other researchers, and finally ended up in quiet rage and a paranoid frenzy. It was the first time, in anyone's recollection, he had been beaten in a public forum. This was done both by solid data, dissecting Kales's 'data', and by a united front from Dement and the company. The 'corridor consensus' was that Kales was finally discredited and would no longer be a force in sleep and hypnotic therapy. I suggest it would be a mistake to let our guard down, however. Paul Leber was present for most of the session. In talking with him it was obvious the FDA would find it difficult to accept Kales's counsel since he was obviously beyond the fringe of the state of the art.*[81]

In 1985, Upjohn got another lift when it was informed that the Crown in The Netherlands, acting on the recommendations of the Dutch Council of State, decided to cancel the decision taken by the Dutch drug regulatory authorities to withdraw the product licence. The Crown also held that the approval of Halcion tablets should not be reinstated under the labelling in force in 1977 and suggested that the company should apply to reregister the product in the 0.25 and 0.5 mg forms.[82] In the same year, sales of the drug reached approximately US$118 million and industry analysts predicted they would reach US$190 million by 1987.[83] In fact, in 1987 Halcion became the world's top-selling sleeping pill, with revenues of around US$220 million for Upjohn.[84] The drug took 46 per cent of the US hypnotic market in 1987, up 16 per cent from 1986.[85] Halcion sales played a major part in helping the company to maintain its sales figures as the third highest for pharmaceuticals in the US in 1987.[86] In short, Halcion had become a phenomenal commercial success.

Conclusion

As early as 1977, unpublished medical research existed showing a 50 per cent incidence of amnesia, anxiety and other serious adverse CNS effects in patients taking 2.0 mg of Halcion per day. By 1979 there were published and unpublished reports of serious adverse psychiatric effects of Halcion in The Netherlands where patients were prescribed daily doses of 1.0 mg. Regulators and Upjohn also knew at about this time that overdose with Halcion could occur at a daily dose of 2.0 mg. Published research did not suggest that Halcion was a therapeutic breakthrough in terms of its effectiveness as a sleeping pill, though it did certainly seem to work at daily doses of 0.5 mg or more. On the other hand, its short half-life, which promised to reduce the 'hangover effect' associated with other sleeping pills, seemed to have the drawback of increasing daytime anxiety in some patients.

Moreover, Halcion's narrow margin of safety with respect to overdose, when prescribed at a daily dose of 1.0 mg, detracted from the comparative safety advantage of benzodiazepines over barbiturates. Yet, Upjohn marketed the drug at this dose in The Netherlands and attempted to do the same in the US. Some regulators in the UK and the US initially expressed concern about Halcion's narrow margin of safety, especially in relation to amnesiac effects on patients. However, the regulatory decision-makers on both sides of the Atlantic put their trust in Upjohn and accepted at face value the company's reassurances that there was no substantial evidence of serious risk associated with the drug at doses as high as 1.0 mg. Suggestions to the contrary were largely dismissed by Upjohn and many regulators as unscientific anecdotes or mass media creations, rather than treated as significant signals of danger. Consequently, regulators on both sides of the Atlantic felt secure in approving Halcion at daily doses below 1.0 mg: 0.25 mg in the UK and 0.5 mg in the US, even though Dutch regulators banned the drug because of concerns about its dangers.

The British and American regulatory authorities reached different conclusions about the efficacy of the drug. The FDA was not convinced of Halcion's effectiveness at low doses of 0.25 and 0.125 mg, while in the UK these were the doses recommended. This implies that British patients might be inclined to take higher doses than those recommended in order for the drug to offer any benefits, thereby increasing their risk of exposure to serious adverse effects. While the labelling in both countries recommended short-term use, the British regulators failed to define this and the FDA implied that it was synonymous with six weeks, even though some medical research had already suggested that Halcion lost its effectiveness within two weeks.

4

Sounding the Retreat: The Accumulation
of Post-Marketing Problems

Introduction

In 1983, one year after Morgan and Oswald reported that Halcion was associated with an increase of daytime anxiety, Kales and his colleagues observed that it was also associated with depression.[1] However, supporters of the drug were not persuaded by these studies. According to Professor Ian Hindmarsh, who was funded by Upjohn to work on Halcion, 40 to 60 per cent of sleep disturbance is psychological in origin.[2] He dismissed claims that Halcion caused depression and argued that the patients were probably already depressed before taking the drug:

> ... there are a lot of patients who are treated as sleep disturbed, who are really depressed. Now, hypnotics don't work as antidepressants... So, the patient comes back and says, 'I'm still not sleeping any better', completely missing the point that sleep is not the problem. The underlying problem is depression. So that patient is still going to present depressive symptoms. The fact that the doctor is not picking them up is not a problem of Halcion, it is a problem of incorrect treatment.[3]

There is no sign that the research by Morgan and Oswald and/or Kales provoked any concern among the British drug regulatory authorities. Yet across the Atlantic, some epidemiologists and other scientists were beginning to analyse the post-marketing reports of adverse reactions to the drug, especially those of a 'psychiatric' kind.

Not what the doctor ordered: amnesia, seizures and hallucinations

In the same month as Halcion was approved in the US, Drs Einarson and Yoder reported two cases of psychosis with hallucinations and amnesia after taking

Halcion.[4] A few months later, Drs Richard Shader and David Greenblatt described four cases of amnesia among healthy subjects who took low doses of Halcion to help ensure they had sound sleep. For example, after two nights of mildly impaired sleep, a lecturer took 0.25 mg of Halcion the night before a presentation. He presented well and gained a project contract later that day; but when phoned about the contract the next day, he had no memory of it. In another case, a traveller took just 0.125 mg of Halcion prior to an overnight flight across the US. A day later, he had no recall of his arrival on the East Coast or the first few hours afterwards.[5]

Amnesia, hallucinations and other central nervous system (CNS) adverse reactions were mentioned on the initial Halcion labelling in the US, but not highlighted in any particular way. Rather, the impression conveyed was that Halcion was similar to other benzodiazepines in those respects. Soon after marketing the drug in the US, that impression began to be challenged within the FDA and beyond.

On 20 March 1984 Theresa Woo, who remained the FDA's medical officer for Halcion, came to review the labelling for the drug. She had been reviewing the spontaneous adverse drug reaction (ADR) data during the first year of marketing: 1983. For a long time, drug regulators had noticed that new drugs often attract the most ADR reports in their first few years on the market because doctors are apparently more inclined to report difficulties with drugs that are new to them. Woo was aware of this phenomenon and took it into account in her review of Halcion and two other benzodiazepine sleeping pills on the market, Dalame and Restoril. She found that, compared with Dalmane and Restoril in their first years of marketing (1970 and 1981 respectively), the FDA had received 339 CNS ADR reports for Halcion, but only 83 for Dalmane and 56 for Restoril.[6] Moreover, she estimated that based on Halcion's share of the market during 1983, it would be expected to be associated with only 35 per cent of the total CNS ADRs; yet preliminary FDA analysis showed that the drug was associated with over 70 per cent.[7]

This worried Woo, so she looked more deeply into the CNS adverse reactions. In her overall evaluation of the drug, she commented:

> *We do* not *agree with the claim that Halcion safety does not differ from other benzodiazepines [emphasis in original]. Serious CNS side effects with Halcion administration include anterograde amnesia and behavioural disturbances such as confusional states, hallucinations, repeated sleepwalking and depersonalization. The disproportionately greater amnesiac effect of Halcion [compared with Dalmane and Restoril] cannot be ascribed to the fact that more ADRs are generated when a drug is first introduced.*[8]

Thus, she recommended that the labelling be revised to warn that 'amnesia of varying severity and paradoxical reactions have been frequently reported following therapeutic doses of Halcion'.[9] Furthermore, she suggested that the label should state that 'Halcion exerts a disproportionately greater amnesiac effect than other benzodiazepines', and that there had been 'reports of withdrawal seizures upon rapid decrease or abrupt discontinuation of Halcion tablets'.[10]

While Purpura at Upjohn dismissed Kales as an 'outsider' whose views had lost credibility with the medical community and the FDA, reports of Halcion's amnesiac effects, the very problem to which Kales had first drawn attention, accumulated within the company. For example, after taking Halcion for the first time, a physician reported that he suffered from amnesia, confusion, loss of coordination, bizarre behaviour, hallucinations and paranoid-schizophrenia. The physician was to perform surgery the next morning, but because of his bizarre behaviour was locked in his house by his girlfriend the next day. However, he found a set of keys and went to work at the hospital. Initially he appeared normal and began surgery, but because of his bizarre behaviour he was physically removed and replaced by another surgeon. He also reported that he had multiple recurrences of bizarre behaviour and amnesia without further exposure to the drug.[11]

Similar problems to those identified by Woo were surfacing at Upjohn's American drug experience unit which, under the directorship of Dr William Barry, collated the ADR reports made to the company. As early as 15 June 1983, Barry compiled a memo comparing the ADR reports of Halcion with Upjohn's other major benzodiazepine, Xanax. He noted that 'a significantly higher proportion of the events reported with Halcion fall into the category "psychiatric"'.[12] In particular, amnesia, confusion, psychosis, hallucination and anxiety featured prominently as adverse events associated much more with Halcion than with Xanax.[13]

According to Barry, one man took Halcion as a suicide attempt. He then had some amnesia, discovered that he had killed his wife and two-year-old daughter and was hospitalized in detention. While in detention, the hospital gave him Halcion and he had another abnormal event. After being given Halcion yet again, he again behaved abnormally by urinating over a neighbouring patient.[14] In another case, a police officer who had taken Halcion claimed that he suffered memory loss and hallucinations, during which time he killed his wife.[15]

By May 1984, Barry had determined that the number of ADR reports received by the company between 1979 and the end of 1983 increased at higher dosages.[16]

Table 4.1 *Number of ADR reports received by Upjohn, 1979–1983, by dose*

Dose	Patients	Reactions	Reactions per patient
<0.125mg/day	2	4	2.0
<=0.25mg/day	46	128	2.8
<=0.5mg/day	102	307	3.0
>0.5mg/day	18	72	4.0

Source: W S Barry, 1984, 'Relationship of medical events to dose of Halcion', internal Upjohn memo, 1 May

This was significant because if the frequency of ADR reports was dose related, then this made it much more likely that the reactions were caused by, and not merely associated with, use of the drug. As Barry himself put it:

> *The purpose of this [analysis] was to see whether there were any changes in the level of the side effects with changes in the amount of the drug taken. This would imply some causality.*[17]

According to Barry, reports of amnesia, anxiety, confusion, hallucinations, impaired coordination and inappropriate behaviour all increased in frequency with increased dose, whereas those of aggressive reactions and being 'spaced out' showed a possible dose relationship, occurring at doses greater than 0.25 mg per day.[18] He formed the view that Halcion seemed to 'unmask underlying psychological pathology' in patients by reducing their 'defence mechanisms'.[19] Moreover, there could be a connection between the amnesiac effects and overdosing. There were some reports of patients taking a Halcion tablet and then taking another one a few hours later, having forgotten about the first one.[20]

It is clear that these findings unsettled Barry; did the Halcion labelling give sufficient prominence to some of these adverse reactions? According to Barry, the drug experience unit at Upjohn had concluded by December 1983 that the labelling for Halcion should mention aggression, amnesia (not merely memory impairment), confusion, delusions, hallucinations and paranoia.[21] This led to some disagreement within Upjohn between Barry and Purpura, especially over whether Halcion had an adverse reaction profile which set it apart from other benzodiazepines. Barry believed that his data suggested that Halcion's 'side-effect profile' was different from other benzodiazepines with respect to the frequency of reports, whereas Purpura emphasized adverse effects of 'Halcion as with other benzodiazepines'.[22]

In particular, Barry felt that the labelling should give more emphasis to the fact that aggression, amnesia, confusion and hallucinations were reported in 'well-controlled clinical studies' as well as during post-marketing. He believed that if the labelling was not changed to give this emphasis, then it might be taken to imply that such adverse reactions were not seen during clinical trials; that the post-marketing data was at odds with the clinical trials data; or even that those types of adverse reactions were not really caused by the drug.[23] Subsequently, Barry testified that he felt that Upjohn did not respond quickly enough to his concerns about Halcion due to a tendency to require confirmation of causality before any mention of an adverse effect:

> *Question: Was Halcion handled the same way as the other drugs that Upjohn marketed with respect to the drug experience unit's recommendations as to labelling?*
>
> *Barry: They were probably processed the same as the other products. The response was different.*
>
> *Question: How was the response different?*

> *Barry: Very few of the side effects that were recommended or that were reported were added early in the marketing after approval of the drug on to the market... There was in general a feeling that even if we could not confirm that the reported medical event was due to the drug, we would include certain events usually with the phrase 'also reported are' to inform the physician of significant or serious events that have been reported even though causality has not been established... Normally, if an event occurred in clinical study even though it may not be statistically significant, and the events were then subsequently found on spontaneous reporting, in most cases this would show up in the package insert at the time of the spontaneous reporting ... normally, if there was some confirming information on voluntary or clinical or animal data, it would show up in the package insert even though there wasn't any confirmation that the event itself was 'caused by' the product.*

> *Question: With respect to other products, significant or serious events that had been reported were included in the package inserts even though causality had not been established. I take it that was not true for Halcion?*

> *Barry: That was not true for Halcion.*[24]

By the end of 1983, Upjohn's drug experience unit felt that amnesia and hallucinations were being caused by Halcion.[25] Soon afterwards, Barry concluded that Halcion could be a contributory factor to, though not the cause of, paranoid or delusional states of mind, aggressive behaviour and even murder, and that 'some information should have been provided in the package insert for physicians prescribing the drug about the association of Halcion with murder, attempted murder or threats of physical violence'.[26] According to Barry, his drug experience unit presented information to Upjohn several times 'that violent or aggressive behaviour, ranging from verbal abuse to murder, occurred' because they 'felt that some warning needed to be in the package insert to better select the patients that the medication was prescribed to'.[27] Barry testified that such persistent collation of adverse effects in the mid 1980s resulted in him being told by Upjohn's marketing division that he was 'killing the product'.[28]

By 1987 the Halcion package insert mentioned amnesia, bizarre behaviour, confusion, hallucinations, paradoxical reactions and agitation.[29] Nevertheless, there remained disagreements between Barry and Purpura about whether the package insert should include the terms 'psychotic disturbance and paranoia'.[30] On 15 March 1988, Barry wrote a memo to Dr Roy Drucker, who was executive director for drug development in the division of medical affairs and co-chair of the package insert committee at Upjohn, saying that the drug experience unit wanted 'delusions' and 'paranoia' to be included in the package insert.[31] Barry's worries about Halcion continued. On 18 September 1989 he wrote a long memo regarding 'populations with increased suscepti-bility to Halcion' in which he recommended that there should be introduced 'a clear and adequate warning in the insert that paranoia and disinhibition can occur, and that dyscontrol in patients with underlying borderline personality disorders may result in aggressive and antisocial behaviour'.[32]

Nevertheless, the FDA was not moved to regulatory action during the mid 1980s. According to Leber, the FDA believed that the adverse events associated with Halcion in The Netherlands were due to excessive dosage, a problem addressed by the American labelling, which emphasized the need for patients to use the lowest effective dose of the drug. On the other hand, contrary to the expectations of Purpura at Upjohn, Leber had come away from the NIH Consensus Development Conference with the view that a lower dose of 0.125 mg per day might be needed for some, or even most, patients:

> *The possibility remains, of course, as suggested at the recent NIH sponsored consensus meeting on hypnotics, that the dose of Halcion recommended in the labelling is on the 'high' side for the typical patient requiring treatment. The possible flaw in dose estimation, again as discussed in the consensus meeting, may relate to the type of patient studied to obtain dose estimates – the chronic insomniac who is especially resistant to the effects of hypnotics. Obviously the firm is aware of this and is in the midst of evaluating a lower dosage formulation (0.125 mg).*[33]

While Leber believed that a wide variety of daily dosages might be required amongst the patient population, he held that the drug was as safe as other benzodiazepines so long as it was not taken at doses *over* 0.5 mg per day. He was not convinced by Woo's analysis, which he belittled by referring to it as 'mere opinion', 'unsupported by either adequate evidence or reason'.[34] Leber preferred to attribute the comparatively high number of ADR reports associ-ated with Halcion to other 'factors unknown' and consequently overruled Woo's recommendation for changes to the labelling:

> *We were not unaware that Halcion might possibly have a differ-ent profile of ADRs than other hypnotics and we hoped to follow the reports of ADRs to determine if Halcion's profile actually differs from that of other marketed benzodiazepine hypnotics. It is not sufficient to have a 'belief or suspicion' about such unique properties. Indeed, even comparisons of ADR type corrected for market share may be biased by factors unknown... It seems totally unfair to hold our response to the sponsor's [Upjohn's] submission hostage to major labelling revision intitiated by Dr Woo. I recommend that ... Dr Woo should find support for her claim that Halcion has a different profile of CNS ADRs than other marketed hypnotics. I am not convinced that the tables attached to Dr Woo's reviews show anything.*[35]

Nevertheless, Leber did request that the FDA's Division of Epidemiology and Surveillance (DES) should conduct a systematic comparison of the ADR experience among the benzodiazpine hypnotics marketed in the US.

Assessing the risks of Halcion: the Food and Drug Administration at war with itself

Within the DES, Drs Diane Wyskowski and David Barash were assigned the task of comparing Halcion's spontaneous ADR reports with those of other benzodiazepines. Although the Wyskowski and Barash analysis was not published until 1991, it was discussed within the FDA as soon as it was completed in late 1986.[36] As early as July 1987, they had drafted a manuscript describing their results, with a view to submitting to a peer-reviewed medical journal for publication.[37] Wyskowski argued that the manuscript should be 'sent as soon as possible to a peer-reviewed journal for publication' because she believed that their findings on Halcion suggested 'an important public health problem', and that adverse reactions experienced by 'thousands of individuals' taking Halcion 'might be prevented in the future' by such publication.[38] However, it was not until two years later that the manuscript was cleared by her superiors at the FDA for submission to a medical journal.[39]

Wyskowski and Barash compared the reports of adverse behavioural effects of Halcion with Dalmane and Restoril for the period of 1980 to 1985. To do this, they used the FDA's spontaneous reporting system (SRS). The five most frequently reported adverse behavioural reactions for Halcion were 133 cases of confusion, 109 cases of amnesia, 59 cases of bizarre or abnormal behaviour, 58 cases of agitation and 40 cases of hallucinations. Wyskowski and Barash found that Halcion had eight to 30 times more of these ADR reports than Dalmane and Restoril combined, depending on the reaction type, as shown in Table 4.2.

Table 4.2 *Number of domestic (US) spontaneous reports with certain adverse behavioural reactions received by the FDA, 1980–1985*

	Halcion		Restoril		Dalmane	
	n	%	n	%	n	%
Confusion	133	15.9	2	1.2	9	5.4
Amnesia	109	13.0	3	1.7	5	3.0
Bizarre behaviour	59	7.0	2	1.2	0	0.0
Agitation	58	6.9	4	2.3	3	1.8
Hallucinations	40	4.8	1	0.6	2	1.2
Cases with any of above reactions	260	31.1	10	5.8	15	9.0
Total cases	837		172		166	

Key: % = per cent of total cases
Source: D K Wyskowski and D Barash, 1991, 'Adverse Behavioural Reactions attributed to Triazolam in the FDA's Spontaneous Reporting System (SRS)', *Archives of Internal Medicine*, vol 151, pp 2003–2008

Thus, according to Wyskowski and Barash, the FDA received 40 times more ADR reports for hallucinations, over 65 times more for confusion, and over 35 times more for amnesia associated with Halcion than with Restoril. These striking quantitative differences existed despite the fact that there were fewer prescriptions for Halcion than for the other two medicines.[40] Wyskowski and Barash reported that, between 1983 and 1985, there were an estimated 13.5 million prescriptions for Halcion, 15 million for Restoril and 26.9 million for Dalmane. Table 4.2 also shows that these CNS ADRs make up a much larger proportion of all ADR cases for Halcion than for Restoril or Dalmane.

Nevertheless, the figures in Table 4.2 require careful interpretation. For example, in general the overall amount of reporting of ADRs is thought to have increased over the years (giving rise to so-called 'secular trends' of reporting). This factor is unlikely to affect the comparison between Halcion and Restoril because they were first marketed in 1983 and 1981 respectively. It could affect comparisons with Dalmane, which was first marketed as early as 1970. However, as Wyskowski and Barash point out, even allowing for a three to fourfold increase in the overall reporting rate over the 12 or so years, there are still over five times as many cases of amnesia and hallucinations associated with Halcion as with Dalmane.

Another factor that needs to be taken into account is the possibility that ADR reporting is greater in the first few years of marketing. This could not affect the comparison between Halcion and Restoril over the period 1980–1985, but could affect comparisons involving Dalmane. Hence, Wyskowski and Barash examined the numbers of reports of adverse behavioural effects associated with Dalmane during its first three years of marketing (1970–1973). These did not exceed the number of such reports associated with Halcion, even when the data was adjusted for a three to fourfold increase in overall reporting over time, and despite the fact that during their first three years of marketing each drug had similar use rates 13.5 million prescriptions for Halcion and 14.7 million for Dalmane. One further reporting factor that could affect the comparison between Halcion and Restoril are contemporaneous differences in reporting between manufacturers. Indeed, Wyskowski and Barash found that, during the 1980s, Upjohn tended to report ADRs about twice as much as Sandoz, the manufacturers of Restoril. Yet this cannot account for the very large differences in the number of reports.

The reality of benzodiazepine use is, of course, that users are sometimes also taking alcohol, other psychoactive medication or even narcotics. They may already suffer from psychiatric problems. Due to tolerance, dependence or for some other reason they may also take more than the maximum recommended dose. Nevertheless, to be as fair as possible to Halcion, these FDA epidemiologists were also careful to exclude all reports concerning Halcion patients who had taken a dose of over 0.5 mg per day (ie overdosing), and to exclude patients with characteristics that could cause adverse behavioural effects, namely concomitant alcohol, narcotic and/or psychoactive drug use and psychiatric disorders. After excluding these cases, Wyskowski and Barash discovered that the number of reports of adverse behavioural effects associated with Halcion were still high: 73 for confusion; 63 for amnesia; 28 for bizarre or abnormal behaviour; 24 for agitation; and 14 for hallucinations.

This implies that even without excluding confounding cases for the other two drugs, the number of ADR reports of amnesia associated with Halcion were 21 times higher than with Restoril and over 12 times higher than with Dalmane. Regarding hallucinations, the figures for Halcion were 14 times higher than for Restoril and seven times higher than for Dalmane. The Halcion to Restoril ratios remained as high as 10.5 and 7.0 for amnesia and hallucinations even when one takes account of Upjohn's tendency to report ADRs twice as much as Sandoz. In fact, having excluded confounding cases for *all three drugs* (including overdosing), Wyskowski and Barash found that the number of reports of adverse behavioural effects associated with Halcion were eight to 14 times larger than those for Restoril and Dalmane *combined*, depending upon the reaction type.

The FDA SRS database suggested that these adverse behavioural effects associated with Halcion were dose related. Since the Halcion labelling in the US suggested that the elderly should *start* at 0.125 mg per day, rather than the recommended dose for other adults of 0.25–0.5 mg per day, Wyskowski and Barash separated their analysis of dose relationship between the under and over 65-year olds. To standardize the crude number of ADR reports associated with different doses (where known), they compared them with the estimated number of prescriptions for each dose using 'dose data' from the National Disease and Therapeutic Index (NDTI).

Table 4.3 *A comparison of doses of Halcion (where known) associated with five specific adverse behavioural reactions from the FDA SRS (1983–1985): strengths of Halcion from prescription mentions (in 1000s) in the NDTI, 1985, for ages under 65 and 65 or over*

< 65 Years	SRS		NDTI	
Dose (mg)	n	%	n (1000s)	%
0.125	0	0.0	24	3.1
0.25	34	27.9	430	54.8
0.5	77	63.1	316	40.3
0.75–1.5	11	9.0	15	1.9
Total	122	100	785	100
= >65 Years	SRS		NDTI	
Dose (mg)	n	%	n (1000s)	%
0.125	1	1.3	28	7.5
0.25	30	39.0	222	59.2
0.375	0	0.0	4	1.1
0.5	42	54.5	101	26.9
0.75–1.5	4	5.2	20	5.3
Total	77	100	375	100

Source: D K Wyskowski and D Barash, 1991, 'Adverse Behavioural Reactions attributed to Triazolam in the FDA's Spontaneous Reporting System (SRS)', *Archives of Internal Medicine*, vol 151, pp 2003–2008

Table 4.3 shows that, for both age groups, the 0.5 mg dose was 'overrepresented' in ADR reports relative to its share of prescriptions. For patients under 65 years, the 0.5 mg dose of Halcion represented 63.1 per cent of the reports of adverse behavioural reactions, whereas that dose only represented 40.3 per cent of the prescriptions. Similarly, for the 65-year olds or over, the 0.5 mg dose was associated with 54.5 per cent of these behavioural ADRs, while taking only 26.9 per cent of the prescription share. By contrast, the 0.125 and 0.25 mg doses were 'underrepresented' in the reports of adverse behavioural effects relative to their overall prescription share. As shown in Table 4.3, this epidemiological research also revealed that a *substantial proportion (about a quarter) of elderly patients were taking Halcion at the high dose of 0.5 mg.*

In her reviews of the drug at the FDA, Woo had consistently argued that Halcion should not be used for long periods partly on safety grounds and partly because she believed it lost its effectiveness over time. Wyskowski and Barash found that 43 per cent of these adverse behavioural reactions associated with Halcion were experienced after the *first dose.* This is important because it suggests that, for many patients, reductions in the recommended *duration* of Halcion therapy would not have protected them from adverse experiences. Furthermore, in only seven cases did withdrawal of Halcion not result in abatement of their reactions and, in another four cases, taking Halcion again was associated with the same adverse behavioural effects ('positive rechallenge').

Wyskowski and Barash concluded:

> *Factors that favour attribution of these adverse behavioural reactions to Halcion include: corroborating reports and studies in the literature; comparisons of the number of reactions with similar benzodiazepine drugs; reports of reactions in otherwise normal individuals; temporal relationship of reactions to initial dose; spontaneous recoveries from reaction with drug withdrawal; and occurrences of positive rechallenge... Because data are from a spontaneous reporting system and neither the extent of underreporting nor the representativeness of reports is known, it is not possible to definitively determine if Halcion is associated with one or more of these adverse behavioural reactions. What we can say from these data is that certain adverse behavioural reactions are being attributed by clinicians to Halcion... Drug sales, manufacturer reporting, concomitant diseases and drugs, and use outside the therapeutic range do not appear to explain away the differences in numbers among Halcion, Restoril and Dalmane.*[41]

Leber remained unconvinced by this analysis and commented that 'the evidence on the existence of a dose-to-behaviour ADR relationship is both epidemiologic and testimonial, but not all that compelling'.[42] Nevertheless, by September 1987, he required Upjohn to amend the labelling so that it recommended a daily dose of 0.25 mg, rather than 0.5 mg for the typical adult.[43] In a tacit acknowledgement that the original labelling had understated the potency of Halcion for the typical patient, the labelling was revised in October 1987 to state that 'a dose of 0.5 mg should be reserved for those patients who do not respond adequately to a lower dose since the risk of several adverse reactions increases with the size of the dose administered'.[44] However, the new label did not state explicitly that the FDA was concerned about the safety of the 0.5 mg dose, even if that is how the US National Institute of Medicine chose to rewrite history a decade later.[45] Referring somewhat sceptically to the research by Wyskowski and Barash, the new labelling continued: 'Specifically, some evidence based on spontaneous marketing reports suggests that confusion, bizarre or abnormal behaviour, agitation and hallucinations may also be dose related, but this evidence is inconclusive'.[46]

Since toxicity is generally dose related, if the 0.25 mg dosage were effective, then it would be therapeutically desirable to limit use of the drug to that lower dose because the 0.5 mg dose could expose patients to an increased risk of adverse effects. One potential problem of the revised labelling was that it assumed that 0.25 mg would be effective for most typical adults. However, as Woo pointed out when Halcion was first approved for marketing in the US, good evidence for the efficacy of the 0.25 mg dose was relatively scarce. Consequently, the number of patients who would 'not respond adequately to a lower dose', that is, 0.25 mg per day, could be large.

Disquiet within the FDA seems to have been detected in the agency's meetings with Upjohn. According to Dr William Barry, director of Upjohn's drug experience unit, during a meeting in 1987 between some FDA and Upjohn staff, several FDA scientists 'expressed their quite strong concern that Halcion was and remained on the market'.[47] Indeed, Barry understood some FDA staff to have said that Halcion should never have been approved.[48] Some months later, Leber and some of his colleagues from the FDA's psychopharmacological drug products division met with senior staff at Upjohn. According to Upjohn's memorandum of this meeting, Leber asked Upjohn to help him show a decrease in ADRs associated with Halcion compared with Restoril, and to assist him 'in the determination of biases or other information to explain the [SRS] data'.[49]

Compromising medicine: safety in doses?

While Halcion may have had an ally in Leber, further criticisms of the 0.5 mg dose were mounting elsewhere. In the mid 1980s, Ian Oswald and his colleague Kirstine Adam, at the Department of Psychiatry in the University of Edinburgh, undertook a study to determine whether regular use of Halcion might cause daytime anxiety. They compared the 0.5 mg dose of Halcion with placebo and another benzodiazepine, known as lormetazepam, by studying their effects over a period of 45 nights on 82 women and 38 men.[50] Adam and Oswald found that:

> *Both drugs improved sleep, but compared with placebo or lormetazepam-takers, Halcion-takers became more anxious on self-ratings, were judged more often to have had a bad response by an observer, more often wrote down complaints of distress,*

and suffered weight loss. After about ten days of regular Halcion
they tended to develop panics and depression, felt unreal and
sometimes paranoid.[51]

Upjohn scientists objected to some of the methods used by Adam and Oswald
in this study, particularly the scales employed to measure the subjects' experiences and anxiety. However, these scales had been used in some of Upjohn's
own clinical studies of Halcion. When those studies showed the drug in a good
light, the company cited them supportively.[52]

Adam and Oswald first presented their findings at a conference in
Philadelphia in September 1985, but it was not until a year later at the Eighth
European Congress on Sleep Research in Hungary that an *abstract* of the
paper was published, stating:

We attribute the daytime anxiety caused by Halcion mainly, but
not wholly, to withdrawal symptoms during each day as a
consequence of its rapid metabolism. The clinical observations
of van der Kroef and our own earlier report are confirmed.[53]

This research threatened to stir up the old worries generated by the van der
Kroef reports of the late 1970s in The Netherlands. Nevertheless, Adam and
Oswald experienced some initial difficulty in getting the full paper published.
They submitted it to the American Medical Association's *The Archives of
General Psychiatry*, but it was rejected on 29 April 1987. The paper had
received mixed reports from referees. One of the unfavourable ones was from
Purpura at Upjohn.[54] We are not suggesting that Upjohn managed to influence
the editorial decisions of journals, but there is evidence that the company
strove 'behind the scenes to discourage the publication of Adam and Oswald'
with 'little, if any, justification'.[55]

For example, an Upjohn document entitled 'Summary of Worldwide
Halcion Committee Activities, March 1986–March 1987' noted:

Oswald's paper indicated a high percentage of Halcion users
have problems. So far we have been successful in having it
stopped. It is scientifically a poor paper.[56]

And an Upjohn memo dated 28 April 1987 commented:

We have learned from another confidential source that the
Oswald paper, critical of Halcion, is now under review at the
third journal, the New England Journal of Medicine. *The paper*
will again receive a negative review.[57]

The full paper finally appeared in *Pharmacopsychiatry* in 1989. Later that
year, an Upjohn memo discussing Oswald's activities stated that 'in recent
months Mr Krzywicki [at Upjohn] has been meeting regularly with editors and
science writers; benzodiazepine stories in the three major newspapers are
beginning to show more balance'.[58]

Others apart from FDA scientists and Adam and Oswald were finding safety problems with Halcion at the 0.5 mg dose. From 1984, the national pharmacovigilance commission in France decided to study some adverse effects associated with benzodiazepine hypnotics, including amnesia, dependence and abuse. As a result of these studies, the 0.5 mg dosage of Halcion was identified as being one of the products most associated with an 'amnesia-automatism syndrome', that is, amnesia together with 'unusual' or 'out-of-character' behaviour. One of these pharmacovigilance studies showed that Halcion was involved in this syndrome in 80 per cent of cases, although to what extent this resulted from doctors reporting more ADRs for Halcion than for the other benzodiazepines is unknown. Nevertheless, the French drug regulatory authorities were persuaded by this evidence and partly for that reason suspended the 0.5 mg form of Halcion in March 1987.[59]

Upjohn did not agree with this decision in France and filed an administrative appeal. Consequently, in September 1987 a group of expert scientists nominated by the French Social Affairs Ministry reviewed the case and endorsed the decision to remove the 0.5 mg form of Halcion from the market.[60] While Upjohn had to comply with this, the company retorted:

> *We remain convinced that the suspension of Halcion 0.5 mg is unfounded both scientifically and medically. Halcion 0.5 mg has been studied in thousands of adult patients, and the safety of this dosage has been well established in clinical trials as well as by ten years of continuous medical use, which have confirmed the benefits of this dosage form in refractory insomniacs.[61]*

Meanwhile, in May 1987 the Italian Health Ministry also suspended the 0.5 mg form of Halcion because in its opinion 'national and international post-marketing surveillance data had shown undesirable side effects, especially with high dosage'.[62] By the beginning of 1988, the German drug regulatory authorities, the Bundesgesundheitsamt (BGA), also announced that they were withdrawing approval of the 0.5 mg strength because of the incidence and severity of dose-related adverse effects. The German authorities elaborated:

> *An adequate hypnotic effect is achieved with doses of 0.25 mg and higher doses are essential only in exceptional cases. Since around two-thirds of the sales of Halcion products come from the 0.5 mg strength, according to the manufacturer's data, it must be assumed that there is a considerable degree of inappropriate use despite the product being available only on prescription. The increased incidence of side effects associated with the inappropriate use is, in the BGA's opinion, not acceptable.[63]*

While Upjohn publicly defended the 0.5 mg tablet in Europe, privately the position at Upjohn headquarters in the US was rather different; by 1987 officials were already resigned to the demise of the 0.5 mg tablet.[64] Indeed, as early as 1973 one Upjohn scientist concluded from a clinical trial that 'doses above 0.5 mg are excessive in many (most?) patients'.[65] Another Upjohn memo in 1982 recounted that:

> *Nicholson, as consultant for Upjohn, is now even more worried than ever about the 0.5 mg dose of Halcion, which he feels is an inappropriate dosage for hypnotic use. He said he has been telling this to Upjohn pharmaceutical research & development people for over two years and considers there is and will be a major attack on this dose.*[66]

In September 1987 an Upjohn memo acknowledged safety problems for the elderly with the 0.5 mg dose, saying:

> *I agree that we [Upjohn] should discontinue the 0.5 formulation. It is clear from the EMIC [epidemiological study in Canada entitled 'Evaluation of Medications for Insomnia'] that the 0.5 mg tablet is being prescribed at a high level even among the elderly. This is in spite of a concerted effort on the company's part to de-emphasize the 0.5 mg dose.*[67]

By this time the company recognized internally that the future of the 0.5 mg *tablet* was bleak and began to plan for its demise, as is evident from the advice of Upjohn's international and regulatory affairs division:

> *... to negotiate the removal of the 0.5 mg tablet with individual countries where there is tangible evidence that they intend to force us to do so. Our objectives are to facilitate registration of the 0.125 mg tablet, to obtain favourable government action regarding pricing and pack size, and to defuse the situation with a minimum of negative publicity.*[68]

On 4 April 1988 Upjohn withdrew the 0.5 mg tablet in the US.[69] The effect of losing the 0.5 mg dose inevitably implied a loss of revenue for the company, but this was to be mitigated by a 5 per cent price rise for the remaining 0.25 mg and 0.125 mg strengths. Upjohn estimated that it would lose 20 per cent of its business to competitive products, but that the remainder would switch to the lower dose strengths.[70] The company strove to put Halcion's problems, including safety problems, in the best possible commercial light. Upjohn representatives were to present the US withdrawal in a positive light as the result of 'wide acceptance of the lower doses and the declining use of the 0.5 mg tablets'. This was to avoid 'bad press indicating that the 0.5 mg was withdrawn for reasons other than the Upjohn company explanation'.[71] Suffice to say that this public representation was less than consistent with Upjohn's own memo in September 1987 about EMIC, which did not imply a 'declining use of the 0.5 mg tablets'.

On 27 June Upjohn sent a letter to American pharmacists, stating:

> *In keeping with good medical practices to encourage the use of*

the lowest effective dosage of Halcion tablets, the Upjohn company has made the decision to no longer manufacture and distribute the 0.5 mg tablet. The continued availability of the 0.125 mg and the 0.25 mg tablets provides adequate dosage flexibility for Halcion tablets. The dosage recommendations remain unchanged: 0.25 mg for most adult patients, 0.125 mg for the elderly or debilitated, and 0.5 mg (ie two 0.25 mg tablets) for those patients who do not respond adequately to a lower dose.[72]

Thus, while the 0.5 mg *tablet* was removed, patients might well continue to take the 0.5 mg *dose* via two 0.25 mg tablets. Yet no explicit mention was made of the concerns of the French, German and Italian drug regulatory authorities about the potential toxicity of the 0.5 mg *dose*.

At the FDA, Leber greeted Upjohn's decision to withdraw the 0.5 mg dose from the US market with disapproval. He was concerned about how this might reflect on the agency's initial decision to market the drug at the 0.5 mg dosage:

Clearly Upjohn's action is driven by pressure from regulatory authorities elsewhere in the world who believe that the 0.5 mg dose is associated with an unacceptable excess of behavioural ADRs ... the decision to cease manufacture of the 0.5 mg dose [meaning tablet] does have a potential downside for us [Leber and his superior at FDA]. It can be interpreted, albeit incorrectly and illogically, as an admission that marketing the 0.5 mg dose was ill advised, even unsafe.[73]

History would show that Leber's concerns were grossly misdirected. In fact, there were already ominous signs that Halcion's problems went much deeper than the safety of the 0.5 mg dose, let alone the 0.5 mg tablet. In October 1985, two Canadian doctors reported paranoid symptoms in an elderly healthy woman after taking just *0.125 mg* of Halcion for 11 days. Three days after withdrawing the drug, her psychosis disappeared and never returned.[74] Much more significantly, in November 1987 Dr John Patterson at the University of Missouri published four case reports of a Halcion 'syndrome' in elderly patients taking a *single dose* of the drug at the *lowest possible dose of 0.125 mg*. None of the patients had any history of psychiatric illness, but after taking the drug they became confused, disoriented, agitated and amnesiac, requiring in some cases to be physically restrained. After discontinuing Halcion, all the patients recovered and completed their stay in hospital uneventfully.[75] Patterson clearly thought that his experiences implied that van der Kroef's findings should have been taken more seriously, even though they related to patients taking Halcion at a high daily dose of 1.0 mg:

Van der Kroef reported on 25 patients with a vast array of symptoms attributed to Halcion... Before these reports, no distinct syndrome due to the oral ingestion of Halcion had been described, and the ramifications of such a syndrome in elderly patients given short-acting benzodiazepines as hypnotics have not been thoroughly appreciated.[76]

Furthermore, as Halcion therapy sounded the retreat from the 0.5 mg dose to the lower doses of 0.25 and 0.125 mg, research began to be published which implied that the drug's effectiveness was compromised at these lower doses. In 1985, Dr Timothy Roehrs and his colleagues at the Sleep Disorder and Research Centre at Henry Ford Hospital in Detroit reported some encouraging findings for Upjohn. In a two-night study with 22 elderly insomniacs, they found that 0.125 mg of Halcion significantly increased total sleep time and decreased number of awakenings compared with placebo.[77] A year later these researchers also conducted a sleep study with 12 healthy normal sleepers taking 0.25 and 0.5 mg of Halcion for six nights. They found that both doses significantly increased total sleep time compared with placebo, and that only the 0.5 mg dose produced rebound insomnia.[78]

This success was short lived. Later in 1986, a group of British researchers conducted a major nine-week study with 53 elderly insomniacs in which 0.125 mg of Halcion was compared with another sleeping pill called chlomethiazole. While Halcion was found to be effective in the first week, its efficacy in increasing total sleep time had disappeared by the third week.[79] These researchers also noted:

> *At week three, significantly more Halcion patients were rated as more restless during the day and they also appeared more hostile, less relaxed, more irritable and more anxious. After withdrawal of Halcion treatment, these adverse reports were reduced.*[80]

The efficacy of even short-term Halcion therapy came under fire. In September 1986, sleep researchers at Stanford and Detroit reported that with short-term (three-day) use 0.25 mg of Halcion was not significantly better than placebo in reversing the sleep loss and consequent daytime sleepiness associated with the shift sleep schedules of 48 healthy subjects.[81]

One month later, Kales and his colleagues published the results of a major 22-night sleep study with 12 insomniacs taking 0.25 mg of Halcion. Their conclusions seriously challenged the viability of the drug:

> *Halcion did not significantly improve any of the major sleep efficiency parameters, and there was a rapid development of tolerance for the drug's slight initial effectiveness. In addition, there were a number of behavioural side effects including amnesia, confusion and disinhibition. Withdrawal of Halcion was associated with sleep and mood disturbances (rebound insomnia and rebound anxiety). Thus, the data in this study shows that 0.25 mg of Halcion, which is being prescribed increasingly, has a profile of side effects that is similar to that of the 0.5 mg dose.*[82]

In 1987, he and other colleagues also questioned Halcion's supposed advantage over other sleeping pills – namely, reduced 'hangover' effect. Kales and Bixler reported that Halcion produced more daytime sedation than Restoril.[83] A few months later, researchers at the Walter Reed Army Institute in Washington DC reported that neither 0.125 nor 0.25 mg of Halcion significantly increased total sleep time or decreased number of awakenings for 49 healthy volunteers.[84]

Blinkering expert advice: the Food and Drug Administration reconsiders Halcion

Taken together, the 1987 labelling changes and the withdrawal of the 0.5 mg tablet were expected to reduce the ADRs associated with Halcion on the assumption that it was the 0.5 mg dose that was primarily responsible for the drug's large number of SRS reports relative to other benzodiazepines. However, in 1988 Dr Charles Anello, the FDA's deputy director of the Office of Epidemiology and Biostatistics informed Leber that an FDA task force reanalysis of SRS data supported the previous conclusions by Wyskowski and Barash at the Division of Epidemiology and Surveillance (DES):

> *The data presented in this reanalysis supports the original DES conclusions that the FDA receives more reports of ADRs, serious ADRs, and the five selected 'behavioural' ADR reports for Halcion compared to Restoril after adjusting for year of marketing, secular trends and the reporting rates of the two firms.*[85]

Moreover, 1988 SRS data indicated twice as many reports of adverse reactions associated with Halcion as had been reported in 1987 or 1986.[86] Significantly, FDA epidemiologists determined that 'the ratio of reporting rates for Halcion compared to Restoril was the same or greater in 1988 than in 1987', as shown in Table 4.4.[87]

Thus, in 1987 there were over five times as many reports of the five adverse behavioural effects, studied by Wyskowski and Barash, associated with Halcion compared with Restoril. Remarkably, in 1988 this figure had grown to over 25 times as many.

Meanwhile, Upjohn had conducted a large post-marketing surveillance study with Halcion in Canada entitled 'Evaluation of Medications for Insomnia in Canada (EMIC)'.[88] The study spanned February 1984 to July 1986 and compared Halcion with Dalmane and Serenid-D (an anxiolytic benzodiazepine). Unlike spontaneous ADR reports, this study involved epidemiological sampling. If willing, patients were recruited to the study cohorts as soon as they presented a prescription for any of the three drugs at a pharmacy which was cooperating with the research. The advantage of this design was that the sizes of the cohorts, among whom ADRs may be reported, were known and results did not depend upon assumptions about ADR reporting rates among physicians. Consequently, estimates of the actual incidence of ADRs could be made with greater confidence. On the other hand, unlike controlled clinical trials, there were no control groups. In total, there were 4753 recruits to the Halcion cohort, 1421

Table 4.4 *Ratios (Halcion:Restoril) of reporting rates for all domestic spontaneous reports*

All reactions	Cases	Serious	Death
1987	6.0	10.9	4.8
1988	6.7	17.4	7.2
Central nervous system (CNS) reactions	Cases	Serious	Death
1987	7.1	12.4	2.6
1988	13.3	15.5	5.7
Amnesia, confusion, bizarre behaviour, agitation and hallucinations	Cases	Serious	Death
1987	5.1	*	*
1988	26.4	*	*

Key: * = ratio not calculable because of absence of Restoril reports
Source: J Freiman, D Graham, D Barash, Medical Epidemiologists, 1989, 'Triazolam (Halcion) adverse reaction reports for 1988', FDA memo to Leber, 12 June, Table 4

to Dalmane and 799 to Serenid-D.[89] Upjohn submitted the results of this report to FDA on 8 December 1988, by which time the Halcion label mentioned 'aggressiveness', 'agitation', 'confusional states', hallucinations', 'inappropriate behaviour' and 'other adverse behavioural effects'.[90]

The results of the EMIC study cannot be compared directly with the SRS analyses by FDA epidemiologists because the former did not include the categories 'bizarre behaviour' and 'agitation', though it did include 'nervousness' and 'paranoia'. No patients on either Dalmane or Serenid-D suffered hallucinations or paranoia, while there were two cases of each among patients taking Halcion. While these reactions represented only 0.1 per cent of the Halcion recruits, which is not a significant difference from zero, the differences *were* detected. As regards 'nervousness', there were 153 (3.2 per cent) cases among Halcion recruits, but only 30 (2.1 per cent) and 24 (3.0 per cent) among the Dalmane and Serenid-D cohorts respectively. Again, in percentage terms these are not significant differences. According to the EMIC, there were 36 (0.8 per cent) Halcion cases of confusion, compared with ten (0.7 per cent) and four (0.5 per cent) among the Dalmane and Serenid-D cohorts respectively. While the EMIC study detected larger percentages of these adverse behavioural effects for Halcion than the other two drugs, the differences are not large. More significantly, the EMIC study reported 34 (0.72 per cent) Halcion cases of memory problems, but only three (0.21 per cent) and two (0.25) cases associated with Dalmane and Serenid-D respectively. These are statistically significant differences which strongly support the FDA's SRS analysis regarding adverse amnesiac effects of Halcion.

Leber responded by convening a meeting of the FDA's Psychopharmaco-logical Drugs Advisory Committee (PDAC) on 22 September 1989 to advise him on what action to take, ranging from total inaction, further labelling changes or removal from the market.[91] The PDAC were asked to consider these options solely on the basis of the SRS post-marketing surveillance and other epidemiological data supplied to it. Although Leber told the PDAC that he did not have 'any prejudged position' about what regulatory action should be taken, over a week prior to the meeting he circulated a document to the committee about how to interpret SRS data, stating:[92]

> *Critically, the voluntary reporting system is* not *capable of deter-mining the* actual incidence *of specific adverse events, and consequently, it is* not *capable of generating reliable estimates of the* relative risk *of various drug products to cause particular types of adverse events (emphases in original).*[93]

In addition, during the discussion in the actual PDAC meeting, Leber asked the committee to confirm his suspicion that taking the drug off the market was an 'absurd position' held by 'people who were alarmists'.[94] These remarks under-line the disagreement between Leber, who generally suspected that the SRS data did not reflect a real risk with Halcion over and above other benzodi-azepines, and senior epidemiological staff at the FDA's DES who suspected that it did.

Leber's approach to the implications of the SRS data for Halcion's safety might be regarded as justifiable scepticism in the context of uncertainty. Yet Leber's scepticism was heavily biased in one direction. When FDA epidemiolo-gists discovered many more ADR reports associated with Halcion than with Restoril or Dalmane, Leber searched relentlessly for ways to explain away those differences. In his circular to the PDAC, Leber implied that there might be more reports with Halcion because of adverse publicity or because doctors were incorrectly attributing their patients' adverse experiences to Halcion rather than to underlying psychiatric illness.[95,96] Indeed, he emphasized:

> *A report of a drug-associated event is in almost every case only a speculation that a causal linkage exists between the occur-rence of the event and the administration of the drug. Admittedly, in many cases, the speculation is sensible, logical and reasonably supported by the circumstances in which the event occurred.*[97]

Whatever the reliability of SRS data, there is no good reason to suppose that Halcion ADR reports were *more* unreliable than those for Restoril or Dalmane. As regards adverse media publicity about Halcion, could that explain the large comparative differences in Tables 4.2 and 4.4 throughout the 1980s? No one really knows, but the FDA's epidemiologists did not believe that it could.

Even after extensive efforts by the FDA to explain these differences by reference to factors other than Halcion failed, Leber remained reluctant to implicate the drug:

> *... our analysis of the reporting rate ratios found that over all years of their joint marketing, more adverse events were reported for Halcion than for Restoril. Aware that the interpretation of the analysis depended, in part, upon the assumption that both drugs were being prescribed in the same manner, for the same use, and in the same populations, we attempted to determine if selective prescribing of Halcion by psychiatrists, or its selective use in a uniquely vulnerable population, or the pattern of its actual usage might account for the results. We also examined the possibility that the relative zeal of Halcion's manufacturer for reporting adverse events might account for the differences in observed reporting rates for Halcion and Restoril.* Each of these analyses failed to identify a factor that might explain Halcion's higher reporting rate, but failure to identify the presence of a source of systematic bias [against Halcion] in an analysis does not preclude the existence of one *(emphasis added)*.[98]

Moreover, he presented *his* thinking behind the epidemiological analysis of the FDA task force on Halcion as follows:

> *Based on our knowledge that Restoril was marketed only two years earlier than Halcion we elected to use it [for presentation to the PDAC ... we reasoned that if we found the reporting rate ratios to be unity [ie no differences between the drugs], the entire issue of Halcion's alleged excess risk would be resolved.*[99]

Evidently, for Leber, only when the data showed substantial differences between the drugs being compared did the validity and reliability of the findings become questionable. The inconsistency of this reasoning was not lost on Leber's boss at the FDA, Robert Temple, who commented during the PDAC meeting:

> *I think it is somewhat disingenuous to say that the [SRS] system is a signalling system and that we do not pay attention to its findings and at least think that it is telling us something. These ratios [of Halcion to Restoril ADR reports of amnesia and seizures] of 40 and 50 are what are knocking people's eyes out* ... it is not easy not to pay attention to those numbers *(emphasis added)*.[100]

According to Leber himself, he sought the advice of the PDAC 'primarily' because the number of ADR reports associated with Halcion in 1988 were double the number received in 1987.[101] Thus, a mere doubling of reports from 1987 to 1988 prompted Leber to consult the PDAC, while dismissing 40-fold differences within the reporting system as invalid! Furthermore, it was the epidemiological analysis of Wyskowski and Barash, showing the dose related-ness of some adverse behavioural effects, that induced Leber to require Upjohn to revise the Halcion labelling to recommend 0.25 mg, rather than 0.5 mg, as the daily dosage for typical adults.[102] Leber acknowledged at least an *apparent* contradiction in his approach and sought to justify it to the PDAC, as follows:

> *... our intra-agency use of comparisons based on the ratio of the reporting rates of Halcion to Restoril may seem implicitly to endorse the ratio of post-marketing adverse reporting rates as a valid estimate of relative drug risk. Not at all! We use reporting rate ratios to explore our large ADR databases for signals of potential problems. We have never advocated that such signals be taken as* compelling proof *of a differential risk associated with two drug products (emphasis added).*[103]

In fact, this comment compounds the contradiction because it reveals a double standard over evidence required to indicate the relative safety or risk of Halcion compared with other drugs in its therapeutic class. When no differences between drugs are found there is an acceptance of safety, but compelling evidence of differences is required to establish danger.

At the beginning of the PDAC meeting, Leber reiterated his critique of the SRS data and implicitly of the analysis of that data by his FDA colleagues in the Division of Epidemiology and Surveillance. His exposition also reinforced the idea that the PDAC should examine regulatory options solely by reference to the SRS data. This was followed by Anello's presentation of the task force's comparative analysis of spontaneous ADR reports for Halcion and Restoril, including all 1988 data. Anello explained to the committee how and why he thought a valid comparison between Halcion and Restoril SRS data had been achieved, and how the task force had taken account of confounding factors.[104] He then presented Halcion to Restoril, reporting rate ratios of 45.6 for amnesia, 8.9 for anxiety and nervousness, 16 for hallucinations and 37.4 for seizures.[105] Clearly, Anello believed that these large differences implied a real drug safety problem with Halcion:

> *Reporting ratios of a magnitude of three or four are not going to be telling us much. You have to decide where you want to draw the line, but I would say that reporting ratios of the order of magnitude of 45 and 37 are something to be concerned about.*[106]

Moreover, Anello argued that adjusting this data to take account of differences in years of marketing, as Wyskowski and Barash had generously done in favour of Halcion, might not be valid because reporting rates are dynamic and may not conform to previous norms.[107] In other words, we cannot apply the fact that there are more ADR reports in early years of marketing for some drugs as a *principle* to other drugs, which do not show such a trend. Relatively more ADR reports with one drug may simply reflect that the drug really is more toxic. Yet, even with all the adjustments that might be legitimate, according to Anello, compared with Restoril, Halcion was associated with ten times more cases of amnesia, nine times more of seizures, four times more of hallucinations and over twice as many cases of anxiety and nervousness.[108]

After hearing the constrasting perspectives of Leber and Anello, the committee heard a presentation by Upjohn representatives who questioned the validity of the SRS data even more than Leber, even though Upjohn's own drug experience unit believed that the kind of analyses conducted by Wyskowski, Barash and Anello were valid.[109] They tried to persuade the PDAC that the number of ADR reports associated with Halcion had been inflated by adverse publicity in the media and the medical literature.[110] The company also presented data from a 1979 post-marketing study in the UK with 3010 outpatients and the EMIC study, discussed earlier. Neither of these studies was large enough to detect seizures occurring at the rate estimated by FDA epidemiologists, but they could provide information about the other adverse behavioural effects under consideration.[111] According to Upjohn, the studies did not reveal significant ADR differences between Halcion and other benzodiazepines, except that Halcion was associated with over three times as many amnesiac effects as comparator drugs in the EMIC study. Dr Roy Drucker closed Upjohn's presentation to the committee with the confident assertion:

> *I would take the position that we have not seen evidence that substantiates that signal [of the FDA task force] this morning and I would also reassure you that there is no information available to the Upjohn company, outside of this meeting, that would tend to substantiate that signal.*[112]

That this PDAC meeting focused entirely on epidemiological and SRS data is highlighted by the fact that, according to the Upjohn representatives, by 'no information' Drucker meant no *epidemiological* data, and that they believed this was the meaning understood by everyone at the meeting.[113] Attention remained on such data throughout the meeting despite one of Upjohn's expert consultants arguing that both experimental clinical studies and epidemiological data needed to be examined.[114] No other experts outside the FDA made a contribution.

The committee members seemed to be swayed by the fact that both the SRS and EMIC data showed that Halcion was significantly more amnesiac than other benzodiazepines. Dr Jeffrey Lieberman of the Albert Einstein College of Medicine seemed to reflect the feeling among the expert committee members when he commented:

> *Our interpretation of the data is also based on our respective clinical experiences in terms of what we have seen with patients, read in the literature and maybe experienced personally in some cases. From that standpoint, given the limitations of the data collected within the spontaneous reporting system, and bearing in mind that the signal can be amplified perhaps inappropriately, we have attempted to adjust for that in our interpretation of the significance of those elevated rates in those different categories of reactions. In terms of concrete concern, it would be most clearly in relation to the cognitive and amnesiac*

events. The others I think fail to reach that threshold but in
terms of seizures and adverse behavioural reactions, they merit
some further discussion.[115]

Leber also acknowledged that observational studies showed excessive association of amnesiac effects with Halcion, while Temple remarked that 'for amnesia
everybody probably believes it [the excessive association with Halcion]
already'.[116,117] However, everybody did not already believe this. On behalf of
Upjohn, Drucker contended: 'I do not think there is anything we have heard
today which would justify a specific patient package insert relating specifically
to Halcion'.[118] On this matter the PDAC decided against Upjohn.

The final recommendation of the PDAC was that Halcion's label should be
revised to warn of the large number of amnesiac effects associated with the
drug compared with other benzodiazepines.[119] Regarding the other 'knock
your eyes out' ADR ratios, such as seizures, anxiety and hallucinations, which
Temple had said were not easy to ignore, the PDAC, in regulatory terms, did
just that, making no specific recommendations about labelling.

The PDAC had been strongly encouraged, if not directed, to take an
extremely sceptical view of the SRS data analysis conducted by the FDA's own
epidemiologists. On the whole, the committee supported the perspectives of
Leber and Upjohn in not finding the SRS data serious or alarming. Leber is a
specialist in psychiatry and clinical pathology and his division concentrates on
evaluating clinical trial data. Like Leber, the membership of the PDAC consisted
almost entirely of specialist clinicians. Yet, these specialists were asked to
review *solely* SRS epidemiological-type data and not clinical data – a mismatch
which seems apparent in Lieberman's above account of how committee
members were likely to draw upon their own clinical experiences, with rather
less emphasis on the data put before them.

The disciplinary and professional coalescence between Leber and PDAC
members may have predisposed the committee to be strongly influenced by
Leber's perspective, especially in taking a sceptical view of epidemiological
data. As Professor Michael Rawlins, a former chairman of the British Committee
on the Safety of Medicines, put it:

If you're a specialist, your life is clinical trials, you're not really
into epidemiology so you don't really understand how much
weight to put on an epidemiological, observational study, and
since it's not clinical trials you assume it's rubbish.[120]

A further explanation for the committee's generous approach towards Halcion
may be the close identification of the members with benzodiazepines.
According to Thomas Moore at George Washington University: 'What we are
really getting [on the PDACs] is a group of people whose lives and careers are
mostly built on drug development'.[121] Indeed, at the PDAC meeting, one of
Upjohn's consultants appealed to just this phenomenon by drawing the
committee's attention to a sense of progress in benzodiazepine therapy represented by Halcion because of its short half-life:

> *The long-acting benzodiazepines such as Dalmane, Valium and so on began to show a number of problems in epidemiologic studies which involved daytime sedation. Because they are long acting, there arose issues of safety in driving, memory problems during the daytime and so on. For that reason, many people, of whom I was one,* and some of the committee members present here today were among the loudest voices saying that we have to develop drugs that act much more rapidly. *Restoril and Halcion were such drugs and, in fact, have largely eliminated this very, very major public health concern (emphasis added).*[122]

That 'social' factors of this kind may have entered into the PDAC's assessment is not an outlandish suggestion even to medical specialists. Leber himself acknowledged that 'risk assessment is always a matter of opinion that depends not only upon expertise and knowledge of "facts", but upon one's personal values and beliefs'.[123]

Whatever the reasons for the PDAC's generosity towards Halcion, it is clear that in September 1989 the committee was concerned about the drug's potential to cause amnesia. Yet Leber's division did not officially propose a labelling change that would strengthen the warning about amnesia until April 1990. Moreover, that proposal represented the degree of concern about amnesia expressed at the PDAC meeting as follows:

> *On September 22 1989 we held a meeting of the PDAC to discuss the excess reporting of various adverse behavioural events for Halcion compared to other benzodiazepines. The committee recommended an additional statement in the Halcion 'warnings' section indicating the* slightly *[emphasis added] greater risk of memory problems with Halcion compared to other benzodiazepines.*[124]

The actual change to the 'warnings' section proposed at that time was the addition of the statement: 'Data from several sources suggest that memory problems may occur at a slightly higher rate with Halcion than with other benzodiazepine hypnotics'.[125] The final regulatory result of the PDAC meeting was that the labelling included the sentence: 'Data from several sources suggests that anterograde amnesia may occur at a higher rate with Halcion than with other benzodiazepine hypnotics'.[126]

Conclusion

As early as 1983, evidence began to emerge that Halcion was associated with more reports of adverse CNS reactions than other benzodiazepines. During the mid 1980s this association was found to be dose related, suggesting a causal link. Some of these reactions were extremely serious. For some reactions, such as amnesia and seizures, Halcion was found to be associated with more than 30 or 40 times the risk of other sleeping pills. This evidence led the FDA's medical officer for Halcion, senior epidemiologists at the FDA and the epidemiologists at Upjohn's own drug experience unit to conclude that Halcion was more likely to cause adverse psychiatric effects, especially at the 0.5 mg dose. Some epidemiologists at the FDA regarded this as a serious public health problem.

The extent of risk implied by spontaneous ADR reports about Halcion was not confirmed by other epidemiological evidence, which suggested that Halcion posed a greater risk than other sleeping pills for some adverse CNS effects (such as amnesia), but at a *much reduced* level. With what some regarded as astonishing complacency about public health, the FDA and Upjohn dismissed the evidence of Halcion's risks as an aberration produced by adverse publicity and other 'factors unknown'. They also persuaded the members of the PDAC, who were mainly clinicians involved in the development of psychotropic drugs, to do the same. As a result, the FDA decided to award Halcion the benefit of the scientific doubt, viewing suggestions that the drug should be taken off the market, as in The Netherlands, as ridiculous. This occurred in the absence of any systematic review of the clinical trial database in the light of the large number of adverse reactions reported to the agency.

Moreover, it involved FDA management overruling their own epidemiologists' interpretation of the data. It seems likely that this resulted from the influence of disciplinary factors and professional interests. Leber's division and the PDAC were predisposed to take a highly sceptical view of spontaneous ADR data because of their disciplinary preconceptions. These were reinforced by professional interests. Leber's division was responsible for the approval of Halcion and any subsequent regulatory action, including removal from the market. Having approved the drug, the division was confronted with evidence of post-marketing risk resulting from that approval, and may not have found it professionally congenial to admit that they made a mistake. As a former chairman of the British Committee on Safety of Medicines told us, 'the people who gave the licence in the first place will defend their decision to the last and that could be to the detriment of the population'.[127] By contrast, the FDA's Division of Epidemiology and Surveillance had no professional interest in supporting the maintenance of Halcion since they were not implicated in approving it.

Upjohn withdrew the 0.5 mg tablet worldwide because of concerns about the *safety* of the 0.5 mg dose in some European countries. As we noted in Chapter 1, the British drug regulatory authorities never permitted the 0.5 mg dose to be marketed in the UK on safety grounds. However, neither Upjohn nor the FDA altered the drug's labelling in the US to warn doctors explicitly that the 0.5 mg *dose* was unsafe. Rather, they simply advised doctors and pharmacists that the 0.5 mg tablet was being removed to encourage use of the lowest effective dose, and that the risk of adverse reactions increased at higher doses. Leber opposed even the withdrawal of the 0.5 mg tablet and became concerned that this might reflect badly on the FDA's official stance that 0.5 mg of Halcion was safe. Thus, American consumers continued to be exposed to the drug at *prescribed* doses as high as 0.5 mg, albeit with two 0.25 mg tablets. The questionable efficacy of the 0.25 mg dose of Halcion made it likely that a lot of patients would ask their doctors for the higher 0.5 mg dose to obtain effective therapy, oblivious of the additional risks of that course of action.

5

Legal Challenge and Loss of Faith: British Medicines Control in Crisis

Introduction

In the UK, where Halcion was licensed at the lower doses of 0.125 and 0.25 milligrammes (mg), no changes were made to labelling (the data sheet) between 1984 and 1988, except to underline the importance of reduced dosages for elderly patients.[1] This message was reinforced in 1989 when the data sheet exhorted:

> *The lowest dose which can control symptoms should be used. It is recommended that the patient be reassessed at the end of no longer than four weeks' treatment and the need for continued treatment to be established.*[2]

By 1990, the problems of dependence and rebound insomnia with Halcion were implicitly acknowledged in the data sheet, which stated that tapering the dose might decrease the extent of 'recurrent insomnia' when discontinuing the drug. Some patients, it was noted, who had taken it for a long time might require the dose to be reduced gradually.[3] The following year this was revised, instructing doctors that 'treatment in all patients should be withdrawn gradually'.[4] Despite the staggering number of central nervous system (CNS) ADR reports received by the FDA about Halcion, in the UK, it was not until 1991 that the data sheet mentioned 'abnormal psychological reactions', such as 'aggressive outbursts', 'hallucinations' and 'inappropriate behaviour – sometimes with amnesia'.[5]

The truth is out there: the Grundberg case

In 1988, Ilo Grundberg, a 57-year-old woman from Utah, killed her 83-year-old mother by shooting her in the head with eight bullets. She was arrested and charged with murder. However, after being subjected to tests by the court-appointed psychiatrists, she was judged to have been 'involuntarily intoxicated' by Halcion when she killed her mother because she had no clear motive for the murder and little memory of it. This evidence was accepted by the prosecution and so the case was dismissed in February 1989 without Grundberg ever having to stand trial. On her release, she embarked on a US$21 million civil suit seeking damages against Upjohn for allegedly failing to warn regulators or the public of Halcion's 'severe and sometimes adverse reactions'.[6] In that case, she claimed that she had been 'involuntarily intoxicated' by the drug. In the US, the Grundberg case began to attract publicity.[7]

Grundberg's lawyers demanded access to Upjohn's data on trials conducted to test the safety and effectiveness of the drug prior to marketing. The company attempted to prevent access to these documents, arguing that under copyright law they were confidential. However, the federal court in the central district of Utah held that the Upjohn copyright was invalid in the Grundberg case. The court also took the view that, even if the copyright were valid, it was an abuse of the copyright to use it in an attempt to hamper opponents in litigation by limiting their copying of documents. Nevertheless, in subsequent cases concerning Halcion, Upjohn pursued this 'copyright strategy' whenever plaintiffs' lawyers sought to negate protective orders of confidentiality over the unpublished data provided. Clearly, the company did not want its confidential data to become public but, for the most part, it did not succeed in preventing its release. No less than 90,000 pages of documentation were released by court order in a case set to trundle on for many months, even years.

It was about the time when the Adam and Oswald paper was published, in *Pharmacopsychiatry* in May 1989, that Oswald agreed to act as an expert in the litigation in Utah between Grundberg and Upjohn. Three months before that, Oswald had written a letter to the *British Medical Journal* claiming that, unlike other commonly prescribed benzodiazepines, Halcion had been shown to cause anxiety in controlled studies. He attributed this in part to its much shorter half-life.[8] In August 1989, he took his criticisms much further, calling for the withdrawal of Halcion from the market in the *Lancet*. Oswald argued that while sleeping pills are mostly taken by the middle aged or older, sometimes for many months, Halcion had been marketed following controlled trials in which only 11 patients over the age of 40 were known to have taken 0.25 mg per day for more than two weeks, and even fewer had received 0.5 mg per day for over two weeks. He acknowledged that, subsequently, there had been three double-blind controlled trials with adequate numbers of subjects aged over 40 and taking the drug for longer than two weeks; but, claimed Oswald, all three of these studies found that taking Halcion regularly caused daytime anxiety. According to Oswald, the shorter studies funded by Upjohn did not allow enough time for the possible development of tolerance and changes in brain function produced by Halcion, which lead to daytime anxiety. He concluded:

> It is now ten years since the Lancet *published a letter from a* Dutch psychiatrist, Dr van der Kroef, *who described anxiety, derealization, paranoid ideas, and other mental changes*

> *associated with triazolam (Halcion)... Van der Kroef was right and the Netherlands have been right to ban triazolam [Halcion]. People who complain of poor sleep are generally anxious people. If after three weeks they are even more anxious, doctor and patient alike easily attribute any change to the patient rather than to the drug. It is a matter for concern that Halcion was marketed on the basis of deficient research. It should no longer be sold.*[9]

By January 1990, he had prepared a critical appraisal of Halcion for Grundberg's lawyers and sent a copy of this to the British drug regulatory authorities, the Medicines Control Agency (MCA).[10] Moreover, in trawling through the enormous quantity of data submitted to them by Upjohn, the expert advisors to Grundberg's lawyers discovered that evidence regarding one important drug trial, known as Protocol 321 (P321) was missing from this material. On 14 June 1991, US District Judge Greene decided whether numerous documents produced by Upjohn and designated as confidential under the terms of a previous court's protective order should continue to be regarded as confidential, and whether Upjohn's claim to copyright in documents should result in restricting their publication. Judge Greene reached the following conclusions:

> *It appears that Upjohn intended to use the copyright laws to thwart accessibility to the public of information contained in documents which may be offered and admitted into evidence in court proceedings ... to whatever extent Upjohn may have a copyrightable interest in the litigation documents, such may not be asserted or maintained to impede or prevent the free use and accessibility of such documents in the context of this [Grundberg] litigation.*[11]

He also ruled that the protective order should be modified so that the documents would be released from its terms once used in the litigation.

On 12 June 1991, Judge Boyce, in charge of the Grundberg case, decided that the reports of P321 might be relevant to the case and overruled Upjohn's objection to the release of underlying raw data concerning a 0.5 mg dose of Halcion during that drug trial. On 16 July 1991, Judge Boyce lifted a ban on the release of a further 8000 pages of evidence to the expert advisors of Grundberg's lawyers, including *all* material from P321: 1.0 mg and 0.5 mg data.[12] In mid August, just two weeks before the case was due to go to trial, Upjohn settled out of court.[13] According to the international pharmaceutical trade journal *Scrip*, 'the case was expected to have generated more publicity for reports of adverse effects associated with the drug'.[14]

Meanwhile, as Halcion was about to face its biggest challenge, the Dutch regulatory authorities reapproved the drug for treatment of insomnia at the lower daily doses of 0.125 mg and 0.25 mg, recommending the lowest possible effective dose for the shortest possible duration. The decision by the Dutch regulators to suspend Halcion's licences in 1979 was opposed by Upjohn, and was eventually referred to The Netherlands State Council. The 'reapproval' resulted, in part, from the fact that the state council had ruled that some of the views of the Dutch regulatory authorities in suspending the product's licences were inappropriate.[15] However, it should be understood that just prior to banning Halcion in The Netherlands in 1980, the Dutch regulatory authorities offered to allow the 0.25 mg tablet to remain on the market with a revised label recommending the reduced dose of 0.25 mg and warning about additional ADRs, but Upjohn refused to accept that offer.[16] Thus, the 'reapproval' was substantially what the company had been offered ten years before.

The hottest data in town: Protocol 321

Protocol 321 was conducted inside Jackson State Prison in southern Michigan between 1972–1973. Upjohn had a special clinic in the prison which it used for drug trials. In the early 1970s, it was quite common for pharmaceutical companies to conduct clinical trials in prison. The P321 study was an early double-blind controlled trial of six weeks' duration, conducted inside the clinic, involving 58 healthy volunteers who were selected for good physical health, no history of mental illness and no recent use of psychotropic drugs. It was the only long-term study that used Halcion at the 1.0 mg dose.[17] As a phase I study, the purpose of P321 was to 'determine the tolerance of normal prison male volunteers to daily administration of U-33,030 [Halcion] for a period of six weeks, and to determine whether this long-term administration would produce any adverse effects'.[18] The principal investigator for the trial was a Dr Harold Oster, who was not employed by Upjohn but had worked for them as a contract physician on clinical research projects since 1957. Most of his contract research for Upjohn was undertaken at the Jackson Prison clinic. According to Oster, a medical/ethical review committee scrutinized the proposal for P321 and approved it.[19]

   In effect, P321 had two parts. In the first part of the trial 30 subjects took 1.0 mg per day of Halcion while 16 took placebo; in the second, eight subjects took 0.5 mg per day while four took placebo.[20] The results of the trial were summarized by Upjohn in a technical report which formed part of the company's New Drug Application to the FDA (and was subsequently forwarded to the UK authorities). The FDA did not include P321 as a pivotal study for Halcion, but some FDA scientists considered it to be an important study because 'it was one of few long-term high dose studies done, was conducted early in Halcion's clinical development [and] took place in a managed environment using normal healthy volunteers'.[21]

   During P321 any medical events, such as ADRs, were recorded on case report forms (CRFs) for each of the subjects and could also be suggested by subjects' responses to questionnaires, which were completed by the prisoners each day that they were on the drug trial. The technical report for the trial was written in two stages. Firstly, summary tables of medical events and subject responses were constructed from the CRFs and the questionnaire data by Upjohn's biostatistical department under Dr Carl Metzler, one of the authors of the report. And secondly, Mr William Veldkamp, the first-named author of the report, constructed the word text, including the summary of the report, from the tables supplied to him by the biostatistical department without referring back to the CRFs.[22]

The validity of Upjohn's technical report for P321 was not questioned until 1991 when, in connection with the Grundberg litigation against Upjohn, Oswald discovered that there were *wholesale omissions of medical events*. Those omissions can be identified by comparing the technical report with the CRFs and the subject questionnaire responses. Upjohn has admitted that the technical report contained 'transcription errors'.[23] In fact, *only 67 per cent of Halcion-related and 79 per cent of placebo-related medical events were contained in the report*.[24] Furthermore, according to Upjohn, these errors and omissions also went unnoticed by anyone in the company until their lawyers discovered them in the same litigation.[25] We do not suggest otherwise.

More specifically, the company reported that two subjects taking placebo became paranoid when, almost certainly, only one did so.[26] In addition, Oswald argued that seven subjects taking Halcion developed symptoms of paranoia, whereas the company reported only two such cases.[27] According to Oswald, this gave the erroneous impression that Halcion was no more likely than a placebo to cause paranoia.[28] Certainly, according to the CRF and subject questionnaire data, as many as nine subjects on 1.0 mg per day reported adverse psychiatric effects, six of them mentioning paranoia, while taking Halcion as summarized in Table 5.1. For example, a nursing note on Subject 16's CRF stated:

Table 5.1 *Upjohn's Protocol 321: side-effect data and technical report*

Subject number	Subject responses recorded on CRFs and questionnaires	What is recorded in the technical report tables
1	nervousness/restlessness	–
8	paranoia, loss of memory	paranoia, loss of memory
9	paranoia, loss of mental ability, restlessness/nervousness	anxiety, abdominal gas, gas in chest
10	paranoia	paranoia, depression, etc
16	restlessness/nervousness weird feeling in head, amnesia	nervousness, lapse of memory, poor concentration
20	paranoia, severe depression, bizarre thoughts	depression, bad dreams, weird thoughts
34	depression, paranoia, severe restlessness/nervousness	–
42	hallucinations, blurred vision, ringing in ears	ringing in ears, blurred vision
47	paranoia, loss of memory	–

Key: – means that the technical report simply omitted the subject altogether for side effects
Sources: Royal Courts of Justice, 1994, 'Judgement between the Upjohn Company and Upjohn Ltd and Professor Ian Oswald and between Dr Royston Frederick Drucker and Professor Oswald and between the Upjohn Company and Upjohn Ltd and the BBC and Tom Mangold before Mr Justice May', Beverley F Nunnery, London, 27 May, pp 57–61; W Veldkamp, A D Rudzik and C M Metzler, 1973, Upjohn Pharmaceutical Research and Development Technical Report, U-33,030: *Six-Week Tolerance Study, SPSM Protocol No 321, Phase II Study*, 27 August

Table 5.2 *Extent of completion and drop-out in Protocol 321*

Number of subjects	Days in study
30	1
27	8
25	15
22	29
17	43

Source: W Veldkamp, A D Rudzik and C M Metzler, 1973, Upjohn Pharmaceutical Research and Development Technical Report, U-33,030: *Six-Week Tolerance Study, SPSM Protocol No. 321, Phase II Study*, 27 August, p 5

> *... refused to take medicine because of undesirable side effects, ie fatigue, but too restless to sleep. Had a weird feeling in head as if pressure was building up inside, then suddenly it seemed to explode and he felt better afterwards but was really scared.*[29]

Subject 20, who dropped out of the trial after 26 days on 1.0 mg of Halcion, complained that he experienced too many side effects such as depression, paranoia, severe restlessness/nervousness, lapse of memory, bad dreams, 'real bizarre thoughts', and feeling like he was going to 'fall off the fourth gallery'.[30]

Not all 30 of the subjects, who began the study on a daily dose of 1.0 mg of Halcion, completed. According to the technical report, only 17 completed the study and three of those had to be dropped to the 0.5 mg dose in order to continue (see Table 5.2).

Regarding the 13 subjects who did not complete this part of P321, the technical report states:

> *... five (subjects 18, 29, 31, 35 and 44) were dropped for disciplinary reasons, three (subjects 1, 9 and 43) were paroled or transferred, four (subjects 16, 28, 34 and 47) asked to be dropped from the study because of side effects and one (subject 17) was dropped by the clinician because the subject complained of chest pains.*[31]

This commentary omitted to mention that Subject 20 dropped out after 26 days because of adverse psychiatric effects.[32] In fact, Subject 28 was on placebo, so that was also incorrect in the text of the report. Moreover, Subject 1 dropped out having complained of restlessness/nervousness; but he was recorded as having dropped out because he was paroled. According to Upjohn, the events were recorded in this way because it was thought that Subject 1 was making up his adverse effects in order to get paroled. The accuracy of Upjohn's version of events about Subject 1's drop out is unknown, but it is known that the technical report did not even mention Subject 1's adverse effects of restlessness/nervousness.[33] Furthermore, the technical report gave little emphasis to reports of amnesia. One of the report's tables entitled 'Symptoms Most Frequently Reported by Subjects in the U-33,030 Group' included 'nausea' as a heading, but not 'amnesia', even though the latter *symptom* was more frequently reported. Although fewer *subjects* reported feelings of amnesia than of nausea, five of the 30 patients taking 1.0 mg of Halcion reported loss of memory.[34]

Oswald took the view that the medical events reported by subjects, on the left of Table 5.1, should have been interpreted as adverse psychiatric effects of Halcion – an interpretation which led him to claim that a major finding of P321 was that the drug caused mental illness.[35] This was not the conclusion of Upjohn's technical report, whose one-page summary listed side effects such as drowsiness, headaches and loss of coordination, but did not mention amnesia, depression or paranoia:

> *The incidence of side effects was greater on U-33,030 [Halcion] than on placebo and included such effects as drowsiness, impaired coordination, headache, restlessness, lightheadedness and nausea. Subjects receiving placebo complained of drowsiness, restlessness, headache and nausea. There was some indication of a development of tolerance to the residual effects of U-33,030 [Halcion] since reports of morning hangover showed a significant decline after the first week on the high dose of U-33,030 [Halcion].*[36]

While some of the omissions in the technical report remain irrational and inexplicable, the evidence suggests that one reason why the report did not highlight adverse psychiatric effects in the ways advocated by Oswald is that the clinical investigators employed or contracted by Upjohn at the time did not regard the subjects' reports on the left of Table 5.1 as serious. Dr Oster, the principal clinical investigator for P321, visited the prison clinic almost every day and he was not greatly concerned about adverse psychiatric effects during the study. Upjohn's three authors of the technical report also held this view.[37] According to Oster, he did not disregard subjects' reports of paranoia and depression during the trial, but he did not think that they were indications of psychiatric disorder. He had not received reports of paranoia in other drug trials, but he felt that psychologically there was nothing abnormal about these reports, given the prison environment.[38] Veldkamp was also aware that there had been reports of paranoia, but he did not think it was unexpected, although it had not been reported on his previous studies that were concerned with other drugs.[39] Indeed, this perspective is reflected in the one and only paragraph within the technical report which mentions paranoia:

> *Approximately half the subjects who had been on U-33,030 [Halcion] considered the drug as non-acceptable and would not be willing to take it again. One reason that may account for the high percentage of non-acceptance among these prison subjects is that most of these men were not insomniacs and were receiving a relatively large dose of U-33,030. This caused them to experience some depression or drowsiness and a feeling of some*

> *loss of mental ability... This gave them a feeling of being less*
> *able to defend themselves if some trouble developed and was*
> *the reason for some subjects reporting feelings of paranoia.*[40]

Professor Hindmarsh at the University of Surrey, who has been a consultant for Upjohn, supported the interpretation contained in the technical report even after the revelations about its errors and omissions. He argued that because the subjects went back to the general prison at night, having spent their days in the special clinic, they returned to their cells with 'a powerful sedative on board', which made them feel less alert and able to cope with the hazards of their immediate environment. Even with the benefit of hindsight in the 1990s, Hindmarsh disputed that P321 showed genuine, clinical incidences of paranoia:

> *Just because someone says they are feeling paranoid does not*
> *mean they're suffering from paranoia... in fact, quite the*
> *reverse. Within Jackson Prison there were something like four*
> *homosexual rapes every month, there were murders, three*
> *guards had been killed, the prisoners were always robbing each*
> *other... Saying, 'man, I feel paranoid' was just part of the*
> *cultural argot of the place.*[41]

The implication of these interpretations of P321 by Oster, Veldkamp and Hindmarsh is that the adverse psychiatric experiences of the subjects were caused by being in prison rather than by Halcion. We do not suggest that those interpretations are, or were, anything other than genuinely held. On the other hand, the fact that Jackson Prison was Upjohn's phase I facility in which the company undertook many other drug studies that did not show such paranoia undermines those interpretations which implicate the prison rather than the drug.[42] Furthermore, the technical report, as produced in 1973, does itself imply that the reported 'loss of mental ability' was *dose related*:

> *All seven subjects who received 0.5 mg of U-33,030 [Halcion]*
> *rated the drug as acceptable and all would be willing to take*
> *the medication again. This is in contrast to approximately half*
> *of the subjects on the 1.0 mg dose who rated the drug as*
> *unacceptable.* This could largely be attributed to the fact that 13
> of 22 subjects on the large dose of U-33,030 [Halcion] reported
> some loss of mental ability during the study, while only one of six
> subjects reported this on the lower dose of drug *(emphasis*
> *added).*[43]

If the 'loss of mental ability' were dose related, then it is likely to have been caused by the drug.

After reviewing P321, Professor Frank Ayd, who had organized the Boston conference on Upjohn's behalf and led the signatories to the *Lancet* letter that discounted the van der Kroef ADR reports, became convinced that the Boston meeting experts had not been given all the relevant documents by Upjohn.[44] He further concluded:

> *Upjohn had information which would have supported some of van der Kroef's criticisms, information which should have been disclosed to the experts in Boston... If I had known then what I know now, I would not have written and signed the [Lancet] letter.*[45]

It is neither known, nor being suggested, that Upjohn deliberately withheld information from the Boston conference experts. What is clear, however, is that, for Ayd, the *Lancet* article undermining van der Kroef's findings in 1979 became invalid in 1991.

The letter in the *Lancet* in 1979 by Ayd and his coauthors at the Boston conference stated that 'studies with doses up to 1.0 mg have not shown the symptoms noted by van der Kroef'.[46] However, patients had reported similar symptoms in P321, but none of the Dutch, British or American regulatory authorities asked for the case report forms (CRFs) for P321 prior to approval and Upjohn did not provide them at that time.[47] Even discounting the errors and omissions in Upjohn's analysis and reporting of P321, the knowledge of this trial, which the company had when van der Kroef reported his findings, could have led them to respond differently to the potential public health problem he raised. Rather than concentrating their efforts on trying to demonstrate that his findings were false, Upjohn scientists could have been more thorough in searching for evidence from trials that might have supported van der Kroef.

Following the van der Kroef reports, Upjohn did review some of its data on Halcion in 1979 and 1980. Indeed, in June 1982, the company wrote to doctors in the UK boasting that:

> *In 1979 and 1980, Upjohn undertook a comprehensive review of all available evidence to determine the truth regarding allegations against Halcion in Holland. These efforts included a complete reanalysis of all available safety data from clinical trials.*[48]

However, according to Upjohn staff, this 'review of all available evidence' did not include a reanalysis of CRFs for Halcion trials.[49] Had it done so, one would expect the company to have discovered the errors and omissions in P321. In any case, although Upjohn reviewed a lot of technical reports on clinical trials with *patients*, the company may not have reviewed even the technical report for P321 because it was a tolerance study with *healthy volunteers*.[50] Evidently, the company's review was not as thorough as it could have been and measures to ensure that is was more complete could have been taken in preference to marshalling efforts to discredit van der Kroef.

Indeed, given the results of P321, as reported in the technical report, not to mention an accurate representation of the results, Upjohn's decision to market the 1.0 mg dose for most patients and the 0.5 mg dose for elderly patients in The Netherlands seems highly questionable. For example, after P321, Veldkamp 'thought that Upjohn had enough data to show that 1.0 mg was a dose that caused *excessive* sleep [emphasis added] and some effects which the subjects did not like'.[51] Furthermore, minutes of an Upjohn meeting as early as 30 July 1974 stated that a detailed examination of the clinical studies with *non*-elderly patients had shown 11 per cent drop outs due to adverse effects on 0.5 mg of Halcion compared with 2.9 per cent on 30 mg of Dalmane.[52] In 1977, when Halcion was marketed at the 0.5 mg dose for the elderly in The Netherlands, Upjohn had only conducted one Halcion study with elderly patients for longer than 14 days, and that was with the 0.25 mg dose.[53] Given that the drug was capable of such excessive and adverse effects in healthy men at the 1.0 mg dose, and non-elderly patients at the 0.5 mg dose, the risk to the sick and elderly, who might also be taking other medications, was likely to be much greater.

Similar comments could be made about the potential amnesiac effects of the drug. The company's determined efforts to 'refute' Kales's 1976 publication, which included his concerns about Halcion's potential to cause amnesia, might have been better directed at an examination of evidence in earlier trials that might have supported his concerns. Among subjects taking 1.0 mg of Halcion in P321, amnesia was reported relatively frequently. At a symposium held in New York on 5 January 1990, even Dr David Greenblatt, generally regarded as a supporter of Halcion, commented:

> *It is now clear that the original dosage recommendations for Halcion were much too high. In many persons, 0.5 mg of Halcion produces coma, which can last for six to 12 hours. There is a large incidence of anterograde amnesia which is very significant clinically... Although 0.25 mg of Halcion has less consistent efficacy, it is considerably safer with regard to the occurrence of these adverse reactions. We do not expect that these reactions will disappear altogether, because 0.25 mg or even 0.125 mg of Halcion can produce amnesia. But we have to put the reports of adverse effects with Halcion in the context of our knowledge that for the first five years or so of use, the dosage recommendations were far too high.*[54]

Enough is enough: the British suspend Halcion

Following Oswald's call for the withdrawal of Halcion in the *Lancet* on safety grounds, the British Committee on Safety of Medicines (CSM) reconsidered the drug. By the end of 1989 the UK Licensing Authority had written to Upjohn drawing its attention to a disturbing number of spontaneous reports concerning Halcion in the UK and the US. However, in January 1990, the CSM concluded that, although there was a signal, it was not proven that severe adverse psychiatric effects were more common with Halcion than with other benzodiazepines. The CSM requested that Upjohn conduct further studies to allay fears about amnesia and psychiatric side effects. The company indicated that they felt there was sufficient evidence on the safety of the drug and that further studies were not warranted. Upjohn officials were eventually persuaded by the chairman of the CSM to change their minds and discussions on early draft protocols began towards the end of 1990.[55] Even at this stage relations between the British regulators and Upjohn concerning Halcion were still on a cooperative footing and the *CSM continued to award the benefit of the scientific doubt to Upjohn and Halcion*.

Nevertheless, serious criticisms of the drug continued to surface in the medical literature. In April 1991 Dr Edward Bixler and his colleagues at Pennsylvania State University College of Medicine published findings in the *Lancet* that Halcion caused frequent memory impairment compared with Restoril or placebo. In controlled double-blind sleep research, Bixler found that five of six subjects taking 0.5 mg of Halcion for five nights reported at least one episode of next-day memory impairment or amnesia. In total there were 12 such episodes on Halcion out of a total of 30 subject-drug nights (ie a rate of 40 per cent). By contrast, in the Restoril group of subjects there were no such episodes of memory impairment. The Pennsylvania researchers concluded:

> *Impairment of delayed recall [evening memory of tasks performed in the morning] was significantly and several times greater [with Halcion] than that in the temazepam [Restoril] or placebo groups. Next-day memory impairment/amnesia after a bedtime dose of triazolam [Halcion] tended to increase with continued or intermittent drug use... A year ago, Oswald proposed that triazolam [Halcion] be withdrawn from the market because of its adverse effects. Considerable and compelling scientific evidence exists (including the findings of this study) to support Oswald's position... In the meantime, the labelling for triazolam should be strengthened to warn patients that its adverse effects are common and severe. Patients should also be told of the likelihood of memory impairment/amnesia, so that they can make an informed decision on whether they wish to take the drug.[56]*

In noting that the recommended daily dose for Halcion had been reduced from 0.5 mg to 0.25 mg since the study began, these researchers warned that memory impairment had been seen at the lower dose of the drug. According to Bixler and his colleagues, neither dose had an adequate benefit-risk ratio, and lowering the dose to 0.25 mg actually decreased this ratio because, they argued, Halcion's efficacy was reduced far more than the adverse effects.

The perspective of the British regulatory authorities towards Halcion changed when, on 3 July 1991, they read about omissions of data in P321 in *Scrip*, a pharmaceutical industry newsletter that was reporting on the Grundberg case.[57] On 14 July 1991 the British regulatory authorities, the MCA, asked Upjohn to provide previously undisclosed data on Halcion which had emerged in the Grundberg case, together with a 'summary of the implications for [Halcion] product licences'.[58] The company had informed the FDA of 'transcription errors' in P321 on 28 June 1991. However, by 12 August 1991,

Upjohn had still not told the MCA about the deficiencies in that drug trial. On that date Dr Susan Wood of the MCA telephoned Upjohn about Halcion data in the Grundberg case and was informed by Upjohn that drug safety information relating to P321 had not been disclosed to the British regulatory authorities at the time of the original Halcion product licence application. A few days later, the MCA wrote to Upjohn stating that it regarded the company's initial omission of safety data as a very serious matter and requested the data, together with evidence in support of the contention that the omissions resulted from 'transcription errors'.[59] Over the next week, the company admitted to the MCA that as a result of litigation in the US they had identified some omissions of medical events due to 'transcription errors' in P321. Nevertheless, Upjohn claimed that the omissions of adverse effects did not alter the risk-benefit assessment of the drug.

On 24 August 1991, Oswald published a letter in the *Lancet* calling on Upjohn to offer the case report forms from P321 for scrutiny by regulatory agencies worldwide.[60] Two weeks later, Keith Krzywicki, the managing director of Upjohn UK Ltd, responded by arguing that Oswald's demands were a 'moot point' because the clinical trial data he asked to be shared with regulatory authorities 'had already been voluntarily provided by Upjohn to the MCA'.[61] Krzywicki further reassured doctors that Upjohn:

> ... *recently became aware of a clerical error from one study done nearly 20 years ago. The transcription error has no bearing on the safety and efficacy of Halcion under the approved use and dosing regimen.*[62]

Krzywicki described the wholesale omissions from P321 as 'a clerical error', even though, on 15 August 1991, Dr Metzler at Upjohn who was investigating the P321 omissions internally found part of the study to be 'grossly in error'.[63] On 22 August 1991, as an internal meeting of Upjohn officials in Kalamazoo convened to discuss a response to Oswald's *Lancet* letter, concern was expressed about the possibility that data had been manipulated.[64] We are *not* suggesting that P321 data *was* manipulated, but that possibility was discussed within Upjohn. Moreover, it was stretching the truth to say that Upjohn had 'voluntarily' provided the P321 clinical trial data to the MCA since it had only submitted the data to the MCA under the compulsion of the 1968 UK Medicines Act when required to do so by the British regulatory authorities.[65]

Despite Upjohn's claims that the revelations about P321 did not change the risk-benefit assessment of Halcion at the licensed doses of 0.25 mg and 0.125 mg, on 2 October the British Licensing Authority suspended all the drug's licences in the UK following the advice of the CSM.[66] Upjohn claimed that 600,000–700,000 patients were being treated with the product when this happened.[67] The news of the data omitted from P321 in the product licence application in the UK had provoked the MCA and the CSM into conducting a review not only of P321, together with all its case report forms (CRFs) for the first time, but also the multidose controlled clinical trials with Halcion and all the post-marketing spontaneous reports of adverse effects associated with the drug in the UK and the US.

The CSM's advice to suspend Halcion's licences was based on these three crucial data sets.[68] The committee's justification for its advice revealed that what Krzywicki referred to as a 'clerical error' in P321 actually consisted of the omission of some 330 medical events regarding the subjects taking the 1.0 mg dose. Extraordinarily, only 27 per cent of the medical events had originally been submitted to the regulatory authorities when the drug was licensed.[69] Prior to UK approval of Halcion in 1978, Upjohn had used the incomplete P321 data to reassure the CSM about the drug's long-term safety, albeit unwittingly.[70] This had a significant influence because P321 was one of the few longer-term trials. According to the CSM, the 'new' complete P321 results 'showed that psychiatric side effects occurred in 14 out of 30 of subjects who took 1.0 mg of Halcion compared to three out of 20 who took placebo'.[71] In fact, there were 11 cases of memory loss, seven cases of depression and seven cases of paranoia. Consequently, the committee found that 'there now appears to be a clear difference between Halcion and placebo in occurrence of psychiatric symptoms and this study [P321] estimates that they occur at a very high frequency of about 50 per cent of patients'.[72]

The CSM's review revealed that approval of Halcion in the UK had been supported by just six controlled clinical trials longer than 14 days, two comparing Halcion with placebo and four comparing it with another hypnotic, Dalmane (flurazepam). Remarkably, in these studies, which had formed an important part of the initial product licence application, almost 20 per cent of the patients taking Halcion withdrew – about three times the rate for placebo or Dalmane. This striking information was available to the British regulatory authorities as early as 1978. Yet, it seems from this CSM review that they did not pursue the reasons for these withdrawals thoroughly prior to approval in 1978:

> *In the original application the reasons for withdrawal were not usually provided on a case-by-case basis and it was therefore uncertain what side effects caused these patients to withdraw and when they first occurred. Upjohn have now provided these data and the reasons for an excess of withdrawals due to side effects in Halcion-treated patients compared to those treated with placebo or Dalmane have been assessed.[73]*

Had the British regulatory authorities demanded this data prior to approval in 1978 they would have found that a substantial number of Halcion withdrawals were due to potentially serious psychiatric adverse effects. In fact, there were 18 such withdrawals among patients taking Halcion, only one among patients taking Dalmane and none among the placebo groups. In short, in controlled clinical studies of greater than 14 days, 'the frequency of withdrawal due to psychiatric side effects was 9.9 per cent on 0.5 mg of Halcion, 1.9 per cent on 30 mg of Dalmane and 0.5 per cent on placebo'.[74] According to the CSM, 'these findings confirm that drug-induced psychiatric side effects similar to those seen in P321 occur at a dose of 0.5 mg of Halcion and in a population of outpatient insomniacs'.[75]

Regarding post-marketing spontaneous reports of adverse drug reactions, it was revealed that over the eight-year period – 1979–1986 – Halcion was often associated with well over ten times as many psychiatric reactions as other benzodiazepines (see Table 5.3).

Table 5.3 *UK spontaneous reports of psychiatric reactions by year for specified benzodiazepines per million prescriptions*

Year	1979	1980	1981	1982	1983	1984	1985	1986
Triazolam (Halcion)	114	44	14	43	20	5.5	1.8	2.5
Flurazepam	0.9	0.9	0.4	1.3	0.5	0.0	2.2	0.0
Nitrazepam	0.1	0.9	0.5	0.0	0.3	0.0	0.8	0.4
Temazepam	4.1	4.5	3.7	1.9	2.2	1.7	1.3	0.4
Lorazepam	2.4	3.3	1.4	2.0	4.3	1.9	6.7	1.9
Diazepam	0.4	0.7	0.1	0.1	0.2	0.4	0.4	1.0

Source: CSM, 1991, 'Confidential' Report to the EU's Committee for Proprietary Medicinal Products (CPMP), Table 5

Table 5.3 shows that throughout the early and mid 1980s spontaneous ADR data in the UK supported the Wyskowski and Barash analysis of FDA SRS data in the US. According to the CSM, in both the UK and the US, 'reporting rates for psychiatric reactions have been consistently and substantially greater for Halcion than any other benzodiazepine' and, in the UK, '161 of 390 reports (41 per cent) for Halcion are of psychiatric reactions and 34 per cent and 53 per cent of these occurred at the low doses of 0.125 mg and 0.25 mg respectively'.[76]

The committee also noted that the large-scale post-marketing EMIC epidemiological study in Canada showed that Halcion was associated with more frequent memory impairment than Dalmane, and that the small controlled clinical trial published by Bixler and his colleagues earlier in 1991 showed that 0.5 mg of Halcion produced frequent memory impairment, unlike Restoril or placebo'.[77] From this review of Halcion data the CSM reached the following conclusions:

1   There is a clear causal association between Halcion and serious psychiatric adverse reactions.
2   The frequency of serious psychiatric adverse reactions is significantly greater than with comparator hypnotics.
3   There is an insufficient margin of safety in relation to dose.
4   The risks of treatment with Halcion outweigh the benefits.[78]

Making up data and other irregularities: disqualified clinical investigators

Generally, when a regulatory agency approves a drug for marketing, the most important data are the controlled clinical trials. It is not an understatement to say that such data forms a central part of the basis for approval of most new drugs and Halcion was no exception. The most important clinical trials submit-

ted in support of the UK product licence application for Halcion in 1978 were
the multiple dose studies comparing the drug with either placebo or another
sleeping pill. There were ten such trials of two weeks or less and six trials of
four weeks or more (see Table 5.4). The six longer trials may be regarded as
particularly important given the tendency for tranquillizers and hypnotics to
be taken for much longer than two weeks (see Chapter 1).

Table 5.4 *Multiple-dose comparative clinical trials submitted with UK Halcion licence application*

Study number	Drugs and dosage	Number of days	Number of patients
Long term			
P6045	Halcion 0.5 mg	28	129
	Placebo		
P6046	Halcion 0.5 mg	28	103
	Dalmane 30 mg		
P6047	Halcion 0.5 mg	42	125
	Placebo		
P6048	Halcion 0.5 mg	42	145
	Dalmane 30 mg		
P6023	Halcion 0.6 mg	84	51
	Dalmane 30 mg		
P6049	Halcion 0.5 mg	91	139
	Dalmane 30 mg		
Short term			
P6041	Halcion 0.5 mg	7	174
	Placebo		
P6042	Halcion 0.5 mg	7	127
	Dalmane 30 mg		
P6009	Halcion 0.5 mg	7	111
	Secobarbital 100 mg		
P6400	Halcion 0.25–0.5 mg	7	102
	Dalmane 15–30 mg		
P6401	Halcion 0.25 mg	7	67
	Placebo		
P6004	Halcion 0.6 mg	7	37
	Dalmane 30 mg		
P6010	Halcion 0.3–0.6 mg	7	83
	Dalmane 15–30 mg		
P6043	Halcion 0.5 mg	14	277
	Placebo		
P6044	Halcion 0.5 mg	14	295
	Dalmane 30 mg		
P6016	Halcion 0.5 mg	14	31
	Dalmane 30 mg		

Source: CSM Report to CPMP, 9 December 1991, Table 2

On 15 November 1982 the FDA produced its summary basis of approval (SBA) for Halcion, which outlined the specific clinical studies on which marketing of the drug in the US was based. The FDA goes further than the British regulatory authorities by defining crucial or 'pivotal' clinical studies in SBAs, together with less vital 'supportive' trials. For Halcion, there were three 'pivotal' and nine 'supportive' studies.(see Table 5.5).

Table 5.5 *Single- and multiple-dose clinical trials in FDA's Halcion SBA*

Study number	Drugs and dosage	Number of days	Number of patients
Pivotal			
P6024	Halcion 0.5 mg (sleep laboratory study)	14	7
P6041	Halcion 0.5 mg Placebo	7	174
P6045	Halcion 0.5 mg Placebo	28	129
Supportive multiple dose			
P6047	Halcion 0.5 mg Placebo	42	125
P6417	Halcion 0.125 mg Placebo	7	60 (elderly)
P6417A	Halcion 0.125 mg Placebo	7	37 (elderly)
Supportive single dose			
P6040	Halcion 0.5 mg Placebo	–	658
P6007	Halcion 0.25 & 0.5 mg Placebo	–	19 & 12
P6013	Halcion 0.25 mg Placebo	–	18
P6087	Halcion 0.25 mg Dalmane 15 mg	–	35
P6097	Halcion 0.25 mg Dalmane 30 mg	–	42
P6060A	Halcion 0.125 mg Placebo	–	42 (elderly)

Source: FDA *Summary Basis of Approval* (Halcion), 15 November 1982, pp 8–11

Thus, the clinical studies listed in Tables 5.4 and 5.5 formed that backbone of clincal data upon which the British and American regulatory authorities, respectively, decided that Halcion was safe and effective enough to go on the market. Yet, a closer examination of this crucial data uncovers breathtaking results. P6024 was one the FDA's three 'pivotal' studies. It was conducted by Professor Anthony Kales and investigated the effects of 0.5 mg of Halcion on seven insomniacs in a sleep laboratory. As is evident from our discussions in earlier chapters, Kales has been consistently sceptical about the safety and effectiveness of Halcion, and by 1991 he was calling for its complete withdrawal from the market. The other two 'pivotal' studies, P6041 and P6045, were the two largest multiple-dose trials with Halcion in the SBA and involved Dr William Franklin in Houston and several other clinical investigators. For P6045, Franklin was the principal clinical investigator. In P6041, Franklin and four other clinical investigators conducted a multidose trial involving 174 insomniacs in five double-blind clinical studies comparing 0.5 mg per day of Halcion with placebo for 28 days; and in P6045, Franklin and three other clinical investigators compared 0.5 mg per day of Halcion with placebo for 28 days in 129 insomniacs in four double-blind multidose clinical trials.[79] Franklin enrolled 52 per cent of the patients in P6045 and 18 per cent of the patients in P6041.[80] He was also involved in P6040, one of the FDA's single dose 'supportive studies'.[81] Overall he contributed 98 out of the 310 patients in all the three pivotal studies and 20 patients out of 1048 in the supportive studies.[82]

As is shown in Table 5.4, P6041 and P6045 were major clinical studies upon which the British regulatory authorities also relied when deciding to license Halcion. Yet, extraordinarily, just nine days after approving Halcion on the US market, the FDA wrote to Upjohn informing the company that, subsequent to FDA investigations of other trials, Franklin had admitted that he submitted false data, failed to maintain adequate and accurate patient case histories and otherwise deliberately violated FDA regulations.[83] Consequently, the agency determined that all of Franklin's data should be regarded as unacceptable and unreliable. In fact, Franklin had been involved in a total of five different clinical trials with Halcion.

P6044, which had also formed a significant part of the UK product licence application, involved a clinical investigator known as Dr Sanguilly. On 1 December 1982, he was also disqualified by the FDA. Some other clinical trials, which were important to approval decisions in the UK and/or the US, also leave something to be desired. Two of the single-dose 'supportive' studies mentioned in the FDA's SBA, P6040 and P6087, involved the Houston-based clinical investigator Dr Louis Fabre.[84] In 1994, the *Houston Chronicle* reported that Upjohn investigated his Halcion trials in the 1970s because of alleged irregularities, such as 'recruiting research patients from a half-way house of alcoholics'.[85] The Upjohn investigator recommended that consideration should be given to deleting the results of his trials from the company's Halcion file. However, he denied the allegations and the Upjohn investigator accepted that ultimately she was unable to verify the allegations against him. According to the *Houston Chronicle*, senior clinical management at Upjohn concluded that 'there was not sufficient evidence to question the validity of the data collected from this site so long ago'.[86]

The clinical trial known as P6047 was one of the FDA's supportive multidose studies and one of the important long-term studies submitted to uphold Halcion's UK licence. Parts of this study involved Dr Lahiri from Detroit and Dr Schlain from Texas. Lahiri enrolled 27 patients on his trial, but all 27 dropped out. He did not maintain records for these drop-outs apparently because he 'misread the protocol' for the study.[87] In effect, all the data on the trial was lost to Upjohn and the study was a complete failure. Although Upjohn did report

Lahiri to the FDA prior to Halcion's approval as a clinical investigator, whose study had been cancelled, he was not mentioned in Upjohn's summary or statistical report on P6047. As for Schlain, he enrolled 63 patients more successfully, but embarked on the highly irregular practice of including himself as one of the subjects as well as his wife.[88]

Two other clinical trials with Halcion, P6415 and P6423, which were not considered to be significant by the British or American regulatory authorities, were conducted by Dr Samuel Fuerst. P6415 had not been regarded as pivotal by the FDA because it compared Halcion with Dalmane, rather than with placebo. Nevertheless, lasting for six months, it was Upjohn's longest double-blind clinical trial with Halcion. But, like Franklin and Sanguilly, Fuerst was disqualified by the FDA.[89] According to Dr Alan Lisook at the FDA's clinical investigations branch, Fuerst just made up his data:

> *Dr Fuerst didn't conduct the trials. As far as we could deter-*
> *mine the trials were not actually done. He submitted to us [the*
> *FDA] case reports forms which were done in his own handwrit-*
> *ing: they described patients who in some cases did not exist; in*
> *other cases the patients did exist but they do not seem to have*
> *ever been in the study. The consent forms were apparently in Dr*
> *Fuerst's own handwriting and were not signed by the patients.*
> *In short, the study was a fictitious study.*[90]

We are not suggesting that Upjohn is, or was, responsible for the conduct of these clinical investigators. Rather, the point is that a substantial and important part of the clinical testing of Halcion for safety and effectiveness, prior to approval, in both the UK and the US left a great deal to be desired, to put it mildly. Upjohn is, of course, responsible for the *company's handling* of the fact that investigators were disqualified and that data was fabricated. It is to this matter that we now turn.

When, on 24 November 1982, the FDA told Upjohn that all Franklin data was unacceptable, they asked the company to consider whether the safety and efficacy claims for Halcion remained justified after the removal of Franklin data. On 30 November 1982 Mr Large, Upjohn's director of drug regulatory affairs, wrote a memo to Dr Robert Straw, Upjohn's director of project management for Halcion, to ascertain whether the trials conducted by Franklin under P6040, P6041 and P6404 were 'pivotal in the evaluation of safety and efficacy' and whether 'their deletion would change any conclusions about safety and efficacy'.[91] At this time Straw was in charge of how clinical trials fed into Halcion's package insert or labelling.

Large's memo did not mention P6045, the pivotal study for which Franklin was the principal clinical investigator. This is because Large himself had *failed to keep adequate and complete files on Franklin.*[92] Upjohn did not receive the FDA's November 1982 summary basis of approval for Halcion until 7 January 1983, so Straw did not have it when he sought to answer Large's queries.[93] That SBA, of course, listed Franklin's central involvement in the pivotal P6045. Having examined data concerning P6040, P6041 and P6404, Straw replied to Large on 7 December 1982 stating that only data from P6040 and P6041 had provided any basis for product labelling and that, because Franklin contributed only 3.6 per cent of Halcion patients in those two trials, it was unlikely that deletion of his data would have a meaningful impact on the overall incidence of reactions.[94]

To obtain full information about the Halcion trials in which Franklin had been involved, Straw merely needed to go to the Upjohn computer to ascertain *all* of Franklin's studies for Upjohn products, or to contact the FDA to obtain this information, but apparently he did neither.[95] *Thus, P6045 was entirely overlooked by both these Upjohn officials.*[96] On 7 April 1983 Upjohn reiterated Straw's assessment in its reply to the FDA with no mention of Franklin's involvement in Protocol 6045 and the reassurance that deletion of his data was insignificant. Evidently, *no one at the FDA checked the validity of Upjohn's assertion for nearly nine years!* On 14 February 1992, the regulatory agency announced:

> *FDA has recently become aware that a clinical investigator who contributed important data to studies of the effectiveness of Halcion had been disqualified by the agency prior to the drug's approval in November 1982. Work of the clinical investigator, Dr William Franklin, was part of two mulitdose, multi-investigator studies identified in FDA's approval documents as 'pivotal'.*[97]

After the FDA had made this discovery, Dr Robert Temple, the agency's director of new drug evaluation, attacked Upjohn's 1983 communication on Franklin, saying: 'The letter is just stunning. It is obviously incomplete, inaccurate in part and generally misleading.'[98] Indeed, the FDA announcement of February 1992 concluded:

> *More troubling are statements made by Upjohn to the effect that Dr Franklin had not played a material role in studies leading to Halcion's new drug application. These statements were made in response to an FDA enquiry shortly after Halcion was approved. Upjohn's statements were incomplete, inaccurate and misleading in that they addressed only his contribution to the safety data and ignored his potentially important role in the evaluation of Halcion's effectiveness.*[99]

If that was troubling, then Upjohn's handling of Fuerst's disqualification is almost beyond belief. On 25 February 1983, Dr Schumann at Upjohn wrote a memo, which went to Straw, noting that earlier that day Lisook at the FDA 'had phoned to say that there were discrepancies in Fuerst's data for P6415, and that Fuerst's explanations for them were "incredible"'.[100] According to the memo, Lisook strongly recommended that Upjohn should undertake a 'rapid and thorough audit' of Fuerst's data.[101] Three days later Straw replied stating that there were no statements on Halcion's labelling derived from P6415.[102] On 27 June 1983 Upjohn wrote to the FDA stating that deletion of the P6415 data 'does not change our conclusions about the safety and efficacy about

Halcion'.[103] Fuerst was found to have fabricated data and on 3 March 1984 the FDA wrote to Upjohn confirming that he was disqualified and asking for reconsideration of claims for safety and efficacy of Halcion with his data removed.[104] However, *according to a 1989 memo by Betty Porter, an Upjohn official, the company did not reanalyse the Halcion data without P6415.*[105] This memo demonstrated that she, at least, was fully aware of Fuerst's disqualification and its relevance to Halcion.

Following the revelations about P321 in the Grundberg litigation, the British regulatory authorities sought more detailed reports about clinical studies with Halcion as a matter of urgency.[106] At a meeting with the MCA on 6 September 1991, Straw provided the authority with copies of the technical reports for various Halcion trials, including P6415, without any mention of the fact that the trial was a fabrication. In this meeting, Upjohn assured the British regulators that the FDA did not have any additional information about the safety of Halcion that would not be given to the MCA. Yet, the MCA was not told about the disqualification of Franklin or Fuerst at that meeting.[107] As a result, the MCA conducted a review of whether it was safe enough for patients to continue to be exposed to Halcion without knowing that some of the data reviewed was unreliable. Even without that knowledge, the MCA still decided the drug was unsafe.

Subsequently, during an interview for the BBC's *Panorama* programme entitled 'Halcion Nightmare' and broadcast on 14 October 1991, Straw relied on P6415 to support the safety and efficacy of Halcion as follows:

Straw: *There are other long-term protocols, some of which have gone on for as long as six months that I am more familiar with than [Protocol 321].*

Mangold: *Which ones?*

Straw: *Protocol 6415.*

Mangold: *And how many patients were on that?*

Straw: *As I remember, there were somewhere in the neighbourhood of 60 or perhaps as high as even 90 patients.*

Mangold: *And what did they take, 1.0 mg or 0.5?*

Straw: *They took 0.5 mg.*

Mangold: *And for how long?*

Straw: *Six months.*

Mangold: *And what were the results on that?*

Straw: *The results on that study were that triazolam [Halcion] was well tolerated for that length of time; it was at least as effective as the comparative drug that was used in that study at the dose at which it was used. There was no tolerance development over that period of time.*[108]

In this interview, Straw never mentioned that Fuerst was disqualified for fabricating data contained in P6415.

After the *Panorama* broadcast when the MCA asked for an explanation of Upjohn's continued reliance on Protocol 6415, Upjohn sent the authority a reassuring reply on 1 April 1992, stating:

> *In late 1982, when the FDA disqualified the three investigators [Franklin, Knapp and Sanguilly], the company reassessed specific databases to judge whether their contributions would materially affect the labelling and overall safety and efficacy profile of Halcion. The company arrived at the conclusion that these investigators' contributions, when removed from the database, did not change the overall assessment of safety and efficacy of Halcion. The FDA did not challenge this assessment.*[109]

As the foregoing analysis shows, this reassurance was misleading for two reasons. Firstly, Upjohn's reassessment of the impact of Franklin's disqualification was flawed and incomplete since it did not include P6045. By 1 April 1992, this was known to Upjohn: just four days earlier, the company had sent a letter and documents to the FDA relating to Franklin's involvement in P6045, stating:

> *With reference to the initial Upjohn response to the FDA's notification of ineligibility of Dr W C Franklin, we wish to point out a discrepancy. In our original response of 7 April 1983 to the FDA notification letter we stated that Dr Franklin conducted three studies with triazolam [Halcion]. We cited two by protocol number (6040 and 6041) specifically because they were among the studies used to generate the adverse reactions section of the labelling. The third protocol 6404 was not used for this purpose. In actuality, Dr Franklin conducted five studies with triazolam as reflected in the attachment of this letter. (The other two Franklin studies were protocols 6045 and 6440). We believe identification of only three of the five studies in the 7 April 1983 letter was due to an oversight in the examination of records in 1982–1983 when attempting to identify Dr Franklin's involvement with Halcion.*[110]

The FDA's failure to challenge Upjohn's 'reassessment' had much more to do with the fact that Upjohn had provided them with inaccurate information than it had with the quality of the 'reassessment', which certainly merited challenge. Upjohn's reassurance was also misleading because it implied that some 'reassessment' was relevant to Fuerst's disqualifiaction, when no reanalysis of the database without his contribution actually took place.

An allegation too far: BBC television Mangolds Upjohn

Twelve days after the British regulatory authorities had suspended Halcion's licences, the BBC broadcast their *Panorama* programme 'The Halcion

Nightmare'. It was presented by Tom Mangold. Clearly this programme embar-rassed Upjohn. When Straw cited Fuerst's fictitious Protocol 6415 to support the safety of Halcion, he did so in the full view of the camera, and Mangold was the first to point out to millions of viewers how astonishing it was that Upjohn's medical scientists continued to rely on fabricated data. During the interview, Straw was filmed sitting beside Dr Jeffrey Jonas, another senior scien-tist at Upjohn. At one point both walked off camera. The *Panorama* broadcast gave the impression that they had left to evade further questioning by Mangold, but Upjohn have denied that they left for that reason and have argued that *Panorama*'s representation of that event was unfair.

Much more seriously, from the outset, the programme claimed to show how Upjohn 'possessed information about its [Halcion's] serious side effects before its launch' and 'how despite hundreds of warnings over the next 14 years, they've continued to deny there's anything seriously wrong with Halcion'. Mangold then launched into an analysis of P321 with the obvious implication that the information of serious side effects possessed by Upjohn was P321 data on adverse psychiatric effects. The implication created by the programme was that Upjohn deliberately covered up P321 data from the late 1970s until the Grundberg case. Furthermore, Oswald claimed on the programme that Dr Roy Drucker, speaking on behalf of Upjohn at the FDA's Psychopharmacological Drugs Advisory Committee (PDAC) on 22 September 1989, lied to the FDA when he stated that 'there is no information available to the Upjohn company outside of this meeting that would tend to substantiate that signal [of adverse psychiatric effects of Halcion presented by Anello at the FDA]'.[111] On 20 January 1992, in an article by Gina Kolata, the *New York Times* reported Oswald as saying that Upjohn had known about the extent of Halcion's adverse effects (such as contained in P321) for 20 years and 'concealed these truths from the world'. Oswald was quoted as saying that 'the whole thing has been one long fraud'.[112] Within a few days Upjohn had retali-ated by issuing press releases accusing Oswald of practising 'junk science' even though in 1975 the company had referred to him as 'a world authority on hypnotics'.[113,114]

As a further response, on 24 January 1992 Upjohn took legal actions for libel in the UK against Mangold and the BBC for the above allegations in the *Panorama* programme, and against Oswald for his allegations in *Panorama* and in the *New York Times*.[115] In a related piece of litigation, Drucker also sued Oswald for libel on the *Panorama* programme. Consequently, the BBC, Mangold and Oswald found themselves attempting to prove the allegation that Upjohn had engaged in a 20-year conspiracy to cover up the adverse effects of Halcion and, in particular, that Drucker had lied to the FDA as part of that cover up. This they failed to do.

In May 1994 in the High Court in London, the judge, Mr Justice May, found in favour of Upjohn and Drucker in the cases involving *Panorama* and the *New York Times* article. In other words, the judge found that overall Upjohn had not been involved in a deliberate and dishonest conspiracy to hide the truth about Halcion's adverse effects and that, in particular, Drucker did not lie to the FDA. The allegations above made by the BBC, Mangold and Oswald were found to be unjustified libels. Oswald had also sued Upjohn for accusing him of 'junk science'. In that case the judge found in favour of Oswald – that is, Upjohn's allegation that Oswald's work was 'junk science' was found to be an unjustified libel. We do not challenge Justice May's judgements in these cases in any way whatsoever.[116]

Costs were awarded to Upjohn against Oswald, together with damages of UK£25,000, while Drucker was awarded damages of UK£75,000, leaving Oswald with a bill approaching UK£1 million which was reportedly being met by the British Medical Defence Union. Against the BBC, costs of UK£1.5 million were awarded to Upjohn plus damages of UK£60,000. This litigation was reported to have cost the BBC the equivalent of 13 editions of Panorama. In the 'junk science' case, Oswald was awarded damages of UK£50,000 to be paid by Upjohn.[117] *

In defending his statement to the FDA's PDAC in September 1989, Drucker argued that it needed to be put in its proper context. Justice May ruled that Oswald had libelled Drucker by taking it out of context and then misrepresenting it as a lie. In the context of the PDAC's review of whether the FDA's spontaneous reporting system data signalled various adverse reactions to Halcion, Drucker said:

I think the next step would then be to ask the question: when we look at appropriate additional data, is there anything that substantiates this signal? I would take the position that we have not seen evidence that substantiates that signal this morning and would also reassure you that there is no information available to the Upjohn company, outside this meeting, that would tend to substantiate that signal.[119]

Oswald alleged that his papers with Morgan and with Adam substantiated the signal, and that Drucker certainly knew about them. However, according to Drucker, by 'additional data' he meant epidemiological studies rather than clinical trials of the kind conducted by Oswald. Moreover, another Upjohn scientist at the PDAC meeting testified that no one present at that PDAC meeting could have been in any doubt that this was what Drucker meant.[120] Accepting, as Justice May has done, the latter view of Drucker's statement, then this is further evidence that the 1989 PDAC focused very narrowly on epidemiological data and neglected clinical studies. Indeed, there is some evidence that Upjohn may not have re-examined any raw clinical data in preparation for the 1989 PDAC meeting.[121]

Leaving Drucker aside, the damages awarded to the Upjohn company were relatively small. This may be because the judge was very critical of Upjohn's

---

* There is some convergence between Justice May's finding and that of a Texas jury at least with regard to Upjohn. In November 1992, a jury in Texas found Upjohn partially negligent in a lawsuit brought by William Freeman, who alleged that Halcion caused him to commit murder. In a rather bizarre verdict, the jury assigned 50 per cent of the responsibility for the murder to the plaintiff, 30 per cent to the doctor who prescribed the drug and 20 per cent to Upjohn. Significantly, the jury found that *Upjohn did not exhibit conscious disregard for human safety* and did not act with malice, but did find that the company had been *grossly negligent*, for which it was fined US$200,000 in punitive damages.[118]

behaviour even though he was not convinced, or even close to being convinced, that they had been involved in a dishonest conspiracy. Regarding Upjohn's handling of van der Kroef's claims about Halcion, Justice May concluded:

> *This can be seen in a poor light as an expression of commercial ethic... It suggests that Upjohn believed in their product... It does, however, show that Upjohn were considering cut-throat commercial tactics.*[122]

On Upjohn's conduct of P321, the judge was equally critical. He described Upjohn's technical report for P321 as 'the product of a time when standards and techniques were nothing like as rigorous as they are today and it is also obviously the product of shoddy work even by its own contemporary standards'.[123] According to Justice May, 'the result was a seriously defective report containing wholesale, but unintentional, omissions'.[124] The judge was even more damning of Upjohn's approach to disqualified clinical investigators, which he described as 'thoroughly discreditable', 'extremely careless' and 'reckless', but not 'consciously dishonest'.[125] Justice May felt the need to comment:

> *Leaving aside any obligation to inform authorities, it is an obvious and elementary necessity that the company's own records should be so organized that the fact of disqualification is sufficiently recorded so that the data is not inadvertently used again.*[126]

During the libel case, Straw was required to explain why he continued to cite Fuerst's P6415 in support of Halcion on *Panorama* years after it had been established as a 'fictitious study'. In response, Straw contended that 'in the heat of a stressful interview it [Fuerst's disqualification] slipped his mind'.[127] However, Justice May considered Straw's explanation to be 'scarcely credible' for the following reasons:

> *Dr Straw personally considered the effects of the disqualification in 1984. Betty Porter knew about it in 1989. Dr Straw's reference to it in the interview is seen to be deliberate and, I think, deliberated. He knew and was able to quote details of the protocol.*[128]

In an attempt to justify their criticisms of Oswald's research as 'junk science', Upjohn had criticized his 1982 paper with Morgan in the *British Medical Journal* as invalid. For example, Purpura described it as 'sensational, unsubstantiated and unscientific speculation'.[129] However, the FDA described Oswald as a 'serious person' and even altered the Halcion package insert as a result of his paper with Morgan to refer to 'the appearance of increased signs of daytime anxiety', despite Upjohn's efforts to persuade them not to do so.[130] Upjohn also argued that Oswald's 1989 paper with Adam in *Pharmacopsychiatry* was nonsense because of the scientific method used. Yet, some studies with Halcion, which had been either conducted by Upjohn scientists and/or supportively cited by Upjohn, had used the same method.[131]

Justice May concluded that the Adam and Oswald paper deserved 'proper consideration' and that his 'basic method of analysis is in concept properly scientific' and 'does not merit the criticisms Upjohn advance'.[132,133] Regarding Oswald's work with Morgan, with Adam and in preparing exhibits for the Grundberg case, Justice May judged:

> *I do not consider that it can properly be described as disreputable ... nor do I think that it is, nor that it may justifiably be described as 'junk science'. On the contrary it is, in my judgement, a proper piece of scientific analysis, amenable to criticism no doubt in a number of respects and dependent on opinions which may be challenged, but deserving nevertheless proper consideration.[134]*

The validity of Oswald's research on Halcion was a particularly important issue to Upjohn because the company claimed that the CSM and the MCA had been strongly influenced by Oswald's intervention. Indeed, Upjohn went so far as to suggest that the MCA did not conduct an independent evaluation of Halcion's safety in September 1991 just prior to suspension. Rather, the company claimed that the British regulators had acted against the drug because of pressure from Oswald and worries about media scrutiny, especially from *Panorama*.[135] Professor Ian Hindmarsh, a consultant for Upjohn at Surrey University in England, also took this view:

> *Here you are, you have just had a* Panorama *programme ['The Opren Scandal'] done [in 1983] on you with the Opren [Oraflex drug in the US] and the whole thing [the CSM and the Department of Health] was made to look fools. Here is* Panorama *crawling around again. Here is some professor in Scotland [referring to Oswald] who is saying: 'You know this drug kills people' or whatever the exaggerations were. The Department of Health is a political thing... They were panicked... They were scared witless that they were going to get another visitation from* Panorama. *And this looked as though it was going to be a problem in the making so they acted precipitately... The MCA were panicked by Oswald, they communicated this panic to the CSM and basically said: 'Look, we are not going to let this through [ie keep Halcion on the market] You cannot do this, we were made to look fools last time'. They probably had words with the chairman of the CSM and said: 'Look, you don't want to end up like Goldberg [chairman of the CSM during the the Opren/Oraflex controversy] in a room at the BBC being filmed with Mangold making you say things you don't want to say'.[136]*

However, Patrick Waller, the MCA's principal medical assessor for Halcion, testified that neither Oswald nor forthcoming publicity from *Panorama* affected his regulatory recommendations about the drug:

> Question: *Did the fact that the* Panorama *programme was going to be devoted to Halcion inject increased urgency into the MCA's enquiries?*
>
> Waller: *Not at all. We'd already made a decision on receiving the data from Protocol 321 that we would take it to the next available meeting of the CSM. That decision was based on the importance, as we perceived it, of the new information and it was not influenced by external considerations.*[137]

Thus, he claimed that potential media exposure did not even add to the urgency with which the British regulatory authorities examined the Halcion case. Waller's testimony was fully accepted by the judge over and above Upjohn's challenges.[138]

It is probably unwise to dismiss the possible influence of the mass media. We believe that forthcoming media criticism probably created a sense of urgency within the MCA and the CSM. For example, Waller admitted that just after learning about the *Panorama* programme, the MCA called an 'extraordinary meeting' of the CSM's Subcommittee on Efficacy and Adverse Reactions (SEAR) to consider Halcion.[139] It seems likely that the considerable attention given to Halcion's safety in the mass media heightened the MCA's concerns about the drug's safety. As for the CSM, two expert scientists who had been involved in advising the MCA about Halcion made the following comments:

> *Obviously when you know the media are interested then it makes you more careful to get it right – that's only human. It does keep you on your toes.*[140]

> *I think committees like the CSM are influenced by the knowledge of how the media is likely to react.*[141]

But these comments are a far cry from justifying Upjohn's 'stronger' claim that Oswald and *Panorama* led the MCA and the CSM to suspend the drug's licences.

Upjohn was also concerned that Oswald's perspective on Halcion might influence other regulatory authorities, especially within Europe. An Upjohn memo by Bruno Musch, the director of Upjohn's Brussels office in 22 October 1991, reports that there was a strong possibility that the European Union's drug safety committee, the Committee for Proprietary Medicinal Products, might recommend the withdrawal of Halcion across the EU in December 1991, and that 'powerful' countries were accepting 'Oswald's hypothesis'. Musch proposed to his Upjohn colleagues that the company should engage in 'discrediting Oswald's hypothesis' and 'use experts to convey our [Upjohn's] messages in this respect to [regulatory] authorities'.[142]

Upjohn's appeal to the Committee on Safety of Medicines

As is their right under the 1968 UK Medicines Act, Upjohn challenged the MCA's decision to suspend Halcion's licences in the UK at a formal hearing before the CSM on 3 December 1991. The company asserted that the atmosphere in Jackson Prison in the early 1970s was violent and frightening. This, they argued, could result in misleading interpretations of all types of medical events, including paranoia – an adverse effect which they contended had not occurred in other clinical trials. Indeed, according to Upjohn, the nature of the P321 data and the environment in which it was collected made it impossible 'to arrive at any conclusion about psychiatric side effects in relation to triazolam [Halcion] whether potentially serious or otherwise'.[143] Furthermore, argued Upjohn, the revelations about subjects taking 1.0 mg of Halcion during P321 did not affect the safety profile of the drug at the licensed doses in the UK: 0.25mg and 0.125mg.[144]

Thus, Upjohn now sought to disown its own phase I clinical study in healthy volunteers, which it had previously submitted as a valid trial to the British, American and other regulatory authorities in the late 1970s and early 1980s in order to gain marketing approval for Halcion around the world. The revelations about P321 in the Grundberg case did, of course, discredit Upjohn's original submission of P321 to regulatory authorities, but they did so on the grounds of Upjohn's incomplete and inaccurate reporting of the data. Those revelations did not have any implications for the validity of the *design* of P321. Rather, they implied that when properly and accurately reported, the data showed that Halcion was very frequently associated with reports of adverse psychiatric effects among the trial subjects. Faced with this indisputable finding, Upjohn attacked the validity of the design of its own trial – a trial whose design Upjohn had not challenged until it was found to show its drug in a poor light. The company's line of attack was not enhanced by the fact that Harold Oster, the clinician contracted by Upjohn to oversee P321, claimed that it was passed by a protocol review committee which he thought was very diligent.[145]

As we mentioned earlier in this chapter, in September 1991 the MCA and the CSM determined that in controlled clinical studies of greater than 14 days, the frequency of withdrawal due to adverse psychiatric effects was 9.9 per cent on 0.5 mg of Halcion, 1.9 per cent on 30 mg of Dalmane and 0.5 per cent on placebo. Regarding these multidose clinical trials comparing 0.5mg of Halcion with 30 mg of Dalmane, Upjohn argued that they were no longer equivalent because since 1988 the 0.5mg Halcion dose had been withdrawn worldwide in favour of the 0.25mg dose.* Hence, argued Upjohn, the properly effective doses for Halcion and Dalmane were 0.25 mg and 30 mg respectively.[146] The implication of this argument is that any comparison of 0.5 mg of Halcion with 30 mg of Dalmane is unfair to Halcion because it will overstate the adverse effects of Halcion relative to Dalmane.

Yet again, Upjohn sought to disown its own clinical trials with Dalmane – trials which the company had previously submitted as valid in order to obtain

---

* Of course it was, in fact, the 0.5 mg *tablet* that was withdrawn in the US, where many patients continued to take a 0.5 mg *dose* after 1988.

marketing approval from regulatory authorities. In particular, as Table 5.4 shows, ten out of the 16 multiple-dose comparative clinical trials submitted to the British regulatory authorities in support of approval in 1978 involved comparisons of 0.5 mg of Halcion with 30 mg of Dalmane. Moreover, in the 1973 technical report for P321, 0.5 mg of Halcion was regarded as equivalent to 30 mg of Dalmane, and in P6049 Upjohn actually stated that 0.5 mg of Halcion was equal to 30 mg of Dalmane in its effect on sleep.[147] Prior to the MCA's decision to suspend Halcion's licences, Upjohn had not told the British regulatory authorities that it believed that over half of the key clinical trials in the UK product licence application involved invalid comparisons because 0.5 mg of Halcion was not equivalent to 30 mg of Dalmane.[148] Indeed, as late as September 1989, Upjohn presented, as valid, comparisons of 0.5 mg of Halcion with 30 mg of Dalmane from the EMIC epidemiological study of insomniacs in Canada to the FDA's PDAC, in support of its argument that the frequency of Halcion's adverse effects was not excessive relative to Dalmane.[149] However, when regulators and critics of Halcion interpreted the indisputable results of the controlled Halcion/Dalamane clinical studies in Table 5.4 as evidence of the drug's excessive adverse effects relative to other hypnotic benzodiazepines, Upjohn attacked the validity of their (dosage) design.

As for the post-marketing spontaneous reports of ADRs in the UK and the US, the company concentrated on the general limitations of such data. Specifically, Upjohn argued that such data is unsuitable for quantitative between-drug comparisons and is greatly affected by non-clinical factors such as publicity and reporting rates of prescribing doctors.[150] According to Upjohn, 'spontaneous reporting databases can only generate and cannot confirm signals of possible drug hazards'.[151] The company also presented data from three post-marketing epidemiological studies in Canada, the US and the UK and claimed that those studies did not support the spontaneous reporting in the UK or the US.[152] Nevertheless, the CSM rejected Upjohn's arguments and advised that all Halcion licences should be revoked on grounds of safety.[153]

During the 1960s and 1970s the hypnotic benzodiazepines became the preferred sedatives as they replaced barbiturates. However, since the late 1980s, the growing signs of dependence among patients upon these benzodi-azepines led some regulators to be less sympathetic towards these drugs (see Chapter 1). In 1991, the CSM declared that as a matter of policy the licensing of benzodiazepines would be affected by concerns over the improper use of the drugs:

> *The CSM has recommended restrictions on the use of benzodi-azepines in order to reduce the risk of dependence... To discourage the improper use of benzodiazepines, these products are only licensed for short-term use in patients with severe anxiety and insomnia.*[154]

It seems likely that this regulatory environment affected the CSM's approach to Halcion, whose safety profile had come under major challenge. As one former member of the CSM involved in the Halcion decision put it:

> *I think there was a bigger, deeper issue there [with Halcion]*
> *which couldn't be dealt with, and which was the safety of all*
> *the benzodiazepines. The question was, 'Should all the short-*
> *acting benzodiazepines be phased out? And what is the way of*
> *doing it?'*[155]

Much more importantly, both the MCA (then known as the Medicines Division) and the CSM had been closely involved in the initial licensing of Halcion. In the light of the P321 revelations these regulatory organizations felt that Upjohn's reassurances at the May 1978 hearing before the CSM had been misleading.[156] Upjohn's written submission which was presented to the CSM at that May 1978 hearing stated:

> *Three hundred patients received 1.0 mg of Halcion for periods*
> *of up to 42 days. In all cases the drug was well tolerated and no*
> *serious side effects occurred. Side effects observed were those*
> *usually associated with a CNS depressant... Based on our*
> *experience in 300 patients, it can be concluded that a dose of*
> *1.0 mg of Halcion, twice the highest recommended dose, is a*
> *safe and effective dose for inpatients. Side effects with 1.0 mg*
> *dose in this patient population are minimal... Fourteen subjects*
> *[in P321] received 1.0 mg (two times the highest recommended*
> *outpatient dose [in the UK but not the Netherlands]) for a period*
> *of 42 days. Halcion was an effective hypnotic in these subjects*
> *and there was no indication of deleterious effects on ECG,*
> *laboratory tests, or vital signs.*[157]

Seventeen subjects from P321 were included in the aforementioned 300 patients. This submission was misleading because:

- Substantially more than 17 subjects embarked on 1.0 mg of Halcion in P321.
- Although P321 was a small proportion of the total of 300, the 17 from that protocol were the only people who took 1.0 mg of Halcion for more than 15 days, while 258 of the total were on the drug for only one day.
- The adverse effects in P321 were not minimal.
- Although P321 did not indicate deleterious effects on ECG, laboratory tests or vital signs, there were arguably other deleterious effects which were not referred to at all.[158]

Upjohn disputed that they had misled the CSM in 1978, but Justice May categorically agreed with the CSM and the MCA that the company's submission at that hearing had been misleading, even by reference to the defective, unrevised 1973 technical report for P321.[159] The Judge concluded:

> *I hesitate, as Professor Oswald would not, to label this dishon-*
> *esty. It is rather in a grey area where someone genuinely trying*

to present in its best light a case, which he believes in, produces material which the judgement of hindsight considers to have been less than frank.[160]

Even more importantly for the CSM and the MCA, that incomplete disclosure of P321 data in 1978 was related to safety because it misled them into under-estimating the significance of other alerting hazard signals. As Patrick Waller, the MCA's medical assessor for Halcion, explained:

Had the entire data been presented for this study they would surely have raised the signal that subsequently came from van der Kroef in Holland in 1979. The committee was already concerned about safety in relation to dose and would have required extensive reassurance that such effects were absent or rare at the doses proposed for use in the UK. It seems inconceivable that the committee would have recommended the grant of the licence in 1978 had the true findings of this study been presented.[161]

Thus, a breakdown in the trust between the MCA and the CSM, on the one hand, and Upjohn, on the other, had occurred. The vital result of this was that the MCA and the CSM were no longer willing to give Upjohn or Halcion the benefit of the many scientific doubts about the drug's safety and efficacy.

This is particularly evident in the MCA's handling of Upjohn's claims that the results of P321, and of clinical trials comparing 0.5 mg of Halcion with 30 mg of Dalmane, should be disregarded. Waller forthrightly rebutted the argument that the design of P321 was invalid:

This study was well designed. It had a control group and random allocation to placebo or triazolam [Halcion], which is a highly scientific method. It had what are known as double-blind conditions whereby patients and the evaluating physicians didn't know which treatment they were on. It had appropriate 'exclusion criteria': subjects were not allowed to be entered if they had significant mental disorder and so forth. So I believe it was a valid trial.[162]

Similarly, he argued that it had not been shown that comparing 0.5 mg of Halcion with 30 mg of Dalmane was inappropriate and so the body of evidence comparing these doses remained relevant to the clinical risk assessment of the licensed doses of Halcion:[163]

...[the issue is] not at all clear-cut... and I don't think we can, therefore, be dismissive of data which shows very striking findings on the basis of the possibility that they may not be precisely equivalent doses.[164]

While members of the CSM reached their own conclusions, Waller's report to the committee is bound to have been influential. He had formed very coherent and strongly argued views about the safety and efficacy data on Halcion that became available after the Grundberg litigation in the US. The diversity of disciplines represented on the CSM meant that an equally strong, but opposing, perspective was unlikely to develop. Furthermore, as many of the experts themselves acknowledge, the medical assessor's report on any drug product is usually very influential, though not determining, in the CSM's decision-making. As one member of the CSM put it:

> We read the assessor's report because that gives us a flavour of the drug... I think the role of the [CSM] members increasingly has been one of almost audit. The individuals are saying, 'Has there there been enough scrutiny of these particular issues?' Because there is no way that the individual members can assimilate all the data. That has to be done by the experts of the secretariat [the MCA].[165]

In addition, the CSM did not accept that spontaneous reporting databases cannot generate quantitative inter-drug comparisons, especially when the magnitude of differences between drugs is large.[166] The committee was also critical of the methods of Upjohn's three epidemiological studies, such as telephone interviewing in order to ascertain adverse effects, and noted that they were all limited to less than two-weeks long.[167]

Upjohn's appeal to the Medicines Commission

The company then exercised its right of appeal to the Medicines Commission. After a formal hearing in May 1992 the commission concluded that the licence for 0.25 mg of Halcion should be revoked but that the licence for the 0.125 mg product should be allowed to return to the market with some variations.

The MCA declined to accept the conclusions of the commission and on 17 July 1992 wrote to Upjohn recommending the revocation of all Halcion licences and identifying how the commission had reached a different assessment from its own on 'substantially the same evidence' as follows:[168]

- The commission took a less serious view of the number of adverse reactions reported in the UK, stating that these were similar to those associated with other benzodiazepines.
- The commission took a different view of the clinical trials, arguing that young and middle-aged patients with no prior mental illness did not appear to be particularly at risk.
- Where psychiatric reactions were evident the commission took the view that they were neither persistent nor life threatening.
- The commission did not draw any conclusions on the frequency or disabling effects of the drug at different doses when presented with data on patients withdrawing from clinical trials.

The commission recommended continued marketing of the 0.125 mg dose, but this advice was based partly 'on the understanding that 0.125 mg is efficacious in geriatric subjects and in a proportion of non-geriatric subjects'.[169] However, the commission also noted that 'a dose of 0.125 mg was efficacious in only a minority of non-geriatric subjects and that the efficacy of 0.25 mg was more convincing for these patients'.[170] The apparent inconsistency of this was not lost on the MCA, who commented:

> *Thus, the restrictions recommended by the commission would result in treatment of non-geriatric subjects being commenced at a dose which they regard as efficacious in only a minority of such subjects.*[171]

Upjohn's appeal to the panel of appointed persons

Upjohn then decided to exercise its further right of appeal to a special panel of 'persons appointed' by the secretary of state for health. The panel considered 'substantially the same evidence as the CSM and the Medicines Commission' and reported to the Department of Health in April 1993.[172,173] It concluded that both 0.25 mg and 0.125 mg dosages of Halcion should be allowed back on the market with some restrictions in dosage, indications and duration of use. The panel's findings differed from those of the MCA as follows.[174]

- Additional data presented by the company included a post-marketing surveillance study carried out in the UK which allowed the panel to conclude that the 0.125 mg and 0.25 mg doses were efficacious and did not point to any important safety hazard.

  The MCA, on the contrary, found the new study to provide 'insufficient reassurances when considered in the context of evidence from several other sources which indicate an important safety hazard with Halcion'.[175]
- The panel accepted Upjohn's assertion that, when comparing the safety of Halcion with other benzodiazepines, the doses which had been used (0.5 mg of Halcion compared with 30 mg of Dalmane) could not be considered equivalent. Consequently, comparative trials were not based on equivalent doses and could not, therefore, be regarded as useful evidence on which to draw conclusions about the safety of the drug.

  This pointed up a basic and fundamental disagreement with the MCA over the equivalence of doses. The MCA did not accept that the doses used in the comparative Halcion/Dalmane trials were non-equivalent and regarded the findings from these trials as valid.
- The panel also reached different conclusions from the MCA on the degree of efficacy of Halcion at low doses. It recommended a starting dose of 0.125 mg in young/middle-aged patients (rising to 0.25 mg if necessary) and 0.0625 mg in the elderly (rising to not more than 0.125 mg).

  Yet, as the MCA noted, there was little evidence to support the efficacy of the 0.125 mg dose in the non-elderly and no completed studies at all concerning the 0.0625 mg dose.

- The MCA also placed considerable weight on published spontaneous reporting data from the US which indicated that psychiatric ADRs had been reported 22 to 99 times more frequently with Halcion than with a comparator drug. The panel appeared to place no weight on this evidence.
- The panel noted that the information provided by Upjohn relating to P321 was incomplete but accepted Upjohn's argument that this had only marginal relevance to the safety of the lower doses in the UK. Therefore, Upjohn's omissions should not determine whether the licences are revoked.

The Medicines Control Agency decides

Between September 1991 and April 1993, the MCA had received three different recommendations from three different expert advisory committees: the CSM who recommended that all Halcion licences should be suspended and revoked; the Medicines Commission who recommended that the licence for the 0.25 mg dose should be revoked, but that the 0.125 mg dose should be permitted back on the market; and the panel who recommended that both the 0.25 mg and 0.125 mg doses should be permitted back on the market, subject to low start doses.

On 9 June 1993, disregarding the advice from the panel and commission, but upholding the CSM's advice, the UK Licensing Authority finally revoked *all* Halcion's licences.[176] Unlike the MCA and the CSM, neither the Medicines Commission nor the panel had been so close to either general policy matters concerning benzodiazepines or the history of licensing and monitoring Halcion. Both the commission and the panel were much more willing to award the benefit of the many scientific doubts about Halcion to Upjohn. By contrast, a determination to give the benefit of the doubt to patient safety is evident in the Licensing Authority's final decision that it 'remains not reassured of the safety of Halcion products', that 'the first concern must be for patients', and that 'it is right to be cautious'.[177,178]

The sociopolitical and ethical framework defining how the benefit of the scientific doubts about Halcion's safety were awarded was the pivotal factor in determining the regulatory implications of the technical data. The relative generosity of the Medicines Commission and the panel towards Upjohn manifested itself in that they accepted the company's challenges to the validity of spontaneous ADR reports and they were willing to recommend marketing daily doses of 0.125 mg, rising to 0.25 mg, and – in the case of the panel – as low as 0.625mg, despite the fact that there was little or no evidence from controlled trials to support the efficacy of such low doses. In sharp contrast, the MCA considered that such evidence of efficacy was necessary in the interests of patients, and that the higher doses recommended by the Medicines Commission and the panel *did not provide an adequate safety margin* for patients because 'it is well established that benzodiazepines are sometimes used at higher doses and for longer periods than are recommended in data sheets'.[179] Halcion was to receive no benefit of the doubt from the Licensing Authority over safety margins.

As for the crucial Halcion/Dalmane clinical trials, the panel and the MCA were in complete contradiction over the technical equivalence of 0.5 mg of Halcion and 30 mg of Dalmane. Again the panel gave Upjohn the benefit of the doubt, despite the many inconsistencies in the company's treatment of this equivalence issue between 1978 and 1991. Regarding P321, the Medicines Commission and the panel were themselves in direct contradiction. The former generously accepted the company's challenges to the validity of the trial, while the latter concluded that it was valid. However, the panel concluded that the protocol had no relevance for the licensing of the drug at the lower doses because it generously awarded the benefit of the doubt to Upjohn by assuming that a narrow margin of safety for Halcion was adequate. We do not know why the Medicines Commission and the panel reached different conclusions about P321 or why their overall clinical risk assessments differed. The fact that these two appelate bodies reached contradictory views on the validity of P321 and recommended different doses cannot have helped the credibility of their advice in the eyes of the Licensing Authority.

Opponents of the British suspension of Halcion soon made their voices heard. In 1993, Professor Ian Hindmarsh and his colleagues examined the effects of the suspension by surveying retrospectively 163 doctors in the UK who had to switch their patients to another sleeping pill. They found that there were more adverse reactions to Halcion substitutes reported in the three months after suspension than were reported for Halcion in the three months prior to its suspension. Consequently, they concluded:

> *If the rationale for the suspension of Halcion was to ensure the safety of patients using hypnotics, the UK regulators' decision was faulty.*[180]

Within weeks an American research team supported Hindmarsh and reported that after reviewing the records of 184 psychiatric inpatients taking either Halcion or Restoril, they discovered no significant differences in the frequency of behavioural disturbances associated with the two drugs.[181] In May 1993, Upjohn representatives also cited this Hindmarsh study in the *British Medical Journal* to support their contention that the banning of Halcion in the UK had caused a change to the prescribing of 'potentially more harmful alternatives'.[182] However, another group of British researchers challenged the validity and methodology of Hindmarsh's conclusions. Noting that his results were at odds with controlled clinical evidence in 1992, they commented:

> *We have strong reservations about Professor Hindmarsh and his colleagues' report. We do not believe it is safe to conclude from their data that Halcion has a better adverse events profile to the various drugs used than do substitutes for Halcion. The data have serious limitations: they are open, uncontrolled and retrospective... Nor do they mention the doses of drugs used.*[183]

More significantly, in 1995 researchers at the University College London School of Medicine examined whether the sudden withdrawal of Halcion from the market had induced patients to stop their benzodiazepine consumption. To do this they interviewed and examined the medical records of 147 patients in London who had been prescribed Halcion in the 12 months prior to suspension. Among this sample they found that 45 per cent of chronic and 66 per cent of intermittent Halcion users had stopped receiving prescriptions from six months after the revocation of Halcion's licences up to 18 months later. As only 11 per cent of these recalled suffering significant withdrawal effects, the researchers concluded that 'official action to curb prescribing of a benzodiazepine acts as an important stimulus for patients to reduce or stop their use of all psychotropic medication without increasing psychological morbidity or leading to unacceptable side effects'.[184]

Conclusion

Social, political and legal factors have been influential in the struggle to determine whether or not Halcion is safe. The media may have added a sense of urgency to the debate and may also have encouraged British regulators to undertake a more careful and rigorous analysis of the drug's safety than had been previously conducted. Unfortunately, this also provided a forum in which some unnecessary and libellous allegations were made against Upjohn.

The institutional interests of Upjohn were also very much in evidence. These appear to have been expressed by a corporate culture which strongly believed in the value of the Halcion product, both medically and commercially, coupled with a defensive distaste for those who criticised it. A key consequence of this was a pervasive institutional bias in the company's handling of matters concerning the safety and effectiveness of Halcion. While some of Upjohn's senior medical staff took the time to write memos and devote resources to trying to discredit van der Kroef and Oswald, others failed to keep adequate records of disqualified clinical investigators whose clinical research on Halcion had been 'pivotal' to regulators' assessment of its safety and effectiveness. This narrow pursuit of institutional interests provided a framework in which some Upjohn scientists were sometimes reckless with the regulatory process designed to protect patients from unsafe drugs.

This institutional bias struck deep into the heart of Halcion's viability. Upjohn was willing to accept Oster's judgement that P321 did not involve significant adverse psychiatric effects, but challenged those doctors who reported such adverse reactions to Halcion. The technical report for P321 was inadequate; yet Upjohn did not check it thoroughly enough to discover its wholesale omissions before unwittingly presenting its flaws as reassurance of the drug's safety to the British regulatory authorities in 1978. According to Graham Dukes, 'it is inconceivable that the Dutch regulatory agency would have approved Halcion had it been aware of the ADR data known in 1994 to have been in the possession of Upjohn at the time'.[185] We are not suggesting that Upjohn was involved in a deliberate cover up of P321 data. Rather, we are highlighting an institutional bias which downplayed Halcion's risks, while promoting the product at the expense of rigorous checks on safety and efficacy testing. This bias continued into the 1990s when Upjohn scientists attacked the validity of their own trials after British regulators interpreted them as casting doubt on the safety of Halcion. Prior to that, the company had submitted them as valid scientific studies.

Significantly, for many years regulatory authorities on both sides of the Atlantic did not detect the consequences of this bias. For example, the MCA first found out about the omissions from P321 by reading about them in a pharmaceutical trade journal, and about the fabrication of one of Upjohn's clinical trials (by Fuerst) by watching a television documentary! Similarly, the FDA did not check for nine years that another of Upjohn's clinical investigators (Franklin), who was centrally involved in two-thirds of the most pivotal clinical trials with Halcion, was disqualified for submitting false data and deliberately violating regulations. Nor did the MCA or the FDA thoroughly check the case report forms of P321 or main controlled clinical trials involving Halcion until 1991 – 13 years after the drug was approved in the UK!

After conducting such an analysis combined with a review of post-marketing safety data, the British regulatory authorities concluded that Halcion's risks outweighed its benefits. Yet previously the British regulators had not treated post-marketing warning signals about the adverse effects of Halcion with sufficient gravity. When the Dutch regulatory authorities reported very high levels of adverse reactions in 1979, British regulators continued to assume that the drug was safe. However, it is evident that they awarded the benefit of the scientific doubt unduly to Halcion in 1979, especially as their final revocation decision stated that the clinical trials available in 1978 were 'the most significant evidence indicating an important safety hazard with the drug'.[186] In July 1992, the chief executive of the MCA told Upjohn that 'acceptance of triazolam [Halcion] as safe at the licensed doses at that time [1978] must be regarded as flawed'.[187] In other words, by the safety standards of the MCA itself, the British regulatory authorities' inability to detect Upjohn's inadequate handling of Halcion permitted patients to be exposed to an unsafe drug for nearly 13 years.

By 1991, British regulators were not so willing to invest their trust in Upjohn. Consequently, Waller critically and thoroughly analysed safety data on Halcion. This time patients' health, not Upjohn, was to receive the benefit of the scientific doubt. Crucially, the MCA concluded that Halcion had a narrow margin of safety because the evidence for effectiveness was weak at the very low doses that might be safe, and because users of benzodiazepines are vulnerable to increasing their doses in response to tolerance and/or dependence.

6

How the West was Won: Keep Taking the Tablets in the United States

Introduction

In the US, regulation of Halcion had been progressing at a leisurely pace. On 19 April 1990, Public Citizen's Health Research Group (PCHRG), the most significant American public health advocacy group, petitioned the FDA to revise Halcion's labelling so that it included a box warning about the higher level of adverse reaction reports with the drug compared with other benzodiazepine hypnotics, and on its 'ineffectiveness' after two weeks of continuous use.[1] Despite this, in August 1990 the much more modest warnings about amnesia proposed by PDAC back in September 1989 were still being discussed by the FDA and Upjohn.[2]

Meanwhile, the drug's limitations continued to surface in medical studies. Researchers at the University of California found that five patients taking 0.125 mg and 0.25 mg of Halcion for four nights achieved significantly more total sleep time, but not less awakenings.[3] Sleep researchers at the University of Toronto could not find any objective increase in the total sleep time among 30 subjects who took either 0.25 or 0.5 mg of Halcion for one night, while discontinuation of the 0.5 mg dose produced withdrawal effects even when used for just a single night.[4] In September 1990, Dr Martin Scharf and his colleagues at the Cincinnati Centre for Research in Sleep Disorder published findings which supported Kales and cast major doubts over the viability of Halcion. They conducted a double-blind sleep laboratory study with 32 healthy insomniacs who took either 0.125 or 0.25 mg of Halcion or equivalent doses of Restoril for 14 days. Although both drugs showed efficacy in inducing sleep, the 0.125 mg dose of Halcion lost its effectiveness during the 14 days because it did not reduce wake time after the subjects had fallen asleep. Moreover, these researchers found that there was 'clear-cut' rebound insomnia after withdrawal of both the 0.125 and 0.25 mg doses of Halcion. This resulted in increased time to fall asleep, a decrease in total sleep time and an increase in the number of awakenings compared with when the insomniacs started on the drug.[5]

Yet Halcion prospered regardless. In 1990 it was approved in 90 countries where approximately 1.5 million prescriptions were written for it. In 1990, 30 per cent of Upjohn's healthcare sales came from psychopharmacological drugs, including Halcion, and amounted to US$726 million.[6] As 1991 opened, the supposed advantages of Halcion over benzodiazepines with longer half-lives were further challenged. As we discussed in Chapter 3, Upjohn and Halcion's supporters had argued that the drug's short half-life meant that the drug was cleared from the body more completely by morning leaving fewer of the 'hangover' effects associated with sleeping pills with longer half-lives such as Mogadon. However, Dr Deborah Robin and her colleagues at Vanderbilt University in Nashville, found that 0.25 mg of Halcion in six healthy volunteers significantly increased their loss of balance. There was no such increase at the 0.125 mg dose and the researchers concluded that the effect was dose related. The risk of falling is, of course, accentuated by loss of balance. Given the dose relatedness of the effect, elderly patients who are smaller, less efficient at clearing drugs from their body and much more vulnerable to the dangers of falling might experience a similar loss of balance at the smaller dose of 0.125 mg.[7] A few months later, yet another double-blind trial in the US found that 0.25 mg of Halcion did not significantly increase total sleep time – on this occasion in 48 subjects over a period of six nights.[8]

Within ten days of the British suspension of Halcion, the Norwegian, Finnish and Bermudan regulatory authorities followed suit and Jamaica joined them a week later. The chairman of the European expert Committee for Proprietary Medicinal Products (CPMP), Professor Poggiolini, wrote to the regulatory authorities in EU member states asking them not to take any action until a CPMP meeting in mid October, though the German regulatory agency, the BGA, could not resist saying that it was planning to suspend the product.[9] Clearly the EU member states were themselves divided about the safety of Halcion.

In the US, the pace of events began to quicken. The most extensively revised labelling in the history of the product emerged in November 1991. This reiterated that the drug should only be used for 'short-term' treatment, but on this occasion it explicitly defined short term to mean *seven to ten days, not six weeks!* The new labelling was much more frank about the drawbacks of Halcion than before:

> *After two weeks of consecutive nightly administration, the drug's effect on total wake time is decreased and the values recorded in the last third of the night approach baseline [ie pre-drug] levels. On the first and/or second night after drug discontinuance (first or second post-drug night), total time asleep, percentage of time spent sleeping and rapidity of falling asleep frequently were significantly less than on baseline (pre-drug) nights. This effect is often called rebound insomnia... An increase in daytime anxiety has been reported for Halcion after as few as ten days of continuous use... Cases of 'travellers' amnesia' have been reported by individuals who have taken*

> *Halcion to induce sleep while travelling, such as during an*
> *airplane flight... Patients at therapeutic doses given for as few*
> *as one to two weeks can also have withdrawal symptoms.*[10]

For the first time in the US, maximum doses were clearly set: doctors were told not to exceed 0.25 mg for elderly patients and 0.5 mg in other adults, even in exceptional cases. They were also warned more strongly about adverse behavioural effects, such as 'aggressiveness', 'agitation', 'amnesia with or without inappropriate behaviour', 'bizarre behaviour', 'confusional states', 'delusions', 'depersonalization', 'derealization', 'disorientation' and the 'worsening of depression, including suicidal thinking'.[11] The new labelling also had a 'patient package information' leaflet specifically attached to it. This stated baldly that users of benzodiazepine sleeping pills should be aware of the risks and limitations, 'including diminishing effectiveness with continued use and the possible development of dependence (addiction) and possibly mental changes, particularly when the drugs are used for more than a few days to a week'.[12] Nevertheless, Upjohn and the FDA continued to produce a label that did not attribute these adverse effects to Halcion more than to other benzodiazepines.

The CPMP's immediate response to the British suspension was also to strengthen the product's labelling by stating that for many patients 0.125 mg should be sufficient, that 0.25 mg should not be exceeded, and that short-term usage of not more than ten days was of 'absolute importance'. They included the statement: 'Halcion is only indicated when the sleeping disorder is severe, disabling or causing extreme distress'.[13] The CPMP set up a rapporteur group to look into whether the drug should be suspended across the EU.[14] In December 1991, a European rapporteur group recommended that Halcion should be withdrawn from the market across the EU, but the CPMP as a whole did not accept this advice.[15]

This prompted individual European countries to take their own action against the drug. Many followed the Australian approach where only the 0.125 mg dose was approved.[16] In January 1992, the French Health Ministry suspended the 0.25 mg tablet form of Halcion because of safety concerns, though they left the 0.125 mg tablet on the market. The ministry's pharma-covigilance commission conducted a risk-benefit assessment of Halcion and concluded that its risks outweighed its benefits. It recommended that both the 0.25 mg and 0.125 mg licences should be suspended, but the health ministry decided to keep the 0.125 mg tablet on the market because of worries about the adverse effects of sudden withdrawal on dependent patients.[17] Within days in Spain, where Halcion was the most widely prescribed sleeping pill, the health ministry also suspended the 0.25 mg tablet form of Halcion, but not the 0.125 mg tablet, following advice from the Spanish National Pharmacovigilance Commission in November 1991 that Halcion was associated with a higher incidence of adverse psychiatric effects than other hypnotics.[18]

Halcion seemed to spiral into deeper crisis in February 1992 when it took a hammering in front of the German BGA at a public hearing on the safety of the 0.125 and 0.25 mg doses. The German regulators were not impressed with Upjohn's Halcion data and stated this publicly:

Most of the studies are deficient in planning, conduct and evaluation and do not stand up to examination in the light of current methodological requirements, such as the German good clinical practice guidelines of 1987 or the CPMP's recent guideline on the conduct of clinical trials for hypnotics. Apart from the fact that there are no adequate trial protocols, treatment periods are too short, there are no adequate placebo withdrawal and subsequent observation phases, and the numbers of patients used in treatment groups were too small... The fundamental problem is that the risk potential of the 0.125 mg and 0.25 mg doses compared with that for other products with the same indication is difficult to assess from the controlled studies... the limited number of observations in itself does not permit any real certainty in the conclusions.[19]

But Halcion survived because the German Commission for the Review of Medicines produced a report demonstrating that the medical profession in Germany found it a very useful product.[20] Halcion's sales worldwide in 1991 were still a staggering US$237 million.[21]

To examine the basis for Halcion's new labelling in the US, Professor Frank Ayd published extensive appraisals of the risks and benefits of 0.125 mg and 0.25mg of Halcion in the April and May 1992 editions of the *International Drug Therapy Newsletter* respectively. In 1979, his letter in the *Lancet* had helped to rehabilitate Halcion, but in 1992 he delivered damning assessments of the drug. Ayd found eight published studies of the drug's hypnotic efficacy at 0.125 mg comprising 166 patients, 54 of whom took it for only one night; 22 for two nights; five for three nights; 23 for 14 nights; and 21 for between three and nine weeks. He concluded that the validity of these studies was in serious doubt because 'besides methodological flaws, the studies had very few subjects and too short duration of exposure to Halcion'.[22] With regard to the 0.25 mg dose, he reviewed 21 published studies involving 1031 patients in total. However, 906 (87.9 per cent) of these subjects were insomniacs in 'open' (ie non-blinded) trials involving subjective assessments of the drug's effectiveness. Moreover, the duration of exposure was seven nights or less for 97.7 per cent of the subjects. Of the remaining 125 subjects in controlled double-blind studies, only 41 were insomniacs evaluated by objective sleep laboratory measures. According to Ayd, the six clinical studies based largely on subjective estimates showed that 0.25 mg of Halcion improved sleep, but 'of the seven sleep laboratory studies in non-elderly subjects with insomnia or induced insomnia only two showed a significant improvement in sleep'.[23]

Watching the detectives: the Food and Drug Administration's inspection of Upjohn

Following the revelations about P321 and disqualified clinical investigators, on 9 December 1991, the FDA's division of scientific investigations began an inspection of Upjohn. The FDA inspectors reviewed raw data from P321 and other clinical studies together with Upjohn memos, correspondence and minutes of meetings. They also interviewed some Upjohn employees and ex-employees. Although the FDA's official report of this inspection was not made public until April 1994, it was conducted between December 1991 and March 1992 when it was suspended.[24]

A large part of the inspection dealt with Upjohn's handling of P321. According to the inspectors' report, William Veldkamp, one of the authors of Upjohn's technical report for P321, did not remember the subjects of P321 being paranoid, though they were concerned about being able to defend themselves. He told the inspectors: 'effects were observed in the prisoners but we didn't think they were medically significant – we just didn't think they were important'.[25] Similarly, Dr Carl Metzler, another of the authors of the technical report, did not think at the time that the adverse psychological reactions were pertinent to normal clinical practice and even after van der Kroef's experience in The Netherlands, according to Metzler, no one asked whether similar problems had occurred in clinical trials.[26] The inspection report also claimed that Dr Harold Oster, who was contracted by Upjohn to oversee P321, saw paranoia reported in the CRFs, but he thought the subjects made up some of their adverse effects and did not view them as psychotic behaviour.[27] Nevertheless, *Oster also told inspectors that he thought the 1.0 mg dose was too high, and that 0.25 mg of Halcion was the highest dose he ever prescribed in his own practice.*[28]

During the inspection, Upjohn could not account for the omissions in the technical report.[29] The comments attributed to Dr Robert Purpura, formerly the worldwide medical manager for psychopharmacology at Upjohn, are perhaps the most damning. According to the inspection report, Purpura told FDA investigators that if P321 was a high dose study designed to define the maximum dose and treatment period, then adverse effects should have been expected, and he continued: 'Someone should have asked the question: where are the side effects in this study?'[30]

Furthermore, Dr William Barry, formerly at Upjohn's drug experience unit, relayed his perceptions of a company that was too reluctant to warn of Halcion's risks. According to Barry, in 1980–1981, the first batch of adverse reports on Halcion was received from Europe and each of the European countries showed similar data: an increased incidence of psychological adverse effects.[31] Barry's drug experience unit proposed a package insert change and made sure that Upjohn was aware of this at the highest level, but no change was made at that time.[32] Perhaps most stunning of all, according to the inspection report, Barry told the FDA investigators that those in Upjohn who were critical of Halcion or critical of the way in which Upjohn was handling it were gradually marginalised.[33] We do not know whether this is true, but it does seem to have been the perception of Barry, whose line manager at Upjohn, Dr Keith Borden, described him as 'careful, meticulous and compulsive' and a 'good scientist'.[34] During the inspection, Borden said that in the mid 1980s he did not understand why the FDA did not do anything because Upjohn's drug experience unit sent the agency 'all kinds of adverse reaction data'.[35]

The findings listed in the FDA's inspection report are hard hitting. Regarding P321, the investigators acknowledge that their inspection did not indicate that the omissions in the technical report were intentional, but commented:

> *Upjohn has repeatedly characterized the incomplete reporting of P321 as 'transcription errors'. This characterization of the omissions is false and misleading. There was, at minimum, a gross and seminal failure to properly tabulate data. Moreover, the claim [made by Upjohn] that the overall incidence of subjects reporting adverse effects would not change is misleading. In fact, the overall incidence and other numbers did change because the report was roughly 30 per cent incomplete.*[36]

The FDA investigators were also highly critical of Upjohn for seeking approval of the 1.0 mg dose in the US (which they did not get), and for seeking approval for long-term use – that is, beyond 14 days (which they did get – up to one month):

> *Importantly, the last group enrolled in P321 was at the 0.5 mg level, which the protocol amendment states was due to intolerance (unacceptable side effects) at the 1.0 mg level. The firm attempted to obtain approval of the 1.0 mg dose [in the US], even though available evidence (P321 and the Dutch experience) indicated that the 1.0 mg dose was too high... The firm attempted to gain approval for long-term use of the drug even though available evidence indicated that long-term use was both dangerous and medically untenable... The only caution statement regarding usage in the original package insert is the statement: 'It is recommended that Halcion not be prescribed in quantities exceeding a one-month supply'.*[37]

After condemning Upjohn for conducting 'a continuous campaign to neutralize any individual or publication reporting adverse information about Halcion' and for misleading the FDA about the disqualified clinical investigator, Dr William Franklin, the inspection report concludes:

> *Although the focus of the inspection was on P321 which represented the most blatant example of incomplete reporting of Halcion data to the FDA, the core of our findings indicates that the misreporting of P321 was not an isolated incident. We conclude that the firm has engaged in an ongoing pattern of misconduct with Halcion.*[38]

While the findings from the FDA's inspection of Upjohn were not made public until April 1994, they were analysed within the FDA during 1992. The regulatory management branch of the agency halted the inspection in March 1992 because it believed that the evidence available did not show that there had been a 20-year conspiracy to cover up the P321 data. Consequently, on 12 May 1992, a meeting was held at the FDA to decide whether or not the case should be referred to the US Department of Justice for a Grand Jury investigation. This decision was deferred pending an analysis by Paul Leber's reviewing division at the FDA, which had been responsible for the approval of Halcion. The May meeting agreed that referral to a Grand Jury investigation should depend upon whether Leber's division decided that Upjohn's misreporting of facts had been relevant or 'material' to the approval process.[39] The reviewing division concluded that the misreporting of P321 was not material to the approval process because the unusual nature of the subjects, who were prisoners, and the high dosage administered made it of 'marginal significance and importance for decision-making regarding Halcion'.[40] Thus, the regulatory management branch concluded that 'no further action' was warranted and closed the investigation.[41] Upjohn's chairman and chief executive, Theodore Cooper, responded to this decision by saying: 'We believe this exonerates Upjohn and our employees.'[42]

When the inspection report was made public in April 1994, Upjohn was surprised. In response to the findings of the FDA investigators the company commented that it was concerned that single memos or other documents seen out of context should not be perceived as being representative of company policy.[43] Kaye Bennett, an Upjohn spokeswoman, defended her company and Halcion by stating:

> Upjohn puts nothing ahead of patients' health. We stand by the fact that our science is sound and that Halcion remains safe and effective medication when it is used as recommended in the labelling.[44]

Return of the experts: the Psychopharmacological Drugs Advisory Committee, 1992

The events of 1991 also prompted the FDA to reconsider the safety and effectiveness of Halcion by reconvening its Psychopharmacological Drugs Advisory Committee (PDAC) in May 1992. Unlike the PDAC review of Halcion in 1989, the 1992 meeting did not confine its attention to spontaneous adverse drug reaction reports. Safety and efficacy data from clinical trials was also evaluated, though not from P321 because FDA scientists had concluded that it was not relevant to the safety of the drug at lower doses.[45] Nor did the 1992 meeting limit its sources of evidence to the FDA and Upjohn. Public Citizen was also invited to give a presentation and there was a public forum for some other presentations. Most significantly, the FDA also invited guest experts: Professor Frank Ayd, the organizer of the Upjohn Boston conference in 1979 and editor of the *International Drug Therapy Newsletter*; David Greenblatt, Professor of Pharmacology at Tufts New England Medical Centre in Boston, formerly a principal clinical investigator for Upjohn and recipient of major Upjohn grants; Anthony Kales, Professor of Psychiatry at Pennsylvania State University College of Medicine and formerly clinical investigator for Upjohn who subsequently petitioned for the withdrawal of Halcion from the market; Wallace Mendelson, Professor of Psychiatry at the State University of New York, formerly an Upjohn consultant and recipient of Upjohn grants; Ian Oswald, Emeritus Professor of Psychiatry at the University of Edinburgh and expert witness against Upjohn in the Grundberg trial; Dr Steven Paul, Scientific Director of the US National Institute of Mental Health, formerly a recipient of fees from Upjohn for giving speeches; and Dr Tom Roth, head of the sleep disorders division at Henry Ford Hospital in Detroit, an Upjohn stock holder, grant holder and advisor.

A few weeks before the PDAC meeting in May 1992, Leber, the director of the FDA's division of neuropharmacological products, and Dr Thomas Laughren, the group leader of psychopharmacology within that division, acknowledged that the agency's initial decision to approve the 0.5 mg dose of Halcion was a 'failing':

> *In retrospect it is now apparent that the agency's approval action endorsed a recommended dose that was* probably too high *for a substantial proportion of the adult population. Hindsight also indicates that the product's labelling was* insufficiently explicit about the preferred duration of the product's use *(emphasis added).*[46]

Indeed, by this time Leber accepted that the 0.5 mg dose was between two and four times too high.[47] At least one member of the PDAC felt that Halcion had been marketed at 'way too high a dose'.[48] Leber also told the committee that the British regulatory authorities had received spontaneous reports of serious adverse psychiatric effects associated with doses as low as 0.125 mg of Halcion.[49]

While it is clear that the 0.5 mg dose was too high on grounds of *safety*, these senior FDA scientists admitted that their approval decision was influenced by the lack of evidence of efficacy at the lower but safer 0.25 mg dose:

> *Although agency staff were aware at the time they were considering Halcion's approval [in 1982] that the UK's regulatory authorities had set 0.25 mg as the maximum recommended dose for adults, they also knew that post-marketing experience in countries where a 0.5 mg dose had been approved was not at all alarming.* Perhaps more important, evidence of Halcion's effectiveness derived primarily from studies employing a 0.5 mg nightly dose. *Thus, the FDA chose, after extended internal deliberations, to endorse a 0.25 to 0.5 mg dose range rather than to impose the 0.25 mg dose limit that the British had (emphasis added).*[50]

In other words, in 1982 senior FDA staff decided to approve Halcion at the 0.5 mg dose, whose safety was in doubt even then, rather than require Upjohn to produce adequate proof of the effectiveness of the lower but safer dose of 0.25

mg. As we noted in Chapter 3, there is some evidence to suggest that that decision was taken over the objections of the FDA's medical officer for Halcion, Dr Theresa Woo, who had retired by 1992, a decision which now came back to haunt the American regulators.

Thus, when the PDAC came to review Halcion in May 1992, the situation was very different from that in 1989 when they had previously assessed the product. By 1992, not only had Upjohn relinquished 0.5 mg as a safe recommended dose, but Leber and his senior allies at the FDA, who had previously told the American public that the 0.5 mg dose was safe, openly admitted that it was hazardous for a 'substantial proportion' of patients.[51] Furthermore, the British regulatory authorities had suspended even the 0.25 mg and 0.125 mg doses on the grounds that their risks outweighed their benefits. Hence, the issues at stake in the May 1992 meeting were the safety and efficacy of the 0.25 and 0.125 mg doses. To address these issues the FDA conducted an analysis of the safety and efficacy data from Upjohn's clinical trials with Halcion and updated their analysis of post-marketing spontaneous adverse drug reaction reports. They did not, however, systematically review the published literature on Halcion.[52]

On the efficacy front, Upjohn had reduced the recommended starting dose from 0.5 mg to 0.25 mg in the US in 1988, but the FDA never required the company to prove that that lower dose remained effective. Four years later the agency now attempted to do this in front of the PDAC. As Dr David Kessler, the FDA commissioner, explained:

> *The reason we presented the data this morning on effectiveness was that the original application was not based on 0.25 mg. And as we've lowered the dose over the years, it was important to go back and check and make sure as we lowered the dose for the safety profile that there is reason to make sure that the drug is still effective.[53]*

Thus, the FDA permitted certain doses of Halcion on the market for four years without checking if they were effective, in contradiction with the regulatory standards advocated, albeit retrospectively, by the FDA commissioner.

To complicate matters, this question of Halcion's efficacy at the 0.25 mg dose was *not* unrelated to its safety at the 0.5 mg dose. Now that the FDA had admitted that the 0.5 mg dose was unsafe for a substantial number of patients, the effectiveness, or not, of the 0.25 mg dose became an even more pressing problem because if the 0.25 mg dose tended to be ineffective, then patients would be inclined to 'overdose' by taking two 0.25 mg tablets to get an effect, thus exposing them to the risks of the higher dose. While Upjohn acknowledged that *short-term* treatment at the *lowest* effective dose was advisable for all hypnotics, they also envisaged some continued use of the 0.5 mg dose even in 1992:

> *Data are available to support the continued efficacy of the 0.5 mg dose for up to three months. This dose, however, should be reserved for exceptional adult patients who do not respond to the 0.25 mg dose.[54]*

So what was this gathering of scientific expertise to make of the efficacy of Halcion at these lower doses? Daniel Marticello, a mathematical statistician, prepared the FDA efficacy review for the PDAC, but it was a scant effort. He considered the usual key efficacy measures: namely, time to fall asleep (sleep onset), number of awakenings and total sleep time. Four clinical trials were examined and found to support efficacy at the 0.5 mg dose for two weeks.[55] Regarding the efficacy of the 0.25 mg dose in non-elderly patients, Marticello analysed P6401, which was a seven-day controlled comparison with placebo involving patients with insomnia, and a multicentre protocol M/2100/0232 involving placebo control insomniacs for 14 days. He found Halcion to be effective relative to placebo on all three efficacy measures in P6401. For M/2100/0232, he found that there was not a significant difference between placebo and 0.25 mg of Halcion on the first two nights or the last two nights for sleep onset. However, he was willing to attribute this to sample size, and to generously conclude that Halcion was effective relative to placebo in the trial.[56]

Marticello presented an analysis of just two studies regarding the efficacy of the 0.125 mg dose. They were both part of P6417, a 17-day placebo-control with geriatric insomniacs. It involved two clinical investigators. One investigator did not find that Halcion had a significant therapeutic effect, while the other results did not show Halcion to be more effective than placebo in reducing number of awakenings, though there was evidence of its effectiveness on the other efficacy measures.[57] According to Marticello, there were no clinical studies in Upjohn's database which even addressed the efficacy of 0.125 mg in non-elderly patients.[58] The very limited data in support of the effectiveness of the 0.125 mg dose clearly troubled some members of the PDAC. For example, Regina Casper, Professor of Psychiatry at the University of Chicago, commented:

> *We have heard this morning from Dr Marticello about two studies, one which did not find this [0.125 mg] dose effective in the geriatric population, and another one which did. Considering that a large proportion of the American population will be elderly I think this is a very important question... the elderly have many more sleep problems.* So this is a question we really have to answer... I am not convinced that we have seen the data on this lower dose, on the 0.125 mg in geriatric patients. *So I don't believe I can address these questions on the effectiveness in geriatric patients (emphasis added).*[59]

Upjohn, on the other hand, presented a large amount of information concerning the efficacy of Halcion. With regard to the lower doses of the drug, Upjohn concluded from a review of 77 controlled clinical studies that 'the preponderance of the evidence strongly supports the efficacy of Halcion at doses of 0.125 and 0.25 mg'.[60] However, after hearing Upjohn's evidence of effectiveness at the *0.125 mg* dose, one of the committee members, Dr Larry Ereshefsky, Director of Psychiatric Pharmacy at the University of Texas Health Centre, concluded:

> *These two studies are good studies, but they are small sample sizes. One was 44 and the other was nine.* If you were to file an NDA [New Drug Application] with that number of patients it wouldn't fly *(emphasis added).*[61]

The PDAC also heard from Professor Frank Ayd, who reviewed much of Upjohn's efficacy data but disagreed with the company's conclusions. For example, the company's presentation highlighted three 'key' studies in support of Halcion's efficacy at the 0.25 mg dose. According to Ayd, Upjohn's accounts of these studies failed to provide adequate information about how patients were screened for psychiatric illness and use of alcohol, coffee or other drugs. One of these studies made no mention of the patients' 'baseline values' for various efficacy measures, such as time taken to fall asleep, total sleep time and number of awakenings prior to taking Halcion.* Ayd suggested that Upjohn's review was biased, commenting: 'All of these points are deficiencies Upjohn emphasizes in studies that report unfavourably on Halcion.'[63]

His most damning criticisms of Upjohn's representation of these studies concerned a 12-week trial comparing Halcion with placebo and another hypnotic. Upjohn concluded from this study that 'the evidence from clinical studies supports the efficacy of 0.25 mg of Halcion in adult patients in studies up to 84 days' duration'.[64] Ayd described this conclusion as 'completely misleading' because, at weeks ten and 12, Halcion was not significantly more effective than placebo in improving sleep onset.[65] He also noted that *only by the second week* did Halcion significantly improve patients' time taken to fall asleep, which is important because the drug was recommended to be taken for *no more than* seven to ten nights. Most strikingly he revealed: 'The text of Upjohn's summary fails to mention improvement in total sleep time, which was not significantly different from placebo.'[66]

Upjohn cited four trials with 0.125 mg of Halcion in non-elderly subjects, acknowledging that two of these four 'failed to show an effect for Halcion over placebo'.[67] Another of these four studies lasted for 14 days and Upjohn concluded that it 'showed significant improvement from baseline in sleep in seven adult insomniacs'.[68] However, Ayd also regarded this as misleading because, as Upjohn's own tables revealed, 0.125 mg of Halcion was significantly different from baseline for total sleep time only on the first three nights; by the end of the study there was little or no improvement on baseline.[69] Moreover, Upjohn's own data for this study showed that Halcion significantly improved time to sleep onset *only from nights 12 to 14*, yet the drug was recommended to be taken for no more than ten days.[70] Despite this, Upjohn concluded that 'the overall evidence from these clinical studies support the efficacy of 0.125 mg of Halcion in adult patients in studies up to 14 days' duration'.[71]

Regarding the efficacy of 0.125 mg of Halcion in elderly patients, Upjohn cited ten controlled clinical trials as support, half involving objective sleep assessment measures and the other half based on sleep questionnaires to the

---

* In the context of criticizing the work of Kales, Upjohn had noted that 'it is necessary to evaluate baseline characteristics' because 'without such information, very little clinical interpretation can be made of observations presented by the authors'.[62]

patients. A total of just 181 elderly insomniacs participated and at least six of the trials lasted no longer than three days. All five of the trials involving objective sleep assessment found that Halcion was significantly more efficacious than placebo for total sleep time, but only one showed significant improvement for sleep onset and only two found that Halcion reduced the number of awakenings compared with placebo.[72] On the other hand, the sleep questionnaire studies offered more support for effectiveness. Upjohn concluded that the evidence from clinical trials supported the efficacy of the 0.125 mg dose of Halcion, whereas Ayd considered Upjohn's evidence to be incomplete and misleading because it omitted published studies that did not support the company's conclusion.[73,74]

Despite the limitations of the clinical data, most members of the PDAC were willing to conclude that the lower doses of Halcion were effective.[75] For example, David Dunner, Professor of Psychiatry at the University of Washington Medical Centre, reasoned:

> *I think that if these were a new NDA, looking at the dose ranges being described, I think there would be an inadequate number of patients to support efficacy. But I think that, given the clinical use of this drug, the efficacy is supported.*[76]

Similarly, the language of reasoning used by Ereshefsky implies a process of self-persuasion beyond the evidence presented:

> *I think many of us have the* sense *that we are dealing with an effective drug, but* the data that we are looking at isn't satisfying... *I think there's enough data to at least* begin to address that issue... *my sense is that there's enough data out there to suggest that the blood levels achieved in most people at the doses being used is sufficient for sedation (emphasis added).*[77]

Here, Ereshefsky resorts to evidence about blood levels rather than evidence of actual clinical effects in order to convince himself that the 0.125 mg dose is effective.

On the question of safety, the committee first heard the FDA analysis and update of the ADR reports collated in the agency's SRS database. As with its presentation to the committee in 1989, the FDA's Division of Epidemiology and Biostatisitcs presented a comparative analysis of the SRS reports for Halcion and Restoril (temazepam), though this time it involved Drs Stadel, Barash, Graham and Wyskowski. As before, Restoril was chosen because it is another benzodiazepine hypnotic with an approximately similar number of prescriptions and it has been marketed since 1981 – a similar period to Halcion.

The FDA epidemiologists split up the data set into two periods: 1981 to 1987 and 1988 to 1991. They did this partly to update the committee who had not seen the 1988–1991 data before and partly to examine the impact of publicity on the reporting of spontaneous ADRs.[78] In 1987 and 1988 there had been a lot of adverse publicity about Halcion in the US, such as two damning articles in the *California Magazine* and a very critical documentary called *20/20*. In fact, during the period of 1988 to 1991, spontaneous ADR reports for Halcion increased *relative* to Restoril. This led some commentators to think that adverse publicity in the media was causing an 'abnormally' high rate of reporting with Halcion compared to other benzodiazepines – a view which Upjohn nurtured at the meeting.[79] However, Table 6.1 shows that this was an illusion. The *absolute number* of spontaneous ADR reports for Halcion actually decreased in the period after 1987. The increase in Halcion reports *relative* to Restoril was due to the fact that the absolute number of Restoril reports *decreased a lot more than Halcion's*.[80]

This is important because if negative media coverage was responsible for Halcion's high level of spontaneous ADR reports, then the drug may not *really* be more hazardous than other benzodiazepines. In short, we might be seeing a 'media effect' rather than a real effect. The data in Table 6.1 strongly suggests that the 'media effect' is unlikely because it would have been associated with an absolute increase in the number of Halcion reports, whereas it was, in fact, associated with a decrease. On this basis, Stadel categorically rejected the 'media effect' hypothesis.[81] Ominously, he surmised that the actual numbers of these ADRs might be 20 times greater than the numbers reported (in Table 6.1).[82]

Table 6.1 *Adverse event reports to FDA for Halcion and Restoril*

	1981–1987		1988–1991	
	Halcion	Restoril	Halcion	Restoril
All events	1266	231	1037	128
Amnesia	174	3	182	5
Agitation/anxiety	159	17	91	8
Psychosis	174	12	153	7
Confusion	205	16	195	6
Hostility	32	2	69	1
Seizure	38	1	17	0
Depression	66	6	85	3
Deaths	103	26	107	5

Source: Graham, D J, 1992, 'Halcion comparison with temazepam', FDA memo, 8 May, Table 1. Stadel, B V, 1992, 'Adverse drug event reporting for Halcion', FDA memo, 11 May

As they had done before the PDAC in 1989, Upjohn claimed that it was not possible to adjust for the 'quantitative biases' in SRS data. The company reiterated its contention that such data could not be used to make quantitative comparisons between drugs and reminded the committee and the FDA that in 1989 they had rejected such analyses by some of the agency's own epidemiologists:[83]

> As noted in a 3 October 1991 FDA talk paper, 'the committee [PDAC in 1989], after examining the evidence presented, concluded that the excess reports were not, by themselves, evidence of an excess risk, and could well represent the larger

number of prescriptions and a difference in reporting practices
rather than a difference in risks'.[84]

However, the FDA's epidemiologists systematically refuted Upjohn's assertion. After taking account of any differences in the extent of prescription, Stadel and his colleagues adjusted the data to take account of possible changes in general reporting in the US over the years 1981 to 1991 (ie secular trends). It is important to do this in order to be fair to Halcion because Restoril was marketed two years before Halcion and it is believed that over the years the level of reporting of post-marketing ADRs has increased. Table 6.2 shows how Halcion compared with Restoril with and without that adjustment.

Table 6.2 *Reporting rate ratios (Halcion:Restoril) for selected adverse events*

Adverse event	Unadjusted 1981–1991	Adjusted for secular trends 1981–1991	Adjusted for secular trends 1981–1987
Amnesia	34.4	26.3	28.0
Agitation/anxiety	7.7	6.1	6.3
Psychosis	13.3	10.6	9.9
Confusion	14.0	10.7	8.8
Hostility	26.0	23.8	14.6
Seizures	42.5	39.1	34.5
Depression	13.0	9.5	7.7
Dependence	14.5	12.8	9.3
Death	5.2	3.8	2.9

Source: Graham, D J, 1992, 'Halcion comparison with temazepam', FDA memo, 8 May, Tables 3 and 5. Stadel, B V, 1992, 'Adverse drug event reporting for Halcion', FDA memo, 11 May

Remarkably, these enormously high ratios, which FDA epidemiologists first discovered in the mid 1980s, had persisted up to 1992. In other words, Halcion continued to be associated with about 40 times as many seizures, 26 times as many cases of amnesia, 23 times as many cases of hostility, 13 times as many cases of dependence and over ten times as many case of psychosis, *even after adjusting for secular trends in reporting.* Robert Temple, the FDA's director of new drug evaluation, characterized some of these adverse events as 'scary'.[85] To be generous to Halcion, the FDA epidemiology division also adjusted for the year of marketing because it is thought that most reporting of ADRs occurs in the first few years of marketing. However, even on adjusting for secular trends and year of marketing simultaneously, the Halcion to Restoril ratio remains very large for amnesia, dependence, hostility and seizures (see Table 6.3).

This data could not be due to differences in the propensity of Upjohn and Sandoz to report ADRs because they were confined to particular types of ADRs and they appeared in the reports from non-industry sources, such as prescribing doctors.[86] Moreover, in an analysis using statistical methods to adjust for *many factors*, including publicity, time of entry into the market, manufacturers' reporting practices and secular trends in overall reporting rates, among

Table 6.3 *Reporting rate ratios (Halcion:Restoril) for the first three years of marketing*

Adverse event	Unadjusted	Adjusted for secular trends
Amnesia	27.4	14.7
Agitation/anxiety	8.6	5.2
Psychosis	15.5	9.0
Confusion	16.6	8.8
Hostility	>> (23/0)	>>
Seizures	>> (33/0)	>>
Depression	8.8	5.5
Dependence	27.0	22.6
Death	2.5	1.8

Key: >> = 'infinitely large' because there were no cases for temazepam (Restoril).
Source: Graham, D J, 1992, 'Halcion comparison with temazepam', FDA memo, 8 May, Table 4.
Stadel, B V, 1992, 'Adverse drug event reporting for Halcion', FDA memo, 11 May

others, Dr Yi Tsong, from the FDA's biometrics division, found that *large risk ratios remained*.[87] Dr David Graham, from the FDA's epidemiology division, drew the following conclusions from these analyses:

> *Reporting of neuropsychiatric ADRs with Halcion has been far in excess of that with temazepam [Restoril]. Reporting rate ratios were very high for amnesia, seizures and hostility; they were high for dependence, psychosis, depression and confusion; they were elevated but of lesser degree for agitation (anxiety) and death. These findings were not explained away or qualitatively altered by adjusting for secular trends in ADR reporting to FDA, year of product marketing, manufacturer reporting practices, or adverse publicity or other period effects. Although not an actual relative risk, the reporting rate ratios appear to reflect actual differences in risk of neuropsychiatric adverse-effect causation. Halcion appears to have greater intrinsic capacity to provoke a number of adverse effects... Halcion may pose greater risks of inducing true physical dependence than temazepam. The pattern of Halcion use in the US also makes the development of physical dependence a possibility. This risk may be disproportionately experienced among the elderly, who represent nearly half of all Halcion users (emphasis added).*[88]

For the analysis of safety data in *clinical trials*, Drs Thomas Laughren and Hillary Lee, from the FDA's psychopharmacological drug products division, reviewed 116 studies sponsored by Upjohn, of which 108 (93 per cent) were conducted prior to approval in the US in 1982.[89] As a result of the revelations about P321 and disqualified investigators, especially Franklin, the FDA became concerned about the integrity of Upjohn's database for the original New Drug Application in 1982. Consequently, the agency scientists created an entirely new safety database by re-entering the data from all the case report forms from these 116 trials, involving 4870 patients on Halcion, 1377 on the comparator drug Dalmane, and 2266 on placebo. However, for their main analysis they focused on 25 studies that were at least one week long and involved the treatment of patients with insomnia, comparing groups on Halcion with groups taking Dalmane or placebo. In all, this subgroup of 25 studies involved 1168 patients on Halcion, 607 on Dalmane and 566 on placebo. To a first approximation, these studies compared 0.5 mg of Halcion with 30 mg of Dalmane ('high' doses) and/or 0.125/0.25 mg of Halcion with 15 mg of Dalmane ('low' doses). That is, they assumed that 30 mg of Dalmane was equivalent to 0.5 mg of Halcion and 15 mg of Dalmane was equivalent to 0.25 mg of Halcion. In the first part of their safety analysis, FDA scientists also adopted that assumption.

Like the approach of the British MCA, the FDA's review concentrated on drop outs from clinical trials because they are a good indication of the severity and importance of adverse reactions. If a patient can no longer tolerate taking a drug in a trial, then clearly the drug is creating problems for that patient. Table 6.4 shows how Halcion compares with Dalmane in the drop-out analysis for these 25 studies without distinguishing between 'high' and 'low' doses. Taking all the adverse reactions together, there was a statistically significantly higher risk of drop out with Halcion than Dalmane. That risk remained statistically significant; indeed, it was increased when the analysis focused solely on 'psychiatric' adverse effects or 'anxiety' or 'memory impairment' (amnesia).

Table 6.4 *Summary drop-out analysis without sorting for dose*

Adverse event term	Number of drop-out events		Risk ratio Halcion/Dalmane
	Halcion (n=1168)	Dalmane (n=607)	
Any adverse event	145	58	1.3*
All 'psychiatric'	63	15	2.2*
Anxiety	44	9	2.5*
Memory impairment	8	0	>>*

Key: * = statistically significant (p<0.05, 1-sided p-value, Fisher's exact test)
>> = 'infinitely large' and hence 'significant'
Source: Laughren, T and Lee, H, 1992, 'Review of adverse event data in Upjohn-sponsored clinical studies of Halcion', FDA submission to PDAC, 1 May, Table 6.25a

When these studies were broken down according to 'high' and 'low' doses, the FDA found that the risk for drop out remained consistently higher for Halcion than for Dalmane (see Table 6.5). On the whole, this higher risk was statistically significant for the 'high' dose groups. However, a much smaller number of patients took the 'low' doses, so the capacity of those patient groups to generate statistically significant results was compromised. For example, for 'any adverse event' in Table 6.5, the risk for drop out with 'low dose' Halcion was 1.7 times greater than for 'low dose' Dalmane, but this figure was only 1.4 for the 'high' doses. Yet, the latter was statistically significant while the former was not. This apparent anomaly was because of the small size of the samples taking the 'low' doses. Moreover, for both 'anxiety' and 'all psychiatric' adverse effects, the risk for drop out with 'low' dose Halcion was substantially larger than for 'low' dose Dalmane from a subjective standpoint and 'infinitely' larger from a mathematical perspective.

Table 6.5 *Drop-out analysis sorted by dose*

Patient groups	Per cent drop-out		Risk ratio
	Halcion	Dalmane	Halcion/Dalmane
Any adverse event			
Low dose	19/272 (7.0%)	3/71 (4.2%)	1.7
High dose	126/896 (14.1%)	55/536 (10.3%)	1.4*
Anxiety			
Low dose	8/272 (2.9%)	0/71 (0.0%)	>>
High dose	36/896 (4.0%)	9/536 (1.7%)	2.4*
Memory impairment			
Low dose	0/272 (0.0%)	0/71 (0.0%)	—
High dose	8/896 (0.9%)	0/536 (0.0%)	>>
All psychiatric adverse events			
Low dose	9/272 (3.3%)	0/71 (0.0%)	>>
High dose	54/896 (6.0%)	15/536 (2.8%)	2.1*

Key: * = statistically significant ($p < 0.05$, 1-sided p-value, Fisher's exact test)
>> = 'infinitely large' and hence 'significant'
Low dose = 0.125, 0.125–0.25, 0.25 mg of Halcion; 15 mg of Dalmane
High dose = 0.25–0.5, 0.5, 0.6 mg of Halcion; 15–30, 30 mg of Dalmane
Source: Laughren, T and Lee, H, 1992, 'Review of adverse event data in Upjohn-sponsored clinical studies of Halcion', FDA submission to PDAC, 1 May, Table 6.25a

Upjohn argued that SRS data needed to be confirmed by *clinical trials* and that no such confirmation was evident.[90] It was on this basis that the company concluded that 'comparative data shows that the safety margin of Halcion is equal to or greater than other hypnotics'.[91] But the findings in Tables 6.4 and 6.5 supported the trends identified in the spontaneous reporting of ADRs for Halcion (Tables 6.1–6.3), albeit at much lower levels. The signal of risk flagged up by the SRS data was *qualitatively confirmed* and *quantitatively clarified* by the analysis of this *clinical trial* data. Notably, as 93 per cent of the trials for this analysis were submitted to the FDA in 1982, the agency could have undertaken substantially the same review in the mid 1980s when the SRS database first signalled large risks associated with Halcion compared with other benzodiazepine hypnotics!

Yet the PDAC were also presented with a more fuzzy picture. In the second part of their analysis of safety data from these 25 clinical trials, FDA scientists Laughren and Lee made a crucial move. They accepted Upjohn's argument that 30 mg of Dalmane was equivalent to just 0.25 mg of Halcion rather than the 'high' 0.5 mg of Halcion, even though the company had not explained how this equipotency was established, and despite the fact that the trials themselves were based on protocols defining 30 mg of Dalmane as equivalent to 0.5 mg of Halcion.[92,93] To do this, Laughren and Lee had to divorce the individual patient CRFs from the trial protocols of which they were a part; as they accepted, this added to the 'noise' or fuzziness of the data because of the different effects that different investigators in protocols might have on results. Oswald, in particular, rejected this 'averaging out' approach to the data because 'the most striking thing about the data was a wide variability of adverse event rates' across different clinical studies and investigators, which 'made it difficult to derive any meaningful summary data from the total data set'.[94] He argued that some clinical investigators, who wrote scarcely anything down about their patients, were 'insensitive research instruments', whereas 'some investigators did listen to their patients, wrote things down and should be the guide' to safety assessment.[95]

Given that the adverse effects of Halcion are generally dose related, the move based on an acceptance that 30 mg of Dalmane was equipotent with just 0.25 mg of Halcion was guaranteed to lower the risk of Halcion relative to Dalmane. On the assumption that 'low' dose Halcion was equivalent to 'high' dose Dalmane, rather than 'low' dose Dalmane, Laughren and Lee constructed what they called 'appropriately dosed' patient groups. While these patients were certainly real, the 'groups' were a post hoc construction because the actual clinical trials never grouped the patients according to such dosing. In other words, these FDA scientists sought to fit the data into a model based on Upjohn's post hoc rationalization about dose equivalence; but because the clinical trials were never set up that way, the length of time 'appropriately dosed' patients had taken the two drugs was very different and the sample dropped to about a quarter of its original size (see Table 6.6). As we discussed in Chapter 5, Dr Patrick Waller, the medical assessor for Halcion within the British regulatory authorities, did not accept this post hoc rationalization on dose equivalence.

Table 6.6 *Sample size and duration of use features for 'appropriately dosed' subgroups*

Subgroup features	Halcion	Dalmane
Sample size	285 patients	423 patients
Median duration	7 days	14 days

Source: Laughren, T and Lee, H, 1992, 'Review of adverse event data in Upjohn-sponsored clinical studies of Halcion', FDA submission to PDAC, 1 May, unnumbered table

Nevertheless, FDA scientists proceeded to conduct a drop-out analysis on this 'appropriately dosed' sample. The analytical construction shown in Table 6.6 had two important consequences for this analysis. Firstly, the relatively small sample ensured that the analysis lacked the power to translate differences into statistical significance; and secondly, patients were dosed for much longer on Dalmane.[96] This is important in a drop-out analysis because if patients are experiencing an adverse effect they are much more likely to drop out if they expect the trial to continue for another week than if it is due to end in a day or two. For instance, they might tolerate an adverse effect for a few days in order to complete the trial, but not for ten days.[97] As patients in this constructed group tended to be on Dalmane for significantly longer than their Halcion counterparts, the drop-out analysis was skewed in favour of Halcion.

Despite this, even the drop-out analysis of 'appropriately dosed' patients suggested a greater risk associated with Halcion than with Dalmane for psychiatric adverse effects (see Table 6.7), although none of these results were statistically significant. In fact, the risk for drop out due to anxiety was three times higher for Halcion than for Dalmane. This was an even greater relative risk than for the 'high' dose group shown in Table 6.5. There the risk ratio was 2.4, but it was statistically significant because of the larger sample size. This is a very clear example of how the sample size in the 'appropriately dosed' analysis may have compromised significant differences between the two drugs for some adverse effects. As Dr Charles Anello, Acting Director of the Division of Epidemiology and Biostatisitcs, commented:

> *Restricting attention to this subgroup [of 'appropriately dosed' patients] resulted in substantial loss of sample size and [statistical] power. Thus this analysis of these data* leaves unresolved the question of safety *at doses of comparable efficacy (emphasis added).*[98]

Table 6.7 *Summary drop-out analysis for 'appropriately dosed' patients*

Adverse event term	Number of drop-out events Halcion (n=285)	Dalmane (n=423)	Risk ratio Halcion/Dalmane
Any adverse event	20 (7.0%)	31 (7.3%)	1.0
All 'psychiatric'	8 (2.8%)	7 (1.7%)	1.7
Anxiety	8 (2.8%)	4 (0.9%)	3.0
Memory impairment	0	0	—

Source: Laughren, T and Lee, H, 1992, 'Review of adverse event data in Upjohn-sponsored clinical studies of Halcion', FDA submission to PDAC, 1 May, Tables 6.26 and 6.26a

Furthermore, if it took the manufacturers of the drug over 20 years to 'appropriately dose' such a small sample of patients in clinical trials, how realistic could it be to expect prescribing doctors to achieve extensive 'appropriate dosing' in the general population of consumers? This issue is particularly pertinent given the questionable effectiveness of the lower 0.125 and 0.25 mg doses because doctors may be inclined to prescribe, and patients inclined to take, higher than the 'appropriate dose' in order to achieve effects from the drug. However that may be, taking all the adverse effects together, the 'appropriately dosed' analysis suggests a disappearance of any difference in risk for drop out between Halcion and Dalmane. Although it is not known how important the difference in length of time on the drugs may have been in dissolving that difference, Laughren told the committee that this was an important finding and argued that the low frequency of drop outs, 3 per cent or less, suggested that Halcion was tolerated 'well enough'.[99,100]

Public Citizen's Health Research Group was not convinced. It called for Halcion to be banned in the US and worldwide, especially in view of the fact that its dangers seemed to increase with long-term use, common among users of sleeping pills in the US and elsewhere.[101] In 1989, Dr Pamela Tullio at the University of Michigan published startling results which demonstrated the potential dangers of how Halcion was used by doctors and patients. Aware that Halcion was indicated for short-term treatment of insomnia, these researchers examined the medical charts of 72 patients (of whom 50 were elderly), who had received a 30-day prescription for 0.125 or 0.25 mg of Halcion. They found that 75 per cent of the prescriptions had been written for a one-month supply with *five refills* so that the average length of therapy was *6.2 months*.[102] They concluded:

> *The fact that most patients who took Halcion nightly experi-*
> *enced decreased quality of sleep when doses were not taken*
> *could indicate dependence. Over 50 per cent of the patients*
> *experienced problems of rebound insomnia, such as waking*
> *during the night or early in the morning and not being able to*
> *return to sleep... Twenty-three per cent of patients described*
> *periods of dizziness while taking Halcion. This occurred in a*
> *larger percentage of patients taking the higher (0.25 mg) dose.*[103]

Ayd reached similar conclusions and told the committee:

> *When the 0.125 mg and 0.25 mg doses became the recommended*
> *Halcion doses in the US in 1988, data began to emerge indicat-*
> *ing three important facts: lowering Halcion dosage to 0.25 and*
> *0.125 mg did not significantly eliminate many adverse*
> *reactions to this drug; physical dependence and withdrawal*
> *problems have not been eliminated; and the therapeutic efficacy*
> *of these doses are not pronounced and often wane after two*
> *weeks' continuous use... I urge the FDA to remove Halcion from*
> *the US market. There is insufficient scientific justification for*
> *marketing a drug with documented toxicity that FDA data*
> *confirms would be taken primarily by elderly patients, not for a*
> *week or two, but possibly for months or years.*[104]

As for Upjohn, they argued that the adverse effect profile of Halcion was similar to other benzodiazepines, and that the 'central nervous system medical events' reported in controlled clinical trials were either 'typical of benzodiazepines' or 'background symptoms of insomniacs' not attributable to drugs.[105] While Oswald told the PDAC that 'it would be a contrivance contrary to the evidence to pretend that the psychiatric effects of Halcion are those typical of benzodiazepines' and urged patients to avoid the drug, the company asserted that, by 1992, Halcion's package insert mentioned these adverse effects, such as memory impairment, confusion, bizarre behaviour, agitation, aggressiveness and hallucinations, and that with this labelling the drug could be used safely.[106]

As regards drop outs, Upjohn merely acknowledged that 'differential rates of drop outs between Halcion and Dalmane observed in some studies occurred when non-equipotent doses were used, eg 0.5 mg of Halcion versus 30 mg of Dalmane'.[107]

While some members of the PDAC accepted that 'the longer the use, the higher the dose and the more likely there are more serious side effects', most concluded that Halcion was safe enough to remain on the market.[108] They reached this conclusion in spite of the robustness of the SRS data, as Ereshefsky noted:

> *One of the things which I looked at with regard to the spontaneous reporting data, because to me that was the most bothersome of all the data, is this apparently large signal sticking out there, and the agency has done a good job of trying to explain it away and control for variables, and it's still there (emphasis added).*[109]

Even in the closing minutes of the meeting Dr Robert Hamer, Associate Professor of Biostatistics in Virginia, seemed entirely unsure whether the 0.25 mg dose was safe:

> *I haven't particularly seen any evidence in the sense that Halcion's unsafe at 0.25 mg, but I also haven't seen enough evidence to assert that it's safe at 0.25 mg. That's a very imprecise way of saying what I feel, which is: one ought to find out what the lowest possible effective dose is, because since the side effects appear to be dose related, then if one could use a lower dose, it would be safer... I don't believe that there is not safety. I fail to believe that there is safety (emphasis added).*[110]

In similar fashion, both Temple and another member of the PDAC seemed entirely unsure about the safety and effectiveness of the 0.125 mg dose:

> *Dr Paul [PDAC member]:*   *Yes, I would agree with Dr Temple. I don't think we are still quite sure what the exact dose is for this drug.*
> *Dr Temple:*   *Indeed.*
> *Dr Paul:*   *While we know that 0.25 mg, I think, is efficacious and relatively safe given the data we have heard, we are not sure that lower doses aren't. Some of the data I have seen suggests that 0.125 mg is efficacious. Dr Kales would probably argue that it is not. So we don't really know (emphasis added).*[111]

Yet, later that day seven out of eight committee members voted that Halcion was safe and effective at the doses of 0.125 mg and 0.25 mg as recommended in the labelling, while the other member, Linda Hezel, Associate Professor at the School of Nursing in the University of Missouri, voted that Halcion was neither safe nor effective.[112] Armed with this advice the FDA continued to permit the marketing of Halcion.

Conflicts of interest: more than meets the eye

The introductory pages of the proceedings of the 1992 PDAC meeting make astonishing reading. Not only were all of the invited guest experts either former or current advisors to Upjohn, recipients of grants from Upjohn or Upjohn stockholders, but ten out of the 11 members of the committee had conflicts of interest. Nine of those ten were recipients of Upjohn grants and the other one was an Upjohn stockholder. Two of these members excluded themselves because their conflicts of interest were so substantial they did not participate in the meeting and another one participated, but she was a non-voting member. Nevertheless, seven out of the eight voting members had conflicts of interest. In all cases the FDA waived their conflicts of interest on the grounds that their expertise and advice were invaluable to the agency.[113]

We are not suggesting that such conflicts of interest determined the opinions of these experts. In fact, the one expert who voted that Halcion was neither safe nor effective did have a conflict of interest. Nor are we suggesting that their views were not genuinely held. The relationship between expert judgements and interests is not a simple one. But this situation was bound to lead collectively to a much closer association with Halcion's manufacturer than would otherwise be the case. Combined with the fact that the PDAC is a highly specialized body, these conflicts of interest might have produced a *group bias of drug benefit over risk* because all the specialists on the committee had such a close intellectual, professional and even institutional relationship with the benzodiazepines.

This may partly explain why the PDAC was so much more sympathetic to Halcion than the British Committee on Safety of Medicines (CSM). The highly specialized PDAC is convened ad hoc by the FDA to provide advice on solely psychopharmacological drugs, whereas the CSM is a more generalist committee passing mandatory judgements on all kinds of new drugs. Consequently, the CSM may be less inclined to specialist group bias. According to Professor Michael Rawlins, a former chairman of the CSM:

> *[Specialists] are often wedded to particular therapeutic strategies. And if you look back over the years when the CSM has issued a warning or done something about various classes of drug, the specialists have often been up in arms at the time. I think they tend perhaps to be conditioned to the successes which they meet in everyday practice and find it more difficult to grasp overall balance.*[114]

Apparently 'intellectual' conflicts of interest are taken account of in the CSM; a member might not participate in discussion about a particular drug if he or she is thought to be very committed to research on that class of drugs even if there are no direct or indirect financial interests involved.[115] No such system operates within the PDAC and this may be a weakness given that Professor Sheila Jasanoff's sociological research into the FDA's advisory committees has concluded that the US system 'conceives of conflicts of interest in overly narrow terms', and that 'there are more subtle patterns of influence that should legitimately concern policy-makers'.[116] The regulation of Halcion may be a case where just such subtle patterns of influence made themselves felt.

In this context it is also significant that Patrick Waller, the MCA's scientist who was so influential in the British regulatory decision to suspend Halcion, was a generalist with particular interests in spontaneous ADR data. Having obtained an MD in the cardiovascular field, he obtained a Master's degree in epidemiology and public health and then worked for a couple of years on post-marketing drug safety monitoring.[117] Consequently, he adopted a public health perspective on drug safety and was predisposed to treat post-marketing spontaneous ADR data with more gravity than his counterparts at the FDA. Waller took the danger signals from the spontaneous ADR reports and examined clinical trials and P321 for evidence of an accumulation of risk. Thus, he gave considerable weight to the adverse effects recorded in P321 and the controlled clinical trials.

By contrast, the FDA's analysis was much more fragmented. Leber's reviewing division of specialist clinicians was dismissive of the safety implications of P321 and in 1989 had been dismissive of SRS data. Moreover, his division adopted an 'averaging out' approach in its review of clinical trials. This approach ignored the possibility that some trials might be more sensitive detectors of adverse reactions than others. For instance, longer trials might be more sensitive to adverse reactions causing drop out than short ones and so on. This 'experimental' approach to the data is also evident in the construction of the 'appropriately dosed' groups, whose significance to the real world of public health is, arguably, much less than Leber assumed.

Furthermore, institutional interests may also be an important factor in accounting for why the FDA's decision differed from that of the MCA. While the same FDA division is responsible for both approval and post-marketing, the licensing and post-licensing divisions within the British MCA are organizationally separate, staffed by officials with differing expertise. Professor Sir William Asscher, a former chairman of the CSM, considered this to be a strength of the British system because 'the people who gave the licence in the first place will defend their decision to the last and that could be to the detriment of the population'.[118] If Asscher is correct, then these organizational aspects of the British and American regulatory authorities are likely to have made it easier for the British to remove Halcion from the market. This could be particularly relevant in the Halcion case because the scientists at the MCA and the CSM who approved the drug's licences in the UK in 1978 are different from those who suspended those licences in 1991; in the US, however, Leber is the same influential regulator at the FDA who approved Halcion in 1982 and who rejected arguments to remove it from the market throughout the 1990s.

Justice and the Food and Drug Administration's conscience

In April 1994 the commissioner of the FDA requested that an FDA task force on Halcion should be formed to examine matters of criminal misconduct and other regulatory concerns. The task force issued its report in May 1996, which recommended that 'the justice department assess whether the Upjohn company committed crimes by failing to report serious side effects'.[119] The task force did not go as far as to recommend criminal prosecution of the company, but concluded that 'further enquiry into allegations of criminal misconduct by Upjohn is most appropriately the subject of consideration by the Department of Justice'.[120] Furthermore, it asserted that in 1992 the FDA had evidence which should have been referred to the justice department. According to the agency's own task force, the FDA made a mistake when it terminated its investigation into Halcion in 1992. The agency had justified termination by arguing that none of the findings from its inspection of Upjohn were relevant to the approval of Halcion. However, the task force concluded that the errors in the technical report for P321 should have been considered material. In other words, the results of P321 were relevant to the decision to approve Halcion as a safe drug. Yet the results of that trial continued to be sidelined even in the FDA's 1992 reassessment of Halcion's safety.

After analysing other clinical studies in the original New Drug Application for Halcion, the task force found that 'Upjohn did not always accurately and completely collect and summarize the information in the technical reports', and that its supervision of trials was poor.[121] By this time, Upjohn was facing about 100 product liability lawsuits in the US from patients alleging adverse effects from taking Halcion, including violent psychiatric reactions.[122] In one such case, the Californian State Supreme Court ruled that Upjohn should have warned consumers of all 'reasonably scientifically knowable' dangers from Halcion, regardless of whether the FDA had approved labelling not containing such specific warnings.[123] This ruling is notable for its comment on the American courts' growing lack of confidence in the FDA to protect consumers.

A task for the super scientists? The Institute of Medicine analysis

The FDA's decision to refer some of Upjohn's conduct to the US Department of Justice did not put an end to criticisms of Halcion's safety and efficacy. In September 1996, Kales and his colleagues at Pennsylvania State College of Medicine published a critique of Halcion in the *International Journal of Risk and Safety in Medicine* citing 192 references in support of their case. They argued that 'to establish convincingly the efficacy of a hypnotic drug, the vast majority of objective sleep laboratory studies should show significant improvement in the various sleep parameters'. However, for 0.25 mg of Halcion, only about half did so. With regard to the risks, they emphasized the drug's *narrow margin of safety* concerning severe adverse psychiatric reactions, such as aggression, amnesia, hallucinations and psychosis. According to the Kales group:

> *Five elderly patients experienced an organic brain syndrome*
> *characterized by delirium, anterograde amnesia and automatic*
> *movements. In four of the five cases only a single dose of 0.125*
> *mg of Halcion was used, whereas in the fifth case the dose was*
> *0.25 mg.*[124]

The risks associated with a narrow margin of safety were further highlighted by an article in the American journal *Women & Therapy*, claiming that physicians were prone to misattribute the adverse effects of Halcion to other things. Given this, the author questioned the wisdom of broadly marketing a medication with frequent and profound adverse effects, while leaving careful prescribing and monitoring up to individual doctors.[125] Moreover, researchers in Madrid reported that 72 per cent of users of hypnotics were taking them for more than three months. Such long-term use was found to be two to three times more frequent among elderly users, but often without adequate adjustment of dosage.[126] This suggests a substantial problem of dependence. Significantly, another group of Spanish researchers found that out of 153 patients who had become dependent upon benzodiazepines, Halcion was the one most frequently used in high doses by the dependents.[127]

Kales and his colleagues also reiterated that the FDA's data on spontaneous reports documented that Halcion was associated with many more adverse psychiatric effects than other sleeping pills, such as Restoril or Dalmane. In particular, they noted that this data 'showed a total of 27 murders or attempted murders related temporally to benzodiazepine hypnotic use, with 26 of these associated with Halcion use'.[128] Moreover, they pointed to reports that increased anxiety associated with Halcion use can lead to self-medication during the daytime, increased total daily dose and dependency. This, combined with the potential for rebound insomnia on attempting to stop taking the drug after just one night, might account for the much higher numbers of reports of withdrawal and dependency problems – including seizures – associated with Halcion relative to Restoril or Dalmane.[129]

In May 1996, the FDA task force concluded that Halcion was 'safe when prescribed according to labelling' and 'effective in the treatment of insomnia at doses and durations recommended in the labelling'.[130] Yet the task force did not have a great deal of confidence in this conclusion because it recommended that there should be a separate reassessment of the drug's safety and efficacy by a panel of 'independent' experts. Consequently, in April 1997, the FDA contracted the Institute of Medicine (IoM) of the US National Academy of Sciences to assess: the adequacy of the major clinical trials pertaining to Halcion; the quality and quantity of the post-marketing ADR data; the overall confidence in the data on the effectiveness and adverse effects of the drug; and the need for additional studies to clarify its risks and efficacy.[131] By this time, Argentina, Brazil, Denmark, Norway and the UK had removed Halcion from their markets, but the drug remained on the markets of many other European countries, as well as Australia, New Zealand, Canada and, of course, the US.[132]

During 1996 and 1997, medical reports from North America continued to reopen old wounds about Halcion's safety. Researchers at the University of Mississippi suggested that even low doses of Halcion might be associated with more nervousness, restlessness and memory impairment than another sleeping pill, while Health Canada found that Halcion and Dalmane presented a higher risk of falling than other benzodiazepines.[133,134] In potentially related research, Deborah Robin and her colleagues at Vanderbilt University replicated their 1991 findings that Halcion increased loss of balance in patients.[135]

The IoM published its report in November 1997. In the US, 0.25 mg remained the recommended dose of Halcion for adults, except for geriatrics who were to be prescribed 0.125 mg. Thus, the IoM's analysis focused on studies of these doses. To assess the efficacy of these doses, the IoM examined placebo-controlled clinical trials in which patients or subjects responded to questionnaires about how well the drug improved their sleep according to various criteria (known as 'endpoints'), and to sleep laboratory studies (known as polysomnographic studies) which yield more precise objective measures of sleep characteristics to which the patients or subjects may be unaware. The sources of these studies were Upjohn's New Drug Application (NDA) in 1982, post-marketing studies by Upjohn and research published in the medical journals.

The institute reanalysed subjective questionnaire data from the double-blind clinical trials in Upjohn's NDA which it considered adequate. They found 18 trials of 0.25 mg and two of 0.125 mg of Halcion involving geriatrics. According to the IoM's reanalysis, this data showed that, compared with placebo, the 0.25 mg dose was effective in overall help with sleep, in reducing time to fall asleep, in increasing total sleep time and in reducing number of awakenings (see Table 6.8). This is impressive evidence in favour of the efficacy of Halcion at that dose. For example, Table 6.8 shows that 51 per cent of

Table 6.8 *Observed proportions of four primary endpoints for subjects who received 0.25 mg of Halcion versus those for subjects who received placebo*

Endpoint	Treatment	

		Proportion for following effect category				
Endpoint	Treatment	1	2	3	4	5
Overall help with sleep		*None*	*Little*	*Quite a bit*	*A lot*	
	Placebo	0.51	0.21	0.18	0.10	
	Halcion	0.17	0.18	0.35	0.30	
Time to sleep onset		*Slower*	*Same*	*Quicker*		
	Placebo	0.14	0.59	0.27		
	Halcion	0.07	0.30	0.64		
Hours of sleep		*<5h*	*5–6h*	*6.1–7h*	*7.1–8h*	*>8h*
	Placebo	0.25	0.29	0.22	0.15	0.08
	Halcion	0.10	0.17	0.26	0.31	0.16
Number of awakenings		*>6*	*4–5*	*2–3*	*1*	*0*
	Placebo	0.05	0.17	0.41	0.19	0.17
	Halcion	0.02	0.07	0.29	0.36	0.26

Source: Institute of Medicine, 1997, *Halcion: an independent assessment of safety and efficacy data*, National Academy Press, Washington, DC, p 38

subjects felt that placebo did not help at all with their sleep overall, whereas only 17 per cent of those taking Halcion felt that way. At the other end of the spectrum, while 10 per cent of subjects on placebo felt that their sleep was a lot better overall, 30 per cent of the subjects taking Halcion did so.

For geriatrics, the 0.125 mg dose was also significantly better at improving sleep except that it did not reduce their number of awakenings (see Table 6.9). For example, while 47 per cent of the geriatrics taking Halcion had two or three awakenings, so had 44 per cent of those on placebo; and while 7 per cent on placebo did not wake during their night's sleep, only 8 per cent of subjects taking Halcion were similarly untroubled. This evidence supported Halcion's effectiveness at the geriatric dose but was less impressive, especially in view of the fact that the results were based on just two studies.[136]

Table 6.9 *Observed proportions of four primary endpoints for geriatric subjects who received 0.125 mg of Halcion versus those for subjects who received placebo*

Endpoint	Treatment	Proportion for following effect category				
		1	2	3	4	5
Overall help with sleep		None	Little	Quite a bit	A lot	
	Placebo	0.52	0.24	0.14	0.10	
	Halcion	0.28	0.22	0.27	0.23	
Time to sleep onset		Slower	Same	Quicker		
	Placebo	0.12	0.62	0.26		
	Halcion	0.00	0.43	0.57		
Hours of sleep		<5h	5–6h	6.1–7h	7.1–8h	>8h
	Placebo	0.26	0.32	0.26	0.10	0.06
	Halcion	0.09	0.31	0.23	0.22	0.14
Number of awakenings		>6	4–5	2–3	1	0
	Placebo	0.06	0.20	0.44	0.23	0.07
	Halcion	0.03	0.15	0.47	0.27	0.08

Source: Institute of Medicine, 1997, *Halcion: an independent assessment of safety and efficacy data,* National Academy Press, Washington, DC, p 39

The IoM was unable to find any sleep laboratory studies of the 0.125 mg dose in Upjohn's NDA or among Upjohn's unpublished post-marketing research. They did, however, reanalyse three such studies of the 0.25 mg dose: namely, P6014 with six subjects for 14 nights, P6020 with three subjects for seven nights, and M21000232 with 26 patients for 14 nights. In all three studies the key criteria of efficacy were time to sleep onset, total sleep time and number of awakenings. During the early nights of P6014, there was some evidence that Halcion improved sleep, but after this the drug showed no significant effect. Since P6020 involved only three patients, the institute reasonably found it inconclusive. The most important of the three studies was M21000232 because of its size and duration. Data from this study showed that Halcion was significantly more effective than placebo at reducing time to sleep onset; but crucially it was not significantly more effective at increasing total sleep time or reducing number of awakenings.

Oddly and rather ambiguously, the IoM deduced from this that 'despite small sample sizes and few studies, the findings were supportive of the questionnaire findings that sleep latency [ie sleep onset] and total sleep time were *affected* [emphasis added] by the 0.25 mg Halcion dose'. This interpretation is astonishingly generous to Halcion, yet simultaneously does not amount to much as far as significant effectiveness is concerned. The most substantial of Upjohn's sleep laboratory studies of this dose does *not* support the questionnaire findings from clinical trials that Halcion significantly improves total sleep time or reduces awakening, and P6014 is as unsupportive as it is supportive. Therefore, there is a tension between the support for Halcion's effectiveness from Upjohn's subjective clinical trials, on the one hand, and the lack of it from their objective sleep laboratory studies, on the other.[137]

The institute reviewed four placebo-controlled clinical trials from the published medical literature in the mid 1990s. One substantial study, in 1997, with 335 elderly subjects for four weeks found that 0.125 mg of Halcion did not significantly improve sleep onset or total sleep time, and that the subjects found it no better than placebo in helping them with their sleep overall. Two of the clinical trials studied the effects of 0.25 mg of Halcion when taken by the non-elderly adults. The larger and more important one, in 1994, involved an impressive 1507 subjects. Such a large sample promised considerable statistical sensitivity. Despite this, Halcion was not found to produce a significant response in subjects compared with placebo, where a response was defined very modestly as shortening sleep onset by 15 minutes, prolongation of sleep time by 20 per cent *or* reduction of awakenings to three or less. In the other one, in 1997, there were 357 patients but it was merely a one-night study. Halcion was found to significantly improve sleep onset and total sleep time and to reduce nocturnal awakening. The fourth study, in 1993, involved 221 elderly patients taking 0.25 mg of Halcion for three weeks; it also showed that the drug was significantly better than placebo in these respects.[138]

The IoM summarized this evidence as follows:

> *Thus, two of the three studies provide support for the efficacy of Halcion at 0.25 mg in the general population, including elderly subjects. Halcion was not significantly better than placebo in the third study at 0.25 mg. The one study with elderly patients with a 0.125 mg dose does not support efficacy in that population.*[139]

Again, this interpretation is extremely generous to Halcion. This summary does not mention that the 0.25 mg dose is *double the recommended dose for the elderly*. Hence, the 0.25 mg study with elderly patients, which showed efficacy, is of little relevance compared with the other studies and should not be thrown in with them. A more informative summary would be to say that the review of published clinical trials does not support the effectiveness of 0.125 mg of Halcion in the elderly at all, while effectiveness was supported in the less substantial of the two trials, which used 0.25 mg with the non-elderly. Overall this is not an impressive showing of effectiveness for Halcion – nothing like the IoM's reanalysis of Upjohn's NDA clinical trials.

To complete its assessment of efficacy, the institute reviewed the sleep laboratory studies of Halcion published in the literature. At the 0.125 and 0.25 mg doses, this comprised five studies at 0.25 mg in non-elderly adults (five to 28 nights), two studies at 0.25 mg in geriatrics (three to 15 nights), one at 0.125 mg in non-elderly adults (14 nights), one at 0.125 mg in typical geriatric insomniacs, and one at 0.125 mg in geriatrics who suffered insomnia due to periodic limb movements of sleep (12 weeks). With further generosity to Halcion, the IoM commented that 'in all but one study of subjects with insomnia, Halcion significantly improved various objective parameters of sleep on the first three nights'.[140] Yet this could be true even if the vast majority of studies showed that Halcion was consistently ineffective on all efficacy criteria, except for one per study.

In fact, three of the 0.25 mg studies showed that Halcion did not significantly improve sleep on most or all efficacy criteria, three showed that it did, and the other one showed significant improvement only on decreasing number of awakenings. Of the three 0.125 mg studies, one involving insomniacs with periodic limb movements of sleep showed significant improvement in sleep, one showed improvement in total sleep time and the other showed a lack of effectiveness after three nights together with rebound insomnia. This is stronger evidence of Halcion's effectiveness than in the published clinical trials, but it is hardly impressive. Perhaps the most remarkable comment made by the IoM about these studies was that they were unable to find any published polysomonographic sleep studies of typical elderly patients taking 0.125 mg for more than a *few* consecutive nights, even though that dose had been recommended for up to ten nights for such patients for almost a decade in the US and from 1978 to 1991 in the UK.[141]

The institute concluded that the evidence supported the effectiveness of 0.125 and 0.25 mg doses, but admitted that the support for the 0.125 mg dose was 'weak'.[142] It took the view that the published literature 'generally supports the claim that the drug is efficacious'.[143] However, these conclusions are not a good representation of the institute's own analysis. At the very least, it should be added that neither the published clinical trials nor the unpublished sleep laboratory studies that were reviewed supported the efficacy of the drug at 0.125 mg in elderly patients. Furthermore, at the 0.25 mg dose in non-elderly patients this data provides only equivocal support for the drug's effectiveness.

To assess the safety of the 0.125 and 0.25 mg doses of Halcion, the IoM revisited data from clinical trials and the SRS. They reanalysed the 25 clinical trials which the FDA had evaluated before the PDAC in 1992. Like the FDA, the IoM analysed adverse events causing patients to drop out. They found no significant differences between 0.25 mg of Halcion and 30 mg of Dalmane in the number of adverse effects reported in these trials, though they did find a significantly increased incidence of memory impairment with increased duration of Halcion. With regard to adverse events for drop out, the institute found that there were significantly more adverse cases of anxiety and memory impairment among patients taking Halcion than among those on placebo, and more cases than for those taking Dalmane.

Like the FDA, the IoM analysed the adverse events in clinical trials by throwing all the trials together. For example, on this approach they found that the overall incidence of memory impairment was low. We are not arguing that this approach is invalid from a scientific viewpoint; but from a precautionary perspective, which emphasizes patient protection, there may be a case for giving more weight to a disaggregated analysis of the data. One reason for doing this is that some clinical investigators may be more sensitive to reporting adverse effects than others, as Oswald suggested at the PDAC in 1992. For example, when 36 subjects took 0.25 mg of Halcion for a week in P6062 there were no cases of anxiety; but during P6042, when 54 subjects took the same dose for four weeks there were 11 (20 per cent) cases of anxiety. As the IoM acknowledged, disaggregation according to the duration of the studies may also be important. It found that subjects were seven times more at risk of adverse psychiatric effects when taking Halcion in long-term studies than when on placebo.[144]

The institute also reviewed a large post-marketing safety study by Upjohn involving about 8000 subjects. Although there was no placebo, the study did compare 0.125 and 0.25 mg of Halcion with Restoril. Subjects' responses were elicited by telephone after two and four weeks of medication. Significantly more subjects taking Halcion dropped out than did subjects on Restoril.[145] Upjohn also conducted a post-marketing sleep laboratory study involving 240 subjects for two nights at doses of 0.125 and 0.25 mg which, according to the IoM, did not create any serious adverse reactions. With regard to the FDA's SRS data on post-marketing ADR reports, the IoM acknowledged that despite Tsong's statistical adjustments for all conceivable confounding influences, Halcion was associated with many more adverse psychiatric (CNS) effects than Restoril and other benzodiazepine sleeping pills:

The IoM committee is left with what seems to be strongly suggestive evidence from SRS data that, among users of Halcion, there is some group of patients who, by personal characteristics, prescription pattern or medication use, do experience CNS-related adverse events not seen at the same rates as those seen in patients taking comparator drugs. The rates of these adverse events in the Halcion group or among the various groups taking other drugs must be so small as to escape detection statistically in any of the variety of controlled studies mounted so far.[146]

On one reading, this account of the situation is true, but on another reading it is inaccurate because adverse psychiatric effects of Halcion were statistically large relative to comparator drugs in some clinical trials, even if not overall. Hence, one interpretation is that, among *some* clinical trials, there is support for the findings from the SRS data. The other interpretation, preferred by the IoM, is that across all the main clinical trials taken together there is no statistically significant support for those findings.

In conclusion, the institute noted that at least some adverse effects associated with Halcion in spontaneous reports were 'similar to those that had been reported in some of the early clinical trials with higher doses of Halcion and with longer durations of use'.[147] It was also aware of the surveys showing that many people use sleeping pills for longer (often for years) and at higher doses than recommended. However true this may be, it does not fully explain why Halcion should be associated with so many more spontaneous ADR reports than other hypnotics, unless patients are particularly at risk from long-term use of high doses of Halcion. If the latter is true, then this implies that Halcion has a *much narrower margin of safety* than other sleeping pills – one reason why the British regulatory authorities removed the drug from the market. Yet, the IoM shied away from the logical implication of its own discussion, preferring instead to leave aside the real world of patients' drug use and to conclude that Halcion is safe and effective as recommended for use on the label.

Despite these problems, both the FDA and its PDAC endorsed the findings of the IoM at a public hearing on 4 December 1997. Indeed, Robert Temple, chief of the FDA's office of drug evaluation, was motivated to declare: 'We don't believe that there is a clear distinction between this drug [Halcion] and others in the class [of benzodiazepine hypnotics]'.[148]

Conclusion

A catalogue of poor decisions has attended the FDA's regulation of Halcion. In 1988, the 0.5 mg tablet of Halcion was withdrawn in the US and a 0.125 mg tablet introduced. However, the lower doses of 0.125 and 0.25 mg were not then approved as effective by the FDA, except in elderly patients. For four years the FDA trusted Upjohn's judgement about the efficacy of these lower doses without conducting its own review. To assist it in making this judgement the FDA turned to a hearing before the PDAC in 1992; seven out of eight of these members had conflicts of interest. This compromised the perceived, if not the actual, independence of the committee as indicated by the FDA's need to consult another group of 'independent' experts, the Institute of Medicine, in 1997.

At the 1992 hearing, the FDA and the PDAC concluded that the 0.125 and 0.25 mg doses were effective, even though there was insufficient controlled clinical trial data to support this conclusion, especially at the 0.125 mg dose. However, most members of the PDAC were willing to persuade themselves that the lower doses were effective because of *anecdotal evidence from the widespread use of Halcion while on the market*. Even by 1997, the Institute of Medicine could find only weak evidence to support the efficacy of the 0.125 mg dose, and that was assisted by an interpretation of the available data that was generous to Upjohn.

By 1992, scientists at the FDA and elsewhere, who had previously defended the daily dose of 0.5 mg of Halcion as safe, acknowledged that they had probably been mistaken. Notably, FDA inspectors discovered that the principal investigator for P321 had concluded in the 1970s that a daily dose of 1.0 mg was too high and considered 0.25 mg to be the highest prescribable dose.

Eventually, the FDA also acknowledged that it had made a mistake in 1992 when concluding that P321 was not material to the safety of Halcion as approved in the US. It follows from this that P321 should have been scrutinized in the safety assessment put before the PDAC in May 1992, but the FDA neglected to do this.

The safety evidence put before the PDAC revealed that the remarkably high levels of adverse psychiatric reactions reported spontaneously in association with Halcion persisted into the 1990s. Quantitative indicators of these 'scary' risks remained very substantial despite relentless efforts by FDA and Upjohn scientists to explain them away. Some of these risks were confirmed by data collected from controlled trials, but generally at a much lower level. Generously giving Upjohn the benefit of the scientific doubt, FDA scientists accepted Upjohn's argument that the 0.25 mg (rather than 0.5 mg) of Halcion could be regarded as equivalent (or equipotent) to 30 mg of Dalmane in clinical trials – a concession which the British MCA was unwilling to make. This concession enabled a lower dose of Halcion, associated with fewer adverse reactions, to be compared with Dalmane. Consequently, many of the differences in risks between the two drugs were dissolved when taken in aggregate, although there remained significantly more cases of anxiety and memory impairment associated with Halcion. Moreover, some clinical trials showed that even 0.25 mg of Halcion was associated with relatively high levels of adverse psychiatric effects.

Nevertheless, despite the weak evidence from controlled research in support of Halcion's effectiveness at lower doses, and despite the extraordinarily large numbers of ADR reports of Halcion in use, the FDA and its experts gave priority to *anecdotal evidence* about Halcion in use when assessing *efficacy*, but to *controlled clinical trial data* when assessing *safety*. What these technical *inconsistencies* in interpreting data have in common is that they both favoured Upjohn and Halcion. This bias constituted the 'scientific' basis for continuing to expose American consumers to Halcion. Since it cannot be technically justified, it appears to be derived from institutional and professional interests which are especially germane when comparing the British and American approaches to the technical data.

Moreover, the 'scientific' assessments of safety and efficacy by the FDA, the PDAC and the IoM put very little emphasis on Halcion's narrow margin of safety. In other words, they did not integrate the problem of how the drug might be used in practice when conducting their risk-benefit evaluation. In fact, the IoM explicitly avoided such regulatory issues by confining itself to the conclusion that Halcion was safe and effective when used as recommended on the label. This set aside the evidence that, in practice, patients frequently take benzodiazepines at higher doses and for longer periods than recommended, especially if the evidence of effectiveness at the lower doses is not strong. By contrast, the British regulatory authorities integrated this problem within their risk assessment by insisting that such drugs, including Halcion, should have a wide margin of safety.

Prescription for Change: The Science and Politics of Medicines Control

At the time of writing in 1999, the battle over the safety of Halcion continues. After the MCA (acting on behalf of the UK Licensing Authority) revoked Halcion's UK licences, Upjohn appealed against the decision in the British High Court.[1] Thus, the company asked the UK Court of Appeal to rule on whether the MCA was, in fact, correct to have revoked the drug's licences. In particular, Upjohn argued that, because EU directives required a drug product to be harmful before removal from the market, it was up to the appeal court to establish whether this was, in fact, true. On the other hand, the MCA countered that the role of the British High Court should be confined to a review of whether the regulatory decision was procedurally flawed, and that the court should not put itself, by its own process, in the place of the regulatory agency. On 26 October 1995, the UK Court of Appeal stated that it was not persuaded by the arguments of either Upjohn or the MCA and decided to refer the matter to the European Court of Justice.[2]

The momentous question of whether the national courts in the EU have to examine national regulatory authority decisions for *correctness* found its way to the European Court of Justice in the form of the Halcion case in May 1997. The UK Court of Appeal sought judgement from the European Court of Justice (ECJ) on whether EU law requires a national court to decide on the correctness of a regulatory decision rather than on whether it was reasonably reached.[3] Had the ECJ's judgement been in Upjohn's favour, there would have been an extraordinary situation in which the appeal court would be empowered to decide whether Halcion is safe, over and above the judgement of the regulatory agency. However, in January 1999, the ECJ ruled that EU law does not require the Member States (such as the UK) to establish a procedure for judicial review of decisions by national regulatory agencies to revoke marketing authorizations for drugs (such as the MCA's revocation of Halcion's licences). It also ruled that EU law does not empower the courts to substitute their assessment of the facts for those of the national regulatory agency, especially not the scientific evidence supporting the revocation decision. The ECJ noted that, when a national regulatory agency makes complex assessments, it enjoys a wide measure of discretion, the exercise of which is subject to only limited judicial review restricted to examining the accuracy of the findings made by the regulatory agency and verification that the action taken by the agency was 'not vitiated by a manifest error or misuse of powers'.[4] At the time of writing, the case has returned to the UK courts and it remains to be seen whether Upjohn will attempt to argue that the MCA's revocation of Halcion's licences was 'vitiated by a manifest error or misuse of powers'.

Even after the withdrawal of Halcion on safety grounds in the UK, Brazil, Argentina, Norway and Denmark, it continued to command a significant market. In 1995, the drug had sales of US$107.9 million worldwide,[5] despite Upjohn facing about 100 product liability suits alleging adverse effects with Halcion.[6] Thus, the safety and regulation of Halcion are not merely academic matters. By 1998, two basically opposing views had emerged. One, exemplified by Oswald, Public Citizen, Waller and the MCA, is that Halcion is a toxic drug which has no place on the market because its safety margin is too narrow and its risks outweigh its benefits. Diametrically opposed to that view is the conviction that Halcion is, in essence, safe when taken at low enough doses, such as 0.125 mg (as exemplified by the Australian regulatory authorities) or 0.125– 0.25 mg (as exemplified by the FDA, Upjohn and ultimately by the IoM). In other words, it is argued that the large number of spontaneous adverse reactions, relative to other sleeping pills, which continued to be reported in the 1990s were a result of patients taking doses higher and/or for longer than recommended on the label.

When considering the withdrawal of Halcion from the market, it is also important to consider the safety and therapeutic implications for those patients who will be denied the drug as a result. On the whole, the evidence that Halcion users have switched to less safe alternatives seems to be weak. Furthermore, it is not at all obvious that Halcion is a uniquely effective sleeping pill for some group of the population, although some individual patients certainly seem to favour it over alternatives.[7] One response to these worries about withdrawing Halcion might be to permit it on the market as a 'second-line' drug – that is, one which should be prescribed only after all other approved sleeping pills prove ineffective for the patient concerned. However, even this option might be unsafe because of the unpredictability of the drug's apparent severe adverse reactions in some patients.[8]

This brings us to a third view, put forward by Dukes, that Halcion is certainly unsafe at high doses – above 0.25 mg – but that it could be safe at lower doses if it were possible to identify individuals susceptible to serious adverse reactions. According to Dukes, the relatively large number of spontaneous adverse reactions associated with Halcion was not merely a consequence of overdosage but also partly due to the fact that some patients, who are particularly sensitive to the potential toxicity of the drug, were not adequately detected, if at all, in clinical trials. Moreover, it is at present impossible to identify prior to medication which patients, for whom the drug is intended, are likely to be at serious risk. The IoM also recognized this problem but advised that the drug should stay on the market, until or unless Upjohn and/or others confirm it. By contrast, Dukes emphasized the need for caution in the interests of patients' protection:

> *The fundamental problem is that no one has adequate knowl-
> edge as to how (and whether) this drug can be safely used; the
> company [Upjohn]... denied the validity of evidence [of Halcion
> risks] adduced by others, instead of recognizing the phenome-
> non and investigating it; had it done so, it would have been
> possible to determine whether there are conditions under which
> Halcion can be safely used, and if so what these conditions are.
> The ideal solution now would, therefore, be either to withdraw
> this drug permanently from the market, or to suspend this
> licence pending research to answer these questions.*[9]

The problem of safe *use* is accentuated by the drug's narrow margin of safety
which means that, to achieve adequate efficacy, some patients are tempted to
take more than the recommended dose. Unlike the IoM, we believe that
consumers and patients should be given the benefit of the scientific doubts
about Halcion safety, especially since there are alternative medications available. This implies that the drug should not be on the market unless, or until,
there is much better knowledge of how it might be used safely. Significant as
this conclusion is, the Halcion case also suggests important lessons about how
medicines should be controlled in the future. It is to these lessons that we
now turn.

Government regulators often argue that pharmaceutical companies should
be given a certain poetic licence to present their drug products in the most
favourable light. This produces what is sometimes called 'honest bias' and
does not involve deliberate dishonesty. Our examination of Halcion shows
that, where corporate power is concerned, a key feature of 'honest bias' is an
imbalance of commitment to product defence compared to patient safety.
Manufacturers may go to enormous lengths to undermine criticisms and critics
of their drug products, while making only half-hearted efforts to ensure
adequate flows of high quality information about their safety.

Regulators frequently claim that this is not a problem because they take
such 'honest bias' into account when they review companies' New Drug
Applications and other data. Yet the Halcion case vividly demonstrates that the
regulatory authorities did *not* detect Upjohn's 'honest bias' and, therefore, did
not take it into account in their regulatory assessments for years. Indeed, the
British regulatory authorities learned about some of this bias by watching
television and reading a pharmaceutical industry magazine, rather than by
scrutinizing the data supplied to them within the regulatory process!

Upjohn's 'honest bias' included the initial and unintentional failure to
report medical events in P321 adequately; the failure to recheck comprehen-
sively the initial reporting of all human testing when major questions about
the safety of the drug emerged within the medical community; and the failure
to maintain adequate records and checks on clinical investigators conducting
clinical trials of Halcion. As a consequence of the latter, the FDA only became
conscious of the fact that two of the three most important clinical studies
supporting the drug's approval in the US had been conducted by an unreliable
investigator some nine years after approval!

In July 1992, and in the light of the British regulators' reassessment of Halcion's safety after the P321 revelations, the chief executive of the MCA told Upjohn that 'acceptance of Halcion as safe at the licensed doses [in 1978] must be regarded as flawed'.[10] Thus, *by the safety standards of the MCA*, the British regulators' inability to detect this 'honest bias' permitted patients to be exposed to an unsafe drug for nearly 13 years! As late as 1991, the MCA did not detect Upjohn's failure to inform them of the disqualification of some clinical investigators. The inevitable conclusion that we must reach from the Halcion case is that regulators' confidence in their capability to take account of 'honest bias' in assessing New Drug Applications *is misplaced, or at best overestimated*.

One major reason for this is the huge amount of trust which regulatory agencies invest in pharmaceutical companies. The systems for controlling medicines safety in Western Europe and the US are based largely on trust in the manufacturers and their data, rather than on accountability. Hence, drug companies are trusted to conduct and organize all the preclinical and clinical testing of their products. Regulatory agencies do not undertake any independent testing of new drugs. It is also the manufacturers who have control over selection and monitoring of clinical investigators. In effect, the entire drug testing process is managed by pharmaceutical companies, even though this is against a background of government standards, which ultimately have the force of law.

This trust in new drugs, which tends to emphasize benefits over risks, is clearly evident in regulators' increasing tendency to refer to marketing approval as a 'provisional' decision.[11] According to Professor Sir William Asscher, a former chairman of the UK Committee on Safety of Medicines (CSM):

> *... you really cannot judge what a drug is going to be like at the time of licensing. You haven't really got a clue as to what the drug is like... We [the British regulatory authorities] license early in this country [the UK] because we are well aware that you can't really get to know a drug until it is used the way it will be used by doctors in the rough and tumble of clinical practice. Clinical trials are very artificial; patients are carefully selected, the indications are very carefully observed. This is not so in ordinary clinical practice... but don't you start saying that the British public are being used as guinea pigs because they benefit from the early licensing of medicines.[12]*

Guinea pigs or not, one former member of the CSM told us ominously:

> *By far the most usual thing which happens is that on the basis of the clinical trials, because that is all we have to go on, a drug is licensed at a particular dose and over the next couple of years the yellow cards [spontaneous ADR reports] come in showing that people are grossly overdosed, some individuals are much*

> *overdosed, and then the CSM calls the company in and then*
> *everybody agrees that you should go down to a quarter or even*
> *a tenth of the conventional dose.*[13]

It is only after approval, when the drug is on the market, that the manufacturer loses some control over information about its safety and effectiveness because doctors and medical researchers begin to report their findings independently of the industry. However, as the Halcion case highlights, once a drug is on the market, regulators can be reluctant to remove it from the market for several reasons. Professional and institutional interests within regulatory agencies may militate against withdrawal because such action might be seen as admitting that an initial marketing approval was mistaken, in which case very powerful evidence is required to overturn an approval decision. For example, Professor Michael Rawlins, a former chairman of the CSM, told us:

> *You have to have sufficient evidence to make you feel that the*
> *drug should be withdrawn. You don't have an option of saying*
> *you don't know* – if you don't know then you leave the drug on
> the market by and large *(emphasis added).*[14]

In other words, once a drug is on the market the CSM is inclined to give it the benefit of the doubt. The problem, of course, is that there is always some doubt once a drug is on the market because it must have been approved with some supportive preclinical and clinical testing in the first place. The result of this regulatory approach is that *compelling evidence of danger to public health is required before a drug is withdrawn*. Rawlins's comment is a measure of just how extremely serious the CSM regarded the risks of Halcion when they recommended its withdrawal from the market in 1991.

The whole philosophy of drug regulation is, therefore, biased in favour of approving drugs and maintaining them on the market. Regulators give companies the benefit of the scientific doubt about clinical and preclinical testing at the marketing approval stage on the grounds that they cannot really know a drug's risks until it is tried out in the real conditions of general clinical practice. The rationalization for this is that the initial approval decision is 'provisional' in the sense that it can be withdrawn if the drug is found to be unsafe. But then, once the drug is on the market, regulators are in a situation where they feel they must have compelling evidence of lack of safety before they can withdraw it from the market. Hence, they also give companies the benefit of the scientific doubt about spontaneous reports of adverse reactions to the drug.

One lesson from the Halcion case is that committed adversaries of a drug who do *not* trust the manufacturers may be more likely to detect a company's inadequate data. This suggests that patients' and consumers' interests could be better protected if regulatory authorities put *less trust* in the pharmaceutical industry and its products and, like Waller, thoroughly investigated clinical trial submissions, giving patients' interests in safety the benefit of the scientific doubt. To facilitate this more critical drug testing and review there could be a requirement that some clinical investigators must be selected by the regulators so that manufacturers are prevented from mobilizing a preponderance of clinicians who are already sympathetic to the drug being tested.

Moreover, the regulatory agency could identify a *small number of key clinical tests* that are needed, inform the manufacturer that it must pay for their cost, and then conduct them while employing its own government scientists. Thus, the manufacturer's control over the drug testing process would be removed for these few crucial trials. For at least these few clinical tests, regulators would be constructing, handling and analysing the original case reports forms (CRFs) of patients. To avoid duplication of testing on the same product, regulatory agencies in different countries could share their governmental testing by direct communication and/or via a special journal devoted solely to the rapid publication of drug testing by regulatory scientists. This arrangement would improve the quality of medicines regulation because these government scientists would be much closer to the drug safety and effectiveness data than regulators are currently. In the long term, this has the added advantage of increasing medical expertise in drug testing independently of industry.

The Halcion case also shows that neither the British nor American regulators treated post-marketing warning signals about adverse effects with sufficient gravity. When the Dutch regulatory authorities reported very high levels of adverse reactions associated with the drug in 1979, the FDA and the British regulators assumed that the drug was safe except that the Dutch had marketed it at too high a dose. However, it is evident that within the British regulators' own judgemental framework they awarded the benefit of the scientific doubt unduly to Halcion in 1979, especially since their final revocation decision in 1993 stated that they considered the clinical trials available in 1978 'to be the most significant evidence indicating an important safety hazard with the drug'.[15] Similarly, following Leber's lead, the FDA did the same with respect to the 0.5 mg dose by discounting the warning signals from spontaneous ADR reports during the 1980s. The consequences of such permissive regulation may be more widespread than the Halcion case. A former member of a special UK regulatory panel of expert advisors told us that he was concerned that 'there are situations where the CSM appears to behave in a very lenient fashion over some drugs'.[16] A major policy implication, therefore, for both the British and American drug regulatory authorities is to avoid an overoptimistic view of drug benefits which leads to complacency about risks.

Furthermore, the approach to spontaneous ADR reports relative to controlled clinical trial data in the US suggests a disciplinary bias which gives undue weight to safety data derived from the latter. The PDACs, the most influential FDA scientists and ultimately the IoM, who reviewed Halcion, consistently dismissed spontaneous ADR data, choosing to put their trust in the results of controlled clinical trials instead. We must also recognize, therefore, that some of the social interests that influence drug regulation are built around disciplinary power blocks. As Donald Mackenzie, Professor of Sociology at the University of Edinburgh, observed about scientific knowledge:

> *Imagine a group of scientists who have spent a great deal of time and effort acquiring a particular set of skills. Imagine also that the goals exemplified in their science – the way they*

> *innovate, their routine judgements – are such that scientific*
> *approaches that make full use of their skills are favoured, and*
> *those that make their skills redundant are rejected. Then we*
> *might quite reasonably postulate that social interests – group*
> *investment in particular skills – are sustaining the goals*
> *manifest in their science.* [17]

Our analysis of disciplinary bias in FDA regulation of Halcion suggests the need to break up the power block of clinicians within the regulatory process. There needs to be greater direct regulatory input from medical scientists with backgrounds in public health. Moreover, once a drug is marketed in the US, responsibility for its regulation should pass to an FDA division of epidemiology and public health, rather than remain with the clinical reviewing division which approved marketing in the first place.

More fundamentally, drug regulation needs to make a conceptual shift towards safety of *patients* rather than merely safety of medicines. Such a shift could have several important implications for public protection. More emphasis could be given to how medicines are *used in practice* than was evident in the Halcion case. This might result in more concern over the *safety margins* of drugs than was shown by FDA regulators or the IoM regarding Halcion. In this context, spontaneous reports of ADRs could be taken more seriously and used to interrogate clinical trial data more thoroughly by disaggregating the results of clinical trials. Thus, all clinical trial results would not be treated equally in a 'risk-blind' way. Rather, more weight might be given to trials by investigators which confirmed significant spontaneous ADR reports. Such a regulatory science would not, therefore, aim for neutrality, but rather the maximization of patient protection and, of course, benefit in relation to drug effectiveness in treating illness.

This book has shown the complex ways in which social interests and political institutions enter into the ostensibly technical debates about medical science. As we discussed in Chapter 2, the political environment of drug regulation is, of course, vitally important. A most obvious weakness of current regulatory systems on both sides of the Atlantic is that they are far too permissive about conflicts of interest. Their influence was well illustrated in an interview we conducted with a former member of the CSM who defended the secrecy of British drug regulation because it protected government experts from industrial pressures and biases:

> *I think it most important that people on a decision-making*
> *body, which is equivalent of a jury, should make their decision*
> *in secret without pressure. Because, remember that now a very*
> *high proportion of funds for research come from the pharma-*
> *ceutical industry. It's no good saying that people on the*
> *decision-making body mustn't have any contact with the*
> *pharmaceutical industry... Apart from anything else, sometimes*
> *you get people 'spilling the beans' in the sense that they are*
> *somebody who is a consultant to a pharmaceutical company*

and declares an interest and leaves the room. The chairman may say to him, 'Have you got anything to tell us before you leave?' He might say, 'This drug's no bloody use to you at all – what they haven't told you is this, this and this [our question: and it's important that that individual feels that he has the freedom to say that – even if not in public?].' He couldn't. He'd lose his personal consultancy, his department would lose their large grants, the rest of the pharmaceutical industry would blackball him, you know.[18]

On this view, the extent to which medical experts, who advise the regulatory authorities, are willing to criticize pharmaceutical companies publicly is affected by their general financial dependence upon them. However, we challenge the premise that there is no point in requiring expert advisors to be independent of the industry at least during their years of office. Surely there are enough expert medical scientists in the Western world that we can expect the expert advisors on the CSM or the PDAC to be free from conflicts of interest. If necessary, governments should pay these advisors higher fees for their services, passing the costs on to the manufacturers when payment for our proposed government drug testing is made.

Perhaps of greater importance is the extent to which regulators are made accountable for their decisions by democratic representatives. In the Halcion case, this was virtually non-existent. In the UK, the MCA's regulation of the drug was not investigated by a parliamentary committee. Indeed, parliament very rarely establishes committees to examine drug regulation. Under the Democrats during the 1980s, the US Congress was active in investigating the FDA's regulation of drug safety. However, the FDA's regulation of Halcion has never been investigated by a congressional committee. Since 1994, when the Republicans took control of Congress, enthusiasm to probe the FDA's handling of individual drug products has waned in favour of efforts to make the agency approve drugs more quickly. Such lack of democratic accountability is now a serious weakness in drug regulation in the UK and the US. According to Leber, the FDA's tendency to protect public health effectively is strongly influenced by these political factors:

We're acting more as a political body than a scientific one. The standards are dictated by the existing political parties. We're making decisions that we wouldn't have made 20 years ago.[19]

One need look no further than Halcion to see how political oversight might have affected the drug's regulation. While it is unrealistic that a UK parliamentary select committee should be established every time there is concern about a drug's safety, one could have been established in the aftermath of van der Kroef and the Dutch government's withdrawal of Halcion in 1980. This committee might well have discovered some of the critical implications of the clinical trials of Halcion which Waller was to establish over a decade later. Similarly, a US congressional committee in the mid 1980s would probably have exposed the fact that two out of three of the pivotal clinical trials involved a disqualified clinical investigator; it might also have probed P321, discovering Upjohn's inadequate reporting of it much earlier.

Given that all drugs have risks, when regulators make decisions about approving them they are making judgements about acceptable risks. But acceptable for whom? The answer must be acceptable for consumers and patients in relation to some illness and potential benefit. Most people accept that experts in medical science and public health are needed to make regulatory judgements about drugs; but should these decisions be left entirely to scientists when it is patients who will bear the risks? This raises two important policy questions. How much access should the public have to the decision-making process of drug regulatory authorities? Should there be direct public participation within regulatory decision-making? For example, should there be a representative of consumer organizations or 'public interest' groups on the CSM?

In the US, citizens already have the best access in the world to the drug regulatory process, thanks to the American Freedom of Information Act and the fact that expert advisory meetings are almost always held in public. However, such access only comes after a drug has been approved. And the public has no rights of access to information about drugs that are never approved. The Halcion case suggests that greater transparency about pre-approval drug-testing might enhance regulatory decision-making in the public interest. For example, the FDA's initial decision to approve the drug at a recommended dose of 0.5 mg, partly because evidence of efficacy at 0.25 mg was relatively weak, might not have been taken if it had been subjected to external scrutiny at the time.

The pharmaceutical industries would almost certainly object to public access to their drug-testing data on the grounds that it would infringe their intellectual property rights. No doubt they would also argue that it would hamper competitiveness and innovation. We believe that it would be more likely to stimulate innovations in safer and more effective new drugs. In any case, the changes to drug-testing which we have proposed above could enable public access to pre-approval drug-testing data without use of industry data. This is because we have proposed that certain key pre-approval clinical tests ought to be conducted by government scientists under the auspices of the regulatory authorities. Subject to the usual confidentiality procedures to protect the identity of patients/subjects and manufacturing trade secrets, these clinical tests could be open to public scrutiny prior to approval. Consequently, the wider medical profession and consumer organizations could participate in the regulatory process at an earlier stage.

In the UK and most European countries, except for Sweden, public access to information about the drug regulatory process is extremely restricted. A superficial view of the Halcion case might suggest that secrecy is not a problem in the UK because the greater openness of the US did not lead to the withdrawal of the drug there, whereas the British regulatory authorities, secretive as they are, did ban it. But it took the British 13 years to ban Halcion. The drug achieved its UK product licence in 1978 partly because of Upjohn's reassurances about safety from the (flawed) P321 results. It is at least conceivable that if the minutes of meetings between the CSM, the MCA and drug manufacturers (in this case Upjohn) had been publicly available immediately after approval, then the quality of the P321 study might well have been subjected to closer scrutiny earlier.

We did not find a consensus among experts about whether there should be much less secrecy in British drug regulation. However, a significant proportion certainly believe that the existing secrecy is excessive and leads to suboptimal decisions. One former member of a special panel of expert advisors to the MCA told us:

> *I believe transparency actually sharpens people's contribution. I think the chances of making a wrong decision are reduced by making it an open forum where the public can go in and see what is happening... I think it is quite wrong that we don't know the reasons why decisions are taken... that everything is out there in the public domain whatever the particualr issues, I think that's an important part of democracy.*[20]

Just as important, greater openness in decision-making encourages consumers and patients to share responsibility for drug safety. This in itself contributes to the protection of public health because there is a more informed and vigilant citizenry. It is high time that European governments modernized their drug regulatory agencies by introducing extensive freedom of information legislation.

The battle over the safety of medicines will continue. Unfortunately, the commercial, institutional and professional interests involved in medicines development and control do not always converge with the realization of public health. The challenge for the future is social and political as well as technical. It is time for medical scientists to stop treating drug regulation as if it were a scientific peer review process. The best protection of public health is likely to come from a regulatory system which is accountable to citizens and patients via direct access to information about the decision-making process and indirect access via oversight bodies representing the interests of public health.

Methodological Appendix

The purpose of this appendix is to provide interested readers with some elaboration on the methodological framework and research methods used in our social scientific investigation of Halcion. Like many researchers in the fields of sociology and politics of science and medicine, we believe that knowledge about the risks and benefits of science and technology are not solely technical problems; they are also socially produced or, if you prefer, socially constructed. Pre-eminent in this field is Sheila Jasanoff, Professor of Science Policy and Law at Harvard University. She has analysed how expert scientific advice is socially constructed by different regulatory institutions within the US, highlighting the problems for risk assessment of scientific disputes between experts in different institutional contexts.[1]

Other social scientists such as Donald Mackenzie, Professor of Sociology at Edinburgh, and Evelleen Richards, Professor of Science and Technology Studies at Wollongong University in Australia, have emphasized the role of social interests in shaping scientific and medical knowledge – both professional and commercial interests have come under scrutiny.[2] Such interests can often be accessed by examining scientific or technological controversies.[3] Halcion was chosen in its own right because of its substantial policy significance, but also because its intra and international controversial nature could facilitate access to underlying interests and values in the pharmaceutical and regulatory field of psychotropics.

Our research on Halcion began in 1993 and finished in 1998, involving fieldwork in the UK and the US. However, before, during and after the fieldwork a systematic analysis of the relevant scientific medical and pharmaceutical trade literature was undertaken, accessed via the MEDLINE and DIALOG computer databases, among others.

The defining feature of our fieldwork in both countries was the collection of extensive documentary data supplemented by interviews. The main British documentary sources were: official documents produced by the British drug regulatory authority, the Medicines Control Agency (MCA) and its expert advisory body, the Committee on Safety of Medicines (CSM); transcripts of the court proceedings regarding libel charges brought by Upjohn against Ian Oswald, a critic of Halcion, and against the BBC; the pharmaceutical trade journals such as *Scrip*; and parliamentary questions and answers recorded in *Hansard*.

Much more access to data was possible in the US because freedom of information legislation operates there, whereas secrecy legislation in the form of the 1968 Medicines Act and the 1911 Official Secrets Act operates in the UK. The main American documentary sources were: scientific reports of the Food and Drug Administration (FDA), the US drug regulatory agency; internal FDA scientific assessments of the drug; the FDA's clinical guidelines on anti-anxiety drugs and hypnotics which provide technical standards for the conduct of clinical trials; the transcripts of the 1977, 1989 and 1992 meetings of the FDA's Psychopharmacological Drugs Advisory Committees (PDAC) on Halcion; internal FDA memos and minutes of meetings regarding Halcion; an inspection report undertaken by FDA's division of scientific investigations into Upjohn's conduct regarding Halcion; publicly available US product liability databases, relevant publications by the Institute of Medicine of the National Academy of Sciences; petitions to ban Halcion by the Public Citizen Health Research Group (HRG), a US consumer pressure group; and the US pharmaceutical trade journals, such as *FDC Reports*.

This generated a huge amount of material. In preparing and writing this book we have analysed thousands of documents. However, interviewing some of those closely involved with the Halcion controversy, as well as others, who were very knowledgeable about it gave the research an additional human dimension. It also enabled us to gather further information more effectively and to confirm (or not) some inferences from our documentary data.

We interviewed 18 British regulators, including the most recent former chairman of the CSM, the former chairman of the CSM who recommended that Halcion's licence should be suspended in 1991, and Dr Patrick Waller, the principal medical assessor for Halcion at the MCA who also recommended that the drug should be taken off the market. In addition, a major supporter of Halcion and consultant for Upjohn (Professor Ian Hindmarsh at Surrey University), the principal critic of Halcion (Ian Oswald, formerly Professor of Psychiatry at the University of Edinburgh) and a representative of the Association of the British Pharmaceutical Industry were interviewed in the UK.

We interviewed nine people in the US. Among them were three senior scientists from the FDA who were all involved in the regulatory discussions about Halcion in a significant way: Dr Paul Leber, head of Psychopharmacological Products – the reviewing division for Halcion and other benzodiazepines – and acting director of that division from 1981 to the time of writing; a former member of the Division of Epidemiology and Surveillance – the division responsible for tracking the post-marketing adverse reactions to Halcion – who wished to remain anonymous; and a member of the scientific investigations division – the division responsible for conducting the FDA's investigation into allegations of misconduct against Upjohn – who also wished to remain anonymous. The other six US interviewees were: Dr Frank Ayd, Clinical Professor of Psychiatry at West Virginia University and formerly a consultant for Upjohn regarding Halcion and other drugs; Dr Mike Bernstein, Executive Secretary of the PDAC – the expert advisory committee to the FDA on Halcion in 1977, 1989 and 1992; Dr Sidney Wolfe, Director of HRG; Dr Thomas Moore, Senior Fellow at George Washington University and critic of FDA drug regulation; Dr Peter Breggin, psychiatrist and critic of drug treatment for psychiatric illness; and a lawyer litigating Halcion liability cases against Upjohn in Texas.

Our interviews were semistructured and tape recorded except in a few cases when permission to tape was denied. In those few cases, contemporaneous notes were written up instead. An interview with Dr Theresa Woo (now retired), the initial reviewing medical officer for Halcion, was requested but she did not reply. However, we obtained and analysed copies of all her medical officer reports on Halcion while at the FDA. Interviews with Upjohn's director of regulatory affairs in Kalamazoo and vice-president of government affairs in Washington, DC, were requested by letter and by fax, but we received no reply. This mirrors unsuccessful attempts to interview Upjohn in the UK. This is unfortunate and made it impossible for us to question Upjohn representatives about the Halcion controversy. We would have welcomed their cooperation in the research. Nevertheless, we collected and analysed extensive documentary data regarding Upjohn's perspectives and actions.

The methodology of the analysis is that we should first understand the medical, social and political contexts of Halcion, which are discussed in Chapters 1 and 2, before embarking on the in-depth examination of the case study. The purpose of the case study is to reveal more about the social, political *and technical/medical* aspects of drug-testing and regulation than a more general survey of medicines safety might do. We then examine the broader implications of the lessons from the case study.

Notes

Introduction

1   Anon (1995) 'Pharmacia and Upjohn agree merger', *Scrip*, no 2054, 25 August, p 6
2   Interview with former member of the UK Committee on Safety of Medicines (CSM), England, 14 September 1994

Chapter 1

1   Gabe, J (ed) (1991) *Understanding Tranquilliser Use*, Routledge, London, pp 2–3
2   Medawar, C (1992) *Power and Dependence*, Social Audit, London, pp 56–58
3   Breggin, P (1991) *Toxic Psychiatry*, HarperCollins, London, p 303
4   Brown, G and Harris, T (1978) *The Social Origins of Depression*, Tavistock, London
5   Clare, A (1991) 'The benzodiazepine controversy: a psychiatrist's reaction' in J Gabe (ed) *Understanding Tranquilliser Use*, op cit Note 1, p 182
6   Kramer, M (1979) 'Cross-national study of diagnosis of the mental disorders', *American Journal of Psychiatry*, April (supplement)
7   Williams, P and Bellantuono, C (1991) 'Long-term tranquilliser use: the contribution of epidemiology' in J Gabe (ed) *Understanding Tranquilliser Use*, op cit Note 1, p 75
8   Medawar, C (1997) 'The antidepressant web: marketing depression and making medicines work', *International Journal of Risk and Safety in Medicine*, vol 10, pp 75–126
9   Anon (1993) 'Benzodiazepines overused in women', *Scrip*, no 1846, 13 August, p 21
10 Inglis, B (1981) *The Diseases of Civilisation*, Paladin, London, p 108. Thomas J Moore, personal communication, August 1999
11 Clare, A (1991) op cit Note 5
12 Breggin, P, op cit Note 3, p 271
13 Institute of Medicine (1997) *Halcion: An Independent Assessment of Safety and Efficacy Data*, National Academy Press, Washington, DC, pp 1, 10
14 Inglis, B, op cit Note 10, pp 116–117
15 Cohen, S I (1978) 'Are benzodiazepines useful in anxiety?', *Lancet*, 7 November, p 1080
16 Williams, P and Bellantuono, C (1991) op cit Note 7, p 77
17 Gabe, J (1991) 'Personal troubles and public issues: sociology of long-term tranquilliser use' in J Gabe (ed) *Understanding Tranquilliser Use*, p 37, op cit Note 1

18 Chetley, A (1990) *A Healthy Business? World Health and the Pharmaceutical Industry*, Zed Books, London, pp 39–41
19 Ibid, p 43
20 Davis, P (1997) *Managing Medicines: Public Policy and Therapeutic Drugs*, Open University Press, Buckingham, p 10
21 Goodman, L and Gilman, A (eds) (1941) *The Pharmacological Basis of Therapeutics* cited in Medawar (1992) op cit Note 2, p 57
22 Chetley, A (1990) op cit Note 18, p 48
23 Cited in Chetley, A (1990) op cit Note 18, p 52
24 Ibid, pp 41–52
25 Medawar, C (1992) op cit Note 2, pp 65, 85
26 Cited in Medawar (1992) op cit Note 2, p 146
27 Inglis, B, op cit Note 10, p 118
28 Chetley, A (1995) *Problem Drugs*, Zed Books, London, p 309
29 Williams, P and Bellantuono, C (1991) op cit Note 7, pp 75–76
30 Jerome, J and Bilgorri, L (1991) *The Lost Years*, Virgin Books, London, p 24
31 Anon (1993) op cit Note 9
32 Anon (1984) 'Psychotropic market poised for growth', *Scrip*, no 918, 30 July, p 12
33 Chetley, A (1995) op cit Note 28, pp 302–303
34 Breggin, P, op cit Note 3, p 298
35 Inglis, B, op cit Note 10, p 118. Anon (1988) 'UK scripts trends 1976–1986', *Scrip*, no 1296, 1 April, pp 2–3
36 Ray, L (1991) 'The political economy of long-term minor tranquilliser use' in J Gabe (ed) *Understanding Tranquilliser Use*, op cit Note 1, p 140
37 Anon (1991) 'Benzodiazepine prescribing in the UK', *Scrip*, no 1644, 21 August, p 26. Anon (1988) 'UK scripts trends 1976–1986', *Scrip*, no 1296, 1 April, pp 2–3. Collier, J (1989) *The Health Conspiracy*, Century, London, p 73. Breggin, P, op cit Note 3, pp 298–301
38 Medawar, C (1992) op cit Note 2, p 90
39 Ibid p 58
40 Ibid pp 61–62
41 Ray, L op cit Note 36, p 141
42 Medawar, C (1992) op cit Note 2, p 112
43 Winger, G (1983) *Tranquillisers: The Cost of Calmness*, Burke Publishing Company, London
44 Medawar, C (1992) op cit Note 2, pp 95–100
45 Ibid, pp101–101
46 Ibid p 142
47 Ibid p 127
48 Williams, P and Bellantuono, C (1991) op cit Note 7, pp 80–81
49 Medawar, C (1992) op cit Note 2, pp 102–105
50 Chetley, A (1995) op cit Note 28, p 306
51 Breggin, P, op cit Note 3, pp 306–307
52 Williams, P and Bellantuono, C (1991) op cit Note 7, p 74
53 Robin, D W et al (1991) 'Pharmacodynamics and drug action', *Clinical Pharmacology and Therapeutics*, vol 49, p 587
54 Tinetti, M E, Speechley, M and Ginter, S F (1988) 'Risk factors for falls among elderly persons living in the community', *New England Journal of Medicine*, vol 319, pp 1701–1707
55 Ray, W A, Griffin, M R, Schaffner, W, Baugh, B K and Melton, L J (1987) 'Psychotropic drug use and the risk of hip fracture', *New England Journal of Medicine*, vol 316, pp 363–69. Ray, W A, Griffin, M R and Downey, W (1989) 'Benzodiazepines of long and short elimination half-life and the risk of hip fracture', *Journal of the American Medical Association*, vol 262, pp 3303–3307

56   Breggin, P, op cit Note 3, p 307

57   Williams, P and Bellantuono, C (1991) op cit Note 7, p 72

58   Schneider–Helmert, D (1988) 'Why low-dose benzodiazepine-dependent insomniacs can't escape their sleeping pills', *Acta Psychiatrica Scandinavica*, vol 78, p 706

59   Medawar, C (1992) op cit Note 2, p 168

60   Williams, P and Bellantuono, C (1991) op cit Note 7, p 79

61   Anon (1984) 'Benzodiazepines: UK concern', *Scrip*, no 890, 23 April, p 13

62   Busto, U, Sellers, E, Naranjo, C A, Cappell, H, Sanches-Craig, M and Sykora, K (1986) 'Withdrawal reaction after long-term therapeutic use of benzodiazepines', *New England Journal of Medicine*, vol 315, pp 854–59. Petursson, H and Lader, M H (1981) 'Withdrawal from long-term benzodizepine treatment', *British Medical Journal*, vol 283, pp 643–45. Mellor, C S and Jain, V K (1982) 'Diazepam withdrawal syndrome: its prolonged and changing nature', *Canadian Medical Association Journal*, vol 127, pp 1093–96. Schoepf, J (1983) 'Withdrawal phenomena after long-term administration of benzodiazepines: a review of recent investigations', *Pharmacopsychiatry*, vol 16, pp 1–8. Tyrer, P, Owen, R and Dawling, S (1983) 'Gradual withdrawal of diazepam after long–term therapy', *Lancet*, vol I, pp 1402–1406

63   Tyrer, P (1980) 'Dependence on benzodiazepines', *British Journal of Psychiatry*, vol 137, pp 576–77. Edwards, J G, Cantopher, T and Olivieri, S (1984) 'Dependence on psychotropic drugs: an overview', *Postgraduate Medical Journal*, vol 60 (supplement no 2), pp 29–40

64   Anon (1989) 'US controls on benzodiazepines', *Scrip*, no 1374/5, 1/6 January, p 16

Chapter 2

1   Stieb, E W (1966) *Drug Adulteration: Detection and Control in Nineteenth Century Britain*, University of Wisconsin Press, Madison, Milwaukee/London, p 114

2   Hodges, M (1987) 'Control of the safety of drugs, 1868–1968', *Pharmaceutical Journal*, 1 August, p 119

3   Stieb, op cit Note 1, pp 153–154

4   Pharmaceutical Society of Great Britain (PSGB) 1920 'Manchester section', *Pharmaceutical Journal*, 27 March, pp 308–309. PSGB 1920 'Ministry of Health: first annual report', *Pharmaceutical Journal*, 18 September, pp 288–289

5   Bailey, T A (1930) 'Congressional opposition to pure food legislation 1879–1906', *American Journal of Sociology*, vol 36, p 52

6   Burrow, J G (1963) *AMA: Voice of American Medicine*, The Johns Hopkins University, Baltimore, pp 238–42

7   Mann, R D (1984) *Modern Drug Use: an Enquiry Based on Historical Principles*, MTP Press, Lancaster. Tweedale, G (1990) *At the Sign of the Plough: 275 Years of Allen and Hanbury's and the British Pharmaceutical Industry 1715–1900*, John Murray, London

8   Abraham, J (1995) *Science, Politics and the Pharmaceutical Industry: Controversy and Bias in Drug Regulation*, UCL/St Martins Press, London/New York

9   Silverman, M and Lee, P R (1974) *Pills, Profits and Politics*, pp 48–80, University of California Press, Berkeley and Los Angeles, California

10   Public Record Office (PRO), Ministry of Health (MH)58/688 1951 *Review of Drug Legislation*

11   Ibid
12   Harris, R (1964) *The Real Voice*, Macmillan, New York, p 89
13   Ibid p 90
14   Ibid pp 78–79
15   PRO, op cit Note 10
16   PSGB (1959) 'Testing of new drugs', *Pharmaceutical Journal*, 1 August, p 1.
     PSGB (1960) 'Testing of new drugs', *Pharmaceutical Journal*, 20 February,
     p 148. PSGB (1960) 'The Industry Reviews 1959–60', *Pharmaceutical
     Journal*, 7 May, pp 401–440
17   Harris, op cit Note 12, pp 121–22
18   PSGB (1962) 'Toxic hazards of new drugs', *Pharmaceutical Journal*, 10
     February, p 112
19   Temin, P (1980) *Taking Your Medicine: Drug Regulation in the US*, Harvard
     University Press, Cambridge, Massachussetts
20   Harris, op cit Note 12, pp 204–205
21   Sky T (1968) 'Agency implementation of the Freedom of Information Act',
     Administrative Law Journal, vol 20, pp 449–450
22   PSGB (1963) 'Committee on Safety of Drugs: members and terms of refer-
     ence', *Pharmaceutical Journal*, 8 June, p 534
23   PSGB (1963) 'Committee on Safety of Drugs: memo to manufacturers and
     importers', *Pharmaceutical Journal*, 26 October, p 433
24   Twenty–second Report of the Committee on Government Operations (1970)
     The British Drug Safety System, 91st Congress, 2nd Session, US GPO,
     Washington, DC, p 37
25   Wade O L (1983) 'Achievements, problems and limitations of regulatory
     bodies' in D Farrell (ed) *Medicines review worldwide a patient benefit or a
     regulatory burden? Proceedings of the fifth annual symposium of the
     British Institute of Regulatory Affairs*, BIRA, London, p 3
26   Department of Health (1969) *Safety of Drugs: Final Report of the Joint
     Sub–Committee of the Standing Medical Advisory Committees*, HMSO,
     London, p 8
27   Association of the British Pharmaceutical Industry (ABPI) (1971) 'The
     Medicines Act: Committees', *ABPI Annual Report 1970–71*, ABPI, London,
     p 10
28   Collier, J (1985) 'Licensing and provision of medicines in the UK: An
     appraisal', *The Lancet*, 17 August, pp 377–380. Delamothe, T (1989) 'Drug
     watchdogs and the drug industry', *British Medical Journal*, vol 299, p 476.
     Anon (1991) 'UK licensing officials' interests in pharma firms', *Scrip*, no
     1595, 1 March, pp 8–9
29   ABPI (1984) 'New ABPI director stresses importance of two-way flow
     between medicines division and industry', *APBI News*, no 198, p 3
30   Ibid
31   Medicines Control Agency (MCA) (1997) *MCA Annual Report for 1996*, MCA,
     London, pp 81–90
32   Ibid
33   US Congress (1976) 'Use of advisory committees by the FDA', *Eleventh
     Report by the Committee on Government Operations*, 94th Congress, GPO,
     Washington, p 72
34   Crossen, C (1994) *Tainted Truth: The Manipulation of Fact in America*,
     Simon & Schuster, New York, p 166
35   US Congress, op cit Note 33, p 74
36   Ibid p 73
37   US Congress (1976) 'News Release', House of Representatives Committee
     on Government Operations, 26 January
38   ABPI (1972) 'Review of the year: Medicines Act 1968', *ABPI Annual Report
     1971–72*, ABPI, London, p 5

39 Committee on Safety of Medicines (1978) *Annual Report 1977*, HMSO, London, p 28. Committee on Safety of Drugs (1972) *Report for Year Ending 1971*, HMSO, London, p 12

40 Steward, F and Wibberley, G (1980) 'Drug innovation – what's slowing it down?', *Nature*, vol 284, 13 March, p 119

41 Cromie, B J (1980) 'Testing new drugs in the UK', *Journal of the Royal Society of Medicine*, vol 73, May, pp 379–380

42 Griffin, J P and Diggle, G E (1981) 'A survey of products licensed in the UK from 1971–81', *British Journal of Clinical Pharmacology*, vol 12, p 461. ABPI (1977) 'Lessons of a decade', *ABPI News*, no 164, January, p 6

43 ABPI (1980) 'Annual Dinner 1980', *ABPI Annual Report 1979–80*, p 24. ABPI (1981) 'Medical and scientific affairs', *ABPI Annual Report 1980–81*, p 6. Department of Health and Social Security (DHSS) *MLX 130*. DHSS *MAL 62*; Hancher, L (1990) *Regulating for Competition: Government, Law and the Pharmaceutical Industry in the United Kingdom and France*, PhD Thesis, University of Amsterdam, p 99

44 Anon (1988) 'UK Medicines Division – proposed changes', *Scrip*, no 1279, 3 February, p 3

45 Anon (1988) 'Cunliffe/Evans report with UK DHSS', *Scrip*, no 1270/1, 1/6 January, p 24

46 Anon (1991) 'MCA launched as "Next Steps" agency', *Scrip*, no 1635, 19 July, p 2

47 MCA (1991) *MAIL*, no 68, July

48 US Congress (1974) *Examination of the Pharmaceutical Industry (part 7)*, Joint Hearings before the Subcommittee on Health of the Committee on Labour and Public Welfare and the Subcommittee on Administrative Practice and Procedure of the Senate Committee on the Judiciary, GPO, Washington, p 2380

49 Review Panel of New Drug Regulation (1977) *Summary of the Special Counsel's Conclusions*, GPO, Washington, p 16

50 Ibid p 2

51 Ibid p 2

52 US Congress (1982) *The Regulation of New Drugs by the FDA*, Hearings before a Subcommittee of the Committee on Government Operations House of Representatives, GPO, Washington, DC. US Congress (1983) *FDA's Regulation of Zomax*, Hearings before a Subcommittee of the Committee on Government Operations House of Representatives, GPO, Washington, DC. US Congress (1986) *Oversight of the New Drug Review Process and FDA's Regulation of Merital*, Hearings before a Subcommittee of the Committee on Government Operations House of Representatives, GPO, Washington, DC. US Congress (1987) *FDA's Regulation of the New Drug Suprol*, Hearings before a Subcommittee of the Committee on Government Operations House of Representatives, GPO, Washington, DC; US Congress (1988) *FDA's Regulation of the New Drug Versed*, Hearings before a Subcommittee of the Committee on Government Operations House of Representatives, GPO, Washington, DC

Chapter 3

1 Kales, A, Kales, J, Bixler, E O, Scharf, M B and Russek, E (1976) 'Hypnotic efficacy of triazolam: Sleep laboratory evaluation of intermediate-term effectiveness', *Journal of Clinical Pharmacology*, vol 16, p 399

2 Vogel, G, Thurmond, A, Gibbons, P, Edwards, K, Sloan, K B and Sexton, K (1975) 'The effect of triazolam on the sleep of insomniacs',

Psychopharmacologia, vol 41, p 65. Rickels, K, Gingrich, R L, Morris, R J, Rosenfeld, H, Perloff, M M, Clark, E L and Schilling, A (1975) 'Triazolam in insomniac family practice patients', *Clinical Pharmacology and Therapeutics*, vol 18, p 315

3   Wheatley, D (1992) 'Prescribing short-acting hypnosedatives', *Drug Safety*, vol 7, pp 106–115

4   Dement, W C (1983) 'Rational basis for the use of sleeping pills', *Pharmacology*, vol 27 (supplement 2), pp 3–38

5   Hindmarsh, I and Ott, H (1984) 'Sleep, benzodiazepines and performance: issues and comments', *Psychopharmacology*, supplement 1, pp 58–69

6   Roth, T, Kramer, M and Lutz, B A (1977) 'The effects of triazolam (0.25 mg) on the sleep of insomniac subjects', *Drugs Under Experimental and Clinical Research*, vol 1, pp 271–277

7   Reeves, R (1977) 'Comparison of triazolam, flurazepam and placebo as hypnotics in geriatric patients with insomnia', *Journal of Clinical Pharmacology*, vol 17, pp 319–323

8   Lipani, J (1978) 'Reference study of the hypnotic efficacy of triazolam 0.125 mg compared to placebo in geriatric patients with insomnia', *Current Therapeutic Research*, vol 24, pp 397–402

9   Kales et al, op cit Note 1, pp 404–405

10   Ibid p 405

11   Upjohn (1976) 'Minutes of Halcion New Pharmaceutical Product Team (NPPT)', internal memo, 18 October, p 2

12   Upjohn (1976) internal memo from Feldt to Kagan, 11 November

13   Ibid

14   Royal Courts of Justice (1994) *Judgement between the Upjohn Company and Upjohn Ltd and Professor Ian Oswald and between Dr Royston Frederick Drucker and Professor Oswald and between the Upjohn Company and Upjohn Ltd and the BBC and Tom Mangold before Mr Justice May, Beverley F Nunnery*, London, 27 May, p 142

15   Ibid p 143

16   Ibid p 144

17   Upjohn (1979) *Halcion Data Sheet*

18   Ibid

19   Anon (1992) 'Dose crucial in Halcion amnesia', *Scrip*, no 1718, 15 May, p 27

20   Royal Courts of Justice, op cit Note 14, p 183

21   Van der Kroef , K (1979) 'Reactions to triazolam', *Lancet*, 8 September, p 526

22   Ibid

23   Royal Courts of Justice, op cit Note 14, p 148

24   Ibid

25   Anon (1985) 'Upjohn can resubmit Halcion in NL', *Scrip*, no 1014, 8 July, p 1

26   Meyboom, R H B (1992) 'The triazolam experience in 1979 in the Netherlands: a problem of signal generation and verification', in B L Strom and G Velo (eds) *Drug Epidemiology and Post-Marketing Surveillance*, Plenum Press, New York

27   Lasagna, L (1980) 'The Halcion story: trial by media', *Lancet*, 12 April, p 815

28   Royal Courts of Justice, op cit Note 14, pp 151–153

29   Upjohn (1979) internal memo from Kratochvil, European medical affairs director, to Struck, 11 September, p 2

30   Upjohn (1979) internal memo from Kagan to Struck, 14 September, p 1

31   Royal Courts of Justice, op cit Note 14, pp 155–159

32   Ibid p 157

33   Ayd, F J (1992) affidavit, Maryland, 7 December, p 12

34   Ayd, F J et al (1979) 'Behavioural reactions to triazolam', *Lancet*, 10 November, p 1018
35   Upjohn (1979) internal memo, 17 September, p 2
36   Ibid p 3
37   Ibid p 2
38   Barry, W S (1992) Deposition in *Freeman vs the Upjohn Company* in the District Court of Dallas County, Texas, 27 August, pp 57–60
39   Psychopharmacological Drugs Advisory Committee (PDAC) (1977) 'Minutes of the Psychopharmacological Drugs Advisory Committee Meeting', FDA Headquarters, Rockville, Maryland, 21–22 March 1977, pp 23–24
40   Woo, T (1977) 'Halcion', FDA medical officer's review (MOR), 26 January, p 29
41   Ibid
42   Ibid, p 30
43   PDAC (1977) op cit Note 39, p 21
44   Ibid p 23
45   Royal Courts of Justice, op cit Note 14, p 137
46   PDAC (1977) op, cit Note 39, p 24
47   Glocklin, V (1977) 'Halcion', FDA Supervisory Pharmacology Review, 19 August, p 23
48   Crabbs, W C (1977) 'Sleep lab studies and labelling for Halcion', FDA memo of meeting with Kales and Bixler, 15 June
49   Woo, T (1981) 'Halcion', FDA MOR, 26 October, pp 10–11
50   Ibid
51   Leber, P (1982) 'Halcion Approvable Letter', FDA internal memo to M Finkel, associate director, New Drug Evaluation, 23 February, p 1
52   Sigelman, D W (1989) 'Halcion: waking up to the dangers of a sleeping pill', *Trial*, November, p 40
53   Nicholson, A N and Stone, B M (1980) 'Activity of the hypnotics, flunitrazepam and triazolam, in man', *British Journal of Clinical Pharmacology*, vol 9, pp 187–194
54   Ogura, C, Nakazawa, K, Majima, K, Nakamura, K, Ueda, H, Umezawa, Y and Wardell, W M (1980) 'Residual effects of hypnotics: triazolam, flurazepam and nitrazepam', *Psychopharmacology*, vol 68, pp 61–65
55   Fernandez-Guardiola, A, Jurado, J L and Solis, H (1981) 'The effect of triazolam on insomniac patients using a laboratory sleep evaluation', *Current Therapeutic Research*, vol 29, pp 950–958
56   Day, B H, Davis, H and Parsons, DW (1981) 'An assessment of two hypnotics in the elderly', *Clinical Trials Journal*, vol 18, pp 273–279
57   Carskadon, M A, Seidel, W F, Greenblatt, D J, and Dement, W C (1982) 'Daytime carryover of triazolam and flurazepam in elderly insomniacs', *Sleep*, vol 5, pp 361–371
58   Goetzke, E, Findeisen, P and Welbers, I B (1983) 'Comparative study on the efficacy of and the tolerance to the triazolodiazepines, triazolam and brotizolam', *British Journal of Clinical Pharmacology*, vol 16, pp 407S–412S
59   Woo, T, op cit Note 49, p 11
60   Woo, T (1981) 'Halcion', FDA MOR, 10 November, p 2
61   Woo, T (1982) 'Halcion', FDA MOR, 26 January, p 5
62   Woo, T (1982) 'Halcion', FDA MOR, 19 August, p 2
63   Ibid, p 1
64   Upjohn (1982) internal memo from Purpura to Varley, 10 September
65   Ibid
66   Leber, op cit Note 51, p 1
67   Upjohn (1983) letter from Turner to Fletcher, 7 March
68   Barry op cit Note 38, p 336

69   FDA (1994) *Establishment Inspection Report for Upjohn*, Division of Scientific Investigations, FDA, Rockville, Maryland, 15 April, p 12
70   Woo, T (1982) 'Halcion', FDA MOR, 15 October, p 1
71   Upjohn (1982) *Halcion Package Insert*
72   Ibid
73   Upjohn (1983) *Halcion Data Sheet*
74   Morgan, K and Oswald, I (1982) 'Anxiety caused by a short-life hypnotic', *British Medical Journal*, vol 284, 27 March, p 942
75   Ibid
76   Royal Courts of Justice, op cit Note 14, p 262
77   Ibid p 263
78   Ibid
79   *Hansard*, no 1253, 29 July 1982, p 668
80   Anon (1985) 'Benzodiazepine ADRs in UK', *Scrip*, no 987, 3 April, p 5
81   Purpura, R P (1983) 'Trip Report, Washington, DC: NIH Consensus Development Conference on Drugs and Insomnia, Bethesda, Maryland', internal Upjohn memo, 18 November
82   Anon (1985) 'Upjohn can resubmit Halcion in NL', *Scrip*, no 1014, 8 July, p 1
83   Anon (1986) 'Update on Upjohn', *Scrip*, no 1087, 24 March, p 14
84   Anon (1988) 'Top 50 branded products worldwide', *Scrip* (Review Issue), p 20
85   Anon (1988) 'Xanax and Upjohn boost Upjohn's sales', *Scrip*, no 1306, 6 May, p 12
86   Anon (1988) 'Top US companies in 1987', *Scrip*, no 1306, 6 May, p 17

Chapter 4

1   Kales, A, Soldatos, C R, Bixler, E O and Kales, J D (1983) 'Early morning insomnia with rapidly eliminated benzodiazepines', *Science*, vol 220, pp 95–97
2   Interview with Hindmarsh, University of Surrey, 10 October 1994
3   Ibid
4   Einarson, T R and Yoder, E S (1982) 'Triazolam psychosis – a syndrome?', *Drug Intelligence and Clinical Pharmacology*, vol 16, p 330
5   Shader, R I and Greenblatt, D J (1983) 'Triazolam and anterograde amnesia: all is not well in the Z–zone', *Journal of Clinical Psychopharmacology*, vol 3, p 273
6   Woo, T (1984) 'Halcion', FDA MOR, 20 March, Table 1
7   Ibid Table 2
8   Ibid p 4
9   Ibid p 2
10   Ibid p 3
11   Barry, W S (1984) 'First report of a physician with professional incapacitation in association with the use of Halcion tablets', internal Upjohn memo, 26 April
12   Barry, W S (1983) internal Upjohn memo, 15 June
13   Ibid Table 2
14   Barry, W S (1992) Deposition in *Freeman vs the Upjohn Company* in the District Court of Dallas County, Texas, 27 August, pp 120–121
15   Ibid p 122
16   Barry, W S (1984) 'Relationship of medical events to dose of Halcion', internal Upjohn memo, 1 May

17 Barry (1992) op cit Note 14, p 24
18 Ibid p 27
19 Ibid pp 84–87
20 Ibid p 129
21 Ibid pp 47–48
22 Ibid pp 46–47
23 Barry, W S (1984) 'Halcion corporate product statement revision', internal Upjohn memo, 27 April. Barry (1992) op cit Note 14, pp 98–103
24 Barry (1992) op cit Note 14, pp 49–55, 306–307
25 Ibid pp 55–56
26 Ibid pp 132, 133, 136, 170, 171
27 Ibid pp 132–133
28 Ibid pp 250–251, 326–327
29 Ibid pp 205–206
30 Ibid pp 212–213
31 Ibid pp 95–96
32 Royal Courts of Justice (1994) *Judgement between the Upjohn Company and Upjohn Ltd and Professor Ian Oswald and between Dr Royston Frederick Drucker and Professor Oswald and between the Upjohn Company and Upjohn Ltd and the BBC and Tom Mangold before Mr Justice May, Beverley F Nunnery*, London, 27 May, p 226
33 Leber, P (1984) 'Dr Woo's review of Halcion (dated 20/3/84)', internal FDA memo, 8 May, p 1
34 Ibid p 2
35 Ibid pp 1, 3
36 Wyskowski, D K and Barash, D 1991 'Adverse behavioural reactions attributed to triazolam in the FDA's Spontaneous Reporting System (SRS)', *Archives of Internal Medicine*, vol 151, pp 2003–2008
37 Wyskowski, D K (1988) 'Questions and comments concerning Halcion manuscript', FDA internal memo to deputy director, Office of Epidemiology and Biostatistics, 27 April, p 1
38 Ibid p 7
39 Wyskowski, D K (1989) 'Chronology of events concerning Halcion and psychic disturbance issue' FDA internal memo to file, 4 May, p 6
40 Ibid
41 Ibid
42 Leber, P (1988) 'Planned Upjohn announcement to discontinue manufacture of 0.5mg dose of Halcion', internal FDA memo of telecon to director of drug research and review, 1 April, p 1
43 Upjohn (1989) 'Halcion tablets', letter from D J Mason, Executive Director, US Pharmaceutical Regulatory Affairs, to P Leber, Director of Neuropharmacological Drug Products, FDA, 1 January, p 1. Leber, P (1989) 'Interpreting post–marketing surveillance information on Halcion', FDA memo to members of PDAC, 11 September, p 11
44 Upjohn (1987) *Halcion Package Insert*, Kalamazoo
45 Institute of Medicine (1997) *Halcion: An Independent Assessment of Safety and Efficacy Data*, National Academy Press, Washington, DC, p 20
46 Upjohn (1987) *Halcion Package Insert*, Kalamazoo
47 Barry (1992) op cit Note 14, p 344
48 Ibid pp 351–352
49 Upjohn (1989) 'Halcion meeting with FDA on 13 January 1989 to discuss medical event reports', internal memo by K J Bruzewski, 16 January
50 Adam, K and Oswald, I (1989) 'Can a rapidly eliminated hypnotic cause daytime anxiety?', *Pharmacopsychiatry*, vol 22, pp 115–119

51   Ibid p 115
52   Royal Courts of Justice, op cit Note 32, pp 265–270
53   Ibid p 270
54   Ibid
55   Ibid p 272
56   Ibid p 271
57   Ibid
58   Ibid p 272
59   Anon (1987) 'French Halcion withdrawal issues', *Scrip*, no 1234, 26 August, p 4
60   Anon (1987) 'French remain firm on Halcion', *Scrip*, no 1239, 11 September, p 2
61   Quoted in Royal Courts of Justice, op cit Note 32
62   Anon (1987) 'Halcion 0.5 mg suspended in Italy', *Scrip*, no 1207, 22 May, p 26
63   Anon (1988) 'BGA proposes triazolam changes', *Scrip*, no 1270/1, 1/6 January, p 35
64   Barry (1992) op cit Note 14, pp 292–294
65   Upjohn (1973) internal memo by C D Brooks reporting on protocol 321, 1 August
66   Upjohn (1982) internal memo by Goss, 6 May
67   Royal Courts of Justice, op cit Note 32, p 186
68   Upjohn 1987 internal memo by Bost, 29 September
69   Royal Courts of Justice, op cit Note 32, p 18
70   Upjohn (1988) internal memo from Christian to Overmyer, 19 January
71   Ibid
72   Upjohn (1988) 'Dear Pharmacist', Kalamazoo, 27 June
73   Leber op cit Note 42, p 1
74   Schogt, B and Conn, D (1985) 'Paranoid symptoms associated with triazolam', *Canadian Journal of Psychiatry*, vol 30, pp 462–463
75   Patterson, J F (1987) 'Triazolam syndrome in the elderly', *Southern Medical Journal*, vol 80, pp 1425–1426
76   Ibid p 1426
77   Roehrs, T, Zorick, F, Wittig, R and Roth, T (1985) 'Efficacy of a reduced triazolam dose in elderly insomniacs', *Neurobiology of Aging*, vol 6, pp 293–296
78   Roehrs, T, Zorick, F, Wittig, R and Roth, T (1986) 'Dose determinants of rebound insomnia', *British Journal of Clinical Pharmacology*, vol 22, pp 143–147
79   Bayer, A J, Bayer, E M, Pathy, M S J and Stoker, M J (1986) 'A double-blind controlled study of chlomethiazole and triazolam as hypnotics in the elderly', *Acta Psychiatrica Scandinavica*, vol 73 (S329), pp 104–111
80   Ibid p 110
81   Seidel, W F, Cohen, S A, Bliwise, N G, Roth, T and Dement, W C (1986) 'Dose-related effects of triazolam and flurazepam on a ciradian rhythm insomnia', *Clinical Pharmacology and Therapeutics*, vol 40, pp 314–320
82   Kales, A, Bixler, E O, Vela-Bueno, A, Soldatos, C, Niklaus, D E and R L Manfredi (1986) 'Comparison of short and long half-life benzodiazepine hypnotics: triazolam and quazepam', *Clinical Pharmacology and Therapeutics*, vol 40, pp 378–386
83   Bixler, E O, Kales, A, Brubaker, B H and Kales, J D (1987) 'Adverse reactions to benzodiazepine hypnotics: spontaneous reporting system', *Pharmacology*, vol 35, pp 286–300
84   O'Donnell, V M, Balkin, T J, Andrade, J R, Simon, L M, Kamimori, G H, Redmond, D P and Belenky, G (1988) 'Effects of triazolam on performance

and sleep in a model on transient insomnia', *Human Performance*, vol 1, pp 145–160

85 Anello, C (1988) 'Halcion', internal FDA memo to Leber, 17 October

86 Leber, op cit Note 43, p 11

87 Freiman, J, Graham, D, Barash, D (1989) 'Triazolam (Halcion) adverse reaction reports for 1988', internal FDA memo to Leber, 12 June

88 Upjohn (1988) 'Halcion', letter from D J Mason, Executive Director, US Pharmaceutical Regulatory Affairs to Division of Neuropharmacological Drug Products, FDA, 8 December

89 Mariano, J P and Gardner, J S (1988) 'Report to FDA of Medical Events Occurring in Evaluation of Medications in Canada', 2 December, p 1

90 Upjohn (1988) *Halcion Package Insert*, September, Kalamazoo

91 Leber op cit Note 43, p 12

92 PDAC (1989) Transcript of Psychopharmacological Drugs Advisory Committee Meeting, FDA Headquarters, 22 September, p 15

93 Leber, op cit Note 43, p 2

94 PDAC, op cit Note 92, p 134

95 Ibid p 11

96 Ibid p 4

97 Ibid p 3

98 Ibid p 9

99 Ibid p 8

100 Ibid, p 48

101 Ibid p 20

102 Ibid p 19

103 P Leber, op cit Note 43, p 7

104 PDAC, op cit Note 92, pp 25–33

105 Ibid pp 37–39

106 Ibid p 40

107 Ibid p 44

108 Ibid p 51

109 Barry (1992) op cit Note 14, pp 193–194, 201

110 Ibid pp 71–75

111 PDAC, op cit Note 92, p 133

112 Ibid p 100

113 Royal Courts of Justice, op cit Note 32, pp 221–222

114 PDAC, op cit Note 92, p 102

115 Ibid pp 123–24

116 Ibid p 21

117 Ibid p 54

118 Ibid p 147

119 Ibid p 162

120 Interview with Professor Michael Rawlins, University of Newcastle, England, 8 January 1996

121 Interview with Dr Thomas Moore, Washington, DC, 20 September 1995

122 PDAC op cit Note 92, p 96

123 P Leber (1989) 'Interpreting Post-Marketing Surveillance Information on Halcion', FDA memo to members of PDAC, 11 September, p 12

124 Laughren, T P (1990) 'Proposed labelling changes for Halcion', internal FDA memo to file by group leader, Division of Neuropharmacological Drug Products

125 Ibid

126 Upjohn (1991) *Halcion Package Insert*, November, Kalamazoo

127 Interview with Professor Sir William Asscher, London, 23 January 1996

Chapter 5

1   Upjohn (1984–88) *Halcion Data Sheets*
2   Upjohn (1989) *Halcion Data Sheets*
3   Upjohn (1990) *Halcion Data Sheets*
4   Upjohn (1991) *Halcion Data Sheets*
5   Upjohn (1991) *Halcion Data Sheets*
6   Gabe, J and Bury, M (1996) 'Halcion nights: a sociological account of a medical controversy', *Sociology*, vol 30, pp 447–469, 454
7   Anon (1989) 'US FDA committee – no Halcion alarm', *Scrip*, no 1453, 6 October, p 22
8   Oswald, I (1989) 'Risks of dependence on benzodiazepine drugs', *British Medical Journal*, vol 298, 18 February, p 456
9   Oswald, I (1989) 'Triazolam syndrome 10 years on', *Lancet*, 19 August, p 451
10 Royal Courts of Justice (1994) *Judgement between the Upjohn Company and Upjohn Ltd and Professor Ian Oswald and between Dr Royston Frederick Drucker and Professor Oswald and between the Upjohn Company and Upjohn Ltd and the BBC and Tom Mangold before Mr Justice May, Beverley F Nunnery*, London, 27 May, p 18
11 Ibid pp 231–232
12 Ibid p 232
13 Anon (1991) 'Upjohn settles Halcion suit', *Scrip*, no 1644, 21 August, p 27
14 Ibid
15 Anon (1990) 'Halcion reapproved in the Netherlands', *Scrip*, no 1540, 15 August, p 22
16 Royal Courts of Justice, op cit Note 10, pp 18, 150–151
17 FDA (1994) Establishment Inspection Report on Upjohn, Kalamazoo, Michigan, 15 April, p 47
18 Veldkamp, W, Rudzik, A D and Metzler, C M (1973) *Upjohn Pharmaceutical Research and Development Technical Report, U–33,030: Six–Week Tolerance Study, SPSM Protocol No 321, Phase II Study*, 27 August, p 2
19 Royal Courts of Justice, op cit Note 10, p 54
20 Veldkamp et al, op cit Note 18. Woo, T (1977) 'Halcion' FDA MOR, 26 January, pp 3–4
21 FDA (1982) *Triazolam Summary Basis of Approval* (SBA), Rockville, Maryland, 15 November. FDA (1994) op cit Note 17, p 12
22 Royal Courts of Justice, op cit Note 10, pp 61–62, 78–79
23 Ibid
24 Ibid, p 63
25 Ibid p 56
26 Ibid, 57–58
27 Ibid
28 Ibid
29 Ibid p 59
30 Ibid pp 59–60
31 Veldkamp et al, op cit Note 18, p 5
32 Royal Courts of Justice, op cit Note 10, pp 59–60
33 Ibid p 57
34 Veldkamp et al, op cit Note 18, Tables 4, 6
35 BBC (1991) 'The Halcion Nightmare', *Panorama*, 14 October. Royal Courts of Justice, op cit Note 10, pp 23–26
36 Veldkamp et al, op cit Note 18, p 1
37 Royal Courts of Justice, op cit Note 10, pp 53–54, 71
38 Ibid, p 71

39   Ibid p 59
40   Veldkamp et al, op cit Note 18, p 8
41   Interview with Professor Ian Hindmarsh, University of Surrey, England, 10 October 1994
42   FDA (1994) op cit Note 17, p 35
43   Veldkamp et al, op cit Note 18, p 10
44   Ayd, F J (1992) affidavit, Maryland, 7 December, p 12
45   Ibid, pp 15–16
46   Ayd, F J et al (1979) 'Behavioural reactions to triazolam', *Lancet*, 10 November, p 1018
47   FDA (1994) op cit Note 17, pp 22, 24
48   Royal Courts of Justice, op cit Note 10, p 165
49   Ibid p 166
50   Ibid pp 165–166
51   Ibid p 61
52   Ibid p 183
53   Ibid p 184
54   Ibid p 187
55   Ibid p 229
56   Bixler, E O, Kales, A, Manfredi, R L, Vgontzas, A N, Tyson, K L and Kales, J D (1991) 'Next-day memory impairment with triazolam use', *Lancet*, 6 April, pp 827–831
57   Anon (1991) 'Upjohn's Halcion data to be disclosed', *Scrip*, no 1630, 3 July, p 14
58   Royal Courts of Justice (1994) Testimony of Dr Patrick Waller in *Proceedings between the Upjohn Company and Upjohn Ltd and Professor Ian Oswald and between Dr Royston Frederick Drucker and Professor Oswald and between the Upjohn Company and Upjohn Ltd and the BBC and Tom Mangold before Mr Justice May, Beverley F. Nunnery*, London, 25 April, Day 54, p 24
59   Royal Courts of Justice, op cit Note 10, pp 236–237
60   Oswald, I (1991) 'Safety of triazolam', *Lancet*, vol 338, 24 August, pp 516–517
61   Krzywicki, K T (1991) 'Safety of triazolam', *Lancet*, vol 338, 7 September, p 632
62   Ibid
63   Royal Courts of Justice, op cit Note 10, p 230
64   Ibid, pp 239–242
65   Ibid, p 242
66   CSM (1991) 'Dear Doctor', letter from W Asscher, Chairman of Committee on the Safety of Medicines
67   Anon (1991) 'Halcion's UK licence suspended – a bolt from the blue?', *Scrip*, no 1658, 9 October, p 22
68   CSM (1991) Report to EC Committee on Proprietary Medicinal Products (CPMP), 9 December
69   Ibid p 3
70   Wood, S M (1991) MCA report from triazolam's medical assessor to CPMP, 9 December, pp 20–21
71   CSM, op cit Note 68, p 2
72   Ibid p 4
73   Ibid p 5
74   Ibid p 2
75   Ibid p 6
76   Ibid p 2
77   Ibid p 2

78   Ibid p 2
79   FDA (1982) *Halcion Summary Basis of Approval* (SBA), Rockville, Maryland, 15 November, pp 8–9
80   Dyer, C (1992) 'Drug tester barred after Halcion trials', *Guardian*, 13 February
81   Royal Courts of Justice, op cit Note 10, p 190
82   Ibid p 193
83   Ibid p 190
84   FDA, op cit Note 79, p 9
85   Reed, S R (1994) 'Halcion research called into question', *Houston Chronicle*, pp 29–30
86   Ibid
87   Royal Courts of Justice, op cit Note 10, p 85
88   Ibid pp 85–91
89   Ibid p 196
90   BBC, op cit Note 35
91   Upjohn (1982) internal memo from Large to Straw, 30 November
92   Royal Courts of Justice, op cit Note 10, pp 190–192
93   Ibid p 191
94   Ibid p 190
95   Royal Courts of Justice, op cit Note 10, p 191
96   Upjohn (1992) letter from J R Assenzo, Executive Director, US Pharmaceutical Affairs, to FDA Division of Neuropharmacological Drug Products, 26 March
97   FDA (1992) 'Halcion Update', *FDA Talk Paper*, 14 February, p 1
98   Dyer, C (1992) 'Drug tester barred after Halcion trials', Guardian, 13 February
99   FDA, op cit Note 97, p 2
100 Upjohn (1983) internal memo from Schumann to manager, copied to Straw, 25 February
101 Ibid
102 Upjohn (1983) internal memo from Straw to Schumann, 28 February
103 Upjohn (1983) letter from G H Ishier, Director of Medical Regulatory Affairs, to FDA Division of Neuropharmacological Drug Products, 27 June, p 1
104 Royal Courts of Justice, op cit Note 10, p 196
105 Upjohn (1991) 'Lancet Rebuttal', internal memo from Porter to MacLeod, 8 September
106 Royal Courts of Justice, op cit Note 10, p 198
107 Ibid p 197
108 BBC, op cit Note 35
109 Royal Courts of Justice, op cit Note 10, p 194
110 Upjohn, op cit Note 96
111 BBC, op cit Note 35
112 Kolata, G (1992) 'Maker of sleeping pill hid data on side effects, researchers say', *New York Times*, 20 January
113 Anon (1992) 'Upjohn to file suit against Prof Oswald', *Scrip*, no 1687, 29 January, p 6. Royal Courts of Justice, op cit Note 10, p 19
114 Royal Courts of Justice, op cit Note 10, p 47
115 Upjohn (1992) 'Upjohn files suits to defend reputation', news release, 24 January
116 Gabe, J and Bury, M (1996) 'Halcion Nights: A Sociological Account', *Sociology* vol 30, no 3, p 453
117 Ibid pp 453, 458
118 Anon (1992) 'Jury implicates Upjohn in Halcion case', *Scrip*, no 1772, 20 November, p 22

119 Psychopharmacological Drugs Advisory Committee (PDAC) (1989) transcript
     of Psychopharmacological Drugs Advisory Committee Meeting, FDA
     Headquarters, 22 September, p 100
120 Royal Courts of Justice, op cit Note 10, pp 221–223
121 FDA (1994) *Establishment Inspection Report on Upjohn*, Kalamazoo,
     Michigan, 15 April, p 26
122 Royal Courts of Justice, op cit Note 10, p 168
123 Ibid p 62
124 Ibid p 79
125 Ibid pp 198–99
126 Ibid p 195
127 Ibid p 197
128 Ibid p 199
129 Ibid p 262
130 Ibid p 263
131 Ibid pp 264–267
132 Ibid p 276
133 Ibid p 286
134 Ibid p 287
135 Royal Courts of Justice, Testimony of Dr Patrick Waller, op cit Note 58, pp
     45–50. Royal Courts of Justice, op cit Note 10, pp 244–247
136 Interview with Hindmarsh, 10 October 1994
137 Royal Courts of Justice, Testimony of Dr Patrick Waller, op cit Note 58, p 50
138 Royal Courts of Justice, op cit Note 10, p 246
139 Royal Courts of Justice, Testimony of Dr Patrick Waller, op cit Note 58, p 50
140 Interview with former member of CSM, 13 September 1994
141 Interview with former member of Medicines Commission, 14 September
     1994
142 Royal Courts of Justice, op cit Note 10, p 278
143 Ibid p 60
144 Wood, op cit Note 70, p 4
145 FDA, op cit Note 121, p 46
146 Ibid p 8
147 Royal Courts of Justice, op cit Note 10, p 187–188
148 Ibid p 187
149 PDAC, op cit Note 119, pp 79–86
150 Wood, op cit Note 70, pp 8–9
151 Ibid p 9
152 Ibid, 10
153 UK Department of Health (1993) letter in 'Current Problems', 9 June
154 Virginia Bottomley, Secretary of State for Health (1991) 'Psychotropic
     Drugs', *Hansard (Written Answers)*, vol 1568, 18 October, columns 266–267
155 Interview with former CSM member, 1994
156 Jones, K (1992) letter from director and chief executive, MCA, to Lee,
     finance director and secretary, Upjohn, 17 July, p 2
157 Royal Courts of Justice, op cit Note 10, pp 143–144
158 Ibid p 144
159 Ibid p 145
160 Ibid p 145
161 Ibid p 78
162 Ibid p 60
163 Ibid p 188
164 Ibid p 74
165 Interview with current member of CSM, 1994
166 Wood, op cit Note 70, p 8

167   Ibid p 10
168   Jones, op cit Note 156, p 5
169   Medicines Commission (1992) 'Report on Halcion' (not precisely dated), p 5
170   Ibid
171   Jones, op cit Note 156, p 7
172   UK Department of Health, op cit Note 153
173   Anon (1993) 'UK Halcion Hearing set for February 1st', *Scrip*, no 1788, 22 January p 21. Anon (1993) 'UK Panel recommends return of Halcion', *Scrip*, no 1814, 23 April, p 25. Anon (1993) 'Halcion – Why UK Authorities Rejected Panel Advice', *Scrip*, no 1830, 18 June, pp 25–26
174   UK Department of Health, op cit Note 153
175   Ibid
176   Ibid
177   Ibid p 3
178   UK Department of Health (1993) 'Withdrawal of Triazolam', press release, 9 June, p 2
179   Jones, op cit Note 156, p 6
180   Hindmarsh, I, Fairweather, D B and Rombaut, N (1993) 'Adverse events after triazolam substitution', *Lancet*, vol 341, 2 January, p 55
181   Rothschild, A J, Bessette, M P, Carter-Campbell, J and Murray, M (1993) 'Triazolam and disinhibition', *Lancet*, vol 341, 16 January, p 186
182   Burton, G and Carter, C (1993) 'Triazolam condemned by misinformation and selective referencing', *Lancet*, vol 306, 29 May, p 1476
183   Hawley, C J, Walker, M and Roberts, A (1993) 'Adverse events after triazolam substitution', *Lancet*, vol 341, 27 February, p 567
184   Nazareth, I, Ashworth, M, Hammond, J and King, M (1995) 'Withdrawal of triazolam's product licence: effect on patients 18 months later', *Addiction*, vol 90, no7, pp 927–934
185   Royal Courts of Justice, op cit Note 10, p 151
186   UK Department of Health, op cit Note 153, p 2
187   Jones, op cit Note 156, p 3

Chapter 6

1   Anon (1990) 'US petition for Halcion labelling revision', *Scrip*, no 1510, 2 May, p 34
2   Anon (1990) 'Stronger warnings on Halcion amnesia', *Scrip*, no 1541, 17 August, p 23
3   Bonnet, M H, Dexter, J R and Arand, D L (1990) 'The effect of triazolam on arousal and respiration in central sleep apnea patients', *Sleep*, vol 13, no 1, pp 31–41
4   Mamelak, M; Csima, A and Price, V (1990) 'The effects of a single night's dosing with triazolam on sleep the following night', *Journal of Clinical Pharmacology*, vol 30, pp 549–555
5   Scharf, M B, Sachais, B A, Mayleben, D W, Fletcher, K and Jennings, S W (1990) 'A polysomnographic comparison of temazepam 15 and 30 mg with triazolam 0.125 and 0.25 mg in chronic insomnia', *Current Therapeutic Research*, vol 48, no 3, pp 555–567
6   Anon (1991) 'Halcion's UK licence suspended – a bolt from the blue?', *Scrip*, no 1658, 9 October, p 22
7   Robin, D W, Hasan, S S, Lichtenstein, M J, Shiavi, R G and Wood, A J J (1991) 'Dose-related effect of triazolam on postural sway', *Clinical Pharmacology & Therapeutics*, vol 49, pp 581–588

8   Schweitzer, P K, Koshorek, G, Muehlbach, M J, Morris, D D, Roehrs, T,
     Walsh, J K and Roth, T (1991) 'Effects of estazolam and triazolam on
     transient insomnia associated with phase-shifted sleep', *Human
     Psychopharmacology*, vol 6, pp 99–107
9   Anon (1991) 'Halcion – regulatory agencies divided', *Scrip*, no 1659,
     11 October, p 21. Anon (1991) 'Halcion – CPMP sets up working party',
     Scrip, no 1662, 23 October, p 20
10   Upjohn (1991) *Halcion Package Insert*, November, Kalamazoo
11   Ibid
12   Upjohn (1991) 'Patient Information' in *Halcion Package Insert*, November,
     Kalamazoo
13   Anon (1991) 'CPMP suggestions for Halcion', *Scrip*, no 1663, 25 October,
     p 22. Anon (1991) 'CPMP confirms Halcion position', *Scrip*, no 1678, 18
     December, p 26
14   Anon (1991) 'Implications of Halcion suspension', *Scrip*, no 1665, 1
     November, p 21
15   Anon (1991) 'CPMP confirms Halcion position', *Scrip*, no 1678, 18
     December, p 26. Anon (1992) 'German public hearing on Halcion', *Scrip*,
     no 1687, 29 January, p 20
16   Anon (1992) 'Flucloxacillin ADRs in Australia', *Scrip*, no 1710, 17 April, p 26
17   Anon (1992) 'French HM suspends 0.25 mg Halcion', *Scrip*, no 1681, 5
     January, p 27
18   Anon (1992) 'Spain suspends Halcion 0.25 mg', *Scrip*, no 1684, 17 January,
     p 25
19   Anon (1992) 'BGA hearing on Halcion – a cultural divide?', *Scrip*, no 1695,
     26 February, p 22
20   Ibid p 23
21   Anon (1992) 'Upjohn in 1991', *Scrip*, no 1726, 12 June, p 13
22   Ayd, F J (1992)'Triazolam 0.125 mg: risks vs benefits', *International Drug
     Therapy Newsletter*, vol 27, no 4, April, p 15
23   Ayd, F J (1992) 'Triazolam 0.25 mg: a reappraisal', *International Drug
     Therapy Newsletter*, vol 27, no 5, May, pp 22–23
24   FDA (1994) *Establishment Inspection Report on Upjohn*, Kalamazoo,
     Michigan, 15 April , p 1
25   Ibid p 50
26   Ibid pp 22, 47
27   Ibid p 48
28   Ibid
29   Ibid p 23
30   Ibid p 45
31   Ibid p 28
32   Ibid p 31
33   Ibid p 33
34   Ibid p 54
35   Ibid p 53
36   Ibid p 2
37   Ibid pp 2–4
38   Ibid p 8
39   FDA (1992) 'Close out of Halcion Case', internal FDA memo from consumer
     safety officer, Regulatory Management Branch, to deputy director, Division
     of Scientific Investigations, 1 December, p 2
40   Ibid
41   Ibid
42   Anon (1992) 'FDA ends Halcion investigation', *Scrip*, no 1775, 1 December,
     p 13

43   Anon (1994) 'FDA will continue Upjohn enquiry', *Scrip*, no 1922, 13 May, p 21
44   Reed, S R (1994) 'Federal report targets Upjohn for misconduct', *Houston Chronicle*, 1 May
45   Lee, J H (1991) 'Halcion: Review and Evaluation of Clinical Data', FDA internal memo, 29 October
46   Leber, P and Laughren, T (1992) 'The question of Halcion: overview and background for the 18 May 1992 Psychopharmacological Drug Products Advisory Committee Meeting', internal FDA memo, 28 April, p 3
47   Psychopharmacological Drugs Advisory Committee (PDAC) (1992) transcript of Psychopharmacological Drugs Advisory Committee Meeting, FDA Headquarters, 18 May, p 54
48   Ibid p 284
49   Ibid p 65
50   Leber and Laughren, op cit Note 46, pp 3–4. PDAC, op cit Note 47, p 56
51   PDAC, op cit Note 47, p 261
52   Ibid p 69
53   Ibid p 95
54   Upjohn (1992) *The PDAC Brochure on Halcion*, p 24
55   Marticello, D N (1992) 'Statistical review and evaluation of Halcion', FDA internal memo, 13 March
56   PDAC, op cit Note 47, pp 70–85
57   Ibid pp 95, 266–268
58   Ibid p 95
59   Ibid pp 266–267
60   Upjohn, op cit Note 54, p 23
61   PDAC, op cit Note 47, p 271
62   Cited in Ayd, F J (1992) 'An assessment of Halcion', PDAC submission 18 May, pp 7–8
63   Ibid p 7
64   Upjohn, op cit Note 54, p 10
65   Ayd, F J (1992) 'An assessment of Halcion', PDAC submission 18 May, pp 8–9
66   Ibid p 8
67   Upjohn, op cit Note 54, p 13
68   Ibid p 13
69   Upjohn, op cit Note 54, p 11. Ayd, op cit Note 65, p 16
70   Upjohn, op cit Note 54, p 11. Ayd, op cit Note 65, p 16
71   Upjohn, op cit Note 54, p 13
72   Upjohn, op cit Note 54, pp 14–19. Ayd, op cit Note 65, p 17
73   Upjohn, op cit Note 54, p 19
74   Ayd, op cit Note 65, p 18
75   PDAC, op cit Note 47, pp 309, 312
76   Ibid pp 283–284
77   Ibid p 315
78   Graham, D J (1992) 'Halcion comparison with temazepam', internal FDA memo, 8 May, p 2. Stadel, B V (1992) 'Adverse drug event reporting for Halcion', internal FDA memo, 11 May, pp 2–3
79   PDAC, op cit Note 47, pp 228–230
80   Ibid pp 105–111, 119–120
81   Ibid p 106
82   Ibid p 128
83   Ibid p 236
84   Upjohn, op cit Note 54, p 63
85   PDAC, op cit Note 47, p 268
86   Ibid p 102–104

87   Tsong, Y (1992) 'Statistical comparison of ADE reporting rates between triazolam and temazepam', internal FDA memo to chief of epidemiology branch, Office of Epidemiology
88   Graham, op cit Note 78, pp 6–7
89   Laughren, T and Lee, H (1992) 'Review of adverse event data in Upjohn sponsored clinical studies of Halcion', FDA submission to PDAC, 1 May, p 7
90   Upjohn, op cit Note 54, pp 62, 71
91   Ibid p 73
92   PDAC, op cit Note 47, p 279
93   Ibid p 147
94   Ibid p 137
95   Ibid p 32
96   Ibid p 148
97   Ibid p 322
98   Anello, C (1992) 'Analyses of adverse events leading to drop-out in 25 parallel trials of Halcion against Dalmane and placebo', internal FDA memo, 4 May, p 2
99   PDAC, op cit Note 47, p 157
100   Ibid pp 151, 194
101   Public Citizen (1992) Testimony of Sidney Wolfe, Health Research Group, before PDAC, 18 May, p 5. PDAC, op cit Note 47, pp 193, 285–286, 311
102   Tullio, de P L, Kirking, D M, Zacardellie, D K and Kwee, P (1989) 'Evaluation of long-term triazolam use in an ambulatory veterans administration medical center population', *DICP – Annals of Pharmacotherapy*, vol 23, no 4, p 290
103   Ibid p 292
104   PDAC, op cit Note 47, pp 277–278, 282
105   Upjohn, op cit Note 54, p 28. PDAC, op cit Note 47, pp 220–221
106   PDAC, op cit Note 47, pp 32–33
107   Upjohn, op cit Note 54, p 58
108   PDAC, op cit Note 47, pp 286, 311
109   Ibid p 315
110   Ibid p 362
111   Ibid pp 320–321
112   Ibid p 363
113   Ibid pp 7–9
114   Interview with Professor Michael Rawlins, former Chairman of the UK Committee on Safety of Medicines, University of Newcastle, 8 January 1996
115   Ibid
116   Jasanoff, S (1990) *The Fifth Branch: Science Advisers as Policymakers*, Harvard University Press, Cambridge, Massachussetts, p 245
117   Royal Courts of Justice (1994) Testimony of Dr Patrick Waller, in *Proceedings between the Upjohn Company and Upjohn Ltd and Professor Ian Oswald and between Dr Royston Frederick Drucker and Professor Oswald and between the Upjohn Company and Upjohn Ltd and the BBC and Tom Mangold before Mr Justice May, Beverley F Nunnery*, London, 25 April, Day 54, p 42
118   Interview with Professor Sir William Asscher, former chairman of the UK Committee on Safety of Medicines, St George's Hospital, London, 23 January 1996
119   Kales, A, Vgontzas, A N and Bixler, E O (1997) 'A reassessment of triazolam', *International Journal of Risk & Safety in Medicine*, vol 9, no 1, p 10. Institute of Medicine (1997) *Halcion: An Independent Assessment of Safety and Efficacy Data*, p 19, National Academy Press, Washington, DC
120   Anon (1996) 'FDA says Halcion a matter for Justice Department', *Scrip*, no 2135, 7 June, p 17

121   Ibid p 17
122   Ibid p 17
123   Anon (1996) 'Strict liability in California causes confusion', *Scrip*, no 2163, 13 September, p 11
124   Kales et al, op cit Note 119, p 17
125   Shapirobaruch, A (1995) 'The dismissal of female clients reports of medication side effects', *Women & Therapy*, vol 16, no 1, pp 113–127
126   Rayon, P, Serrano-Castro, M, del Barrio, H, Alvarez, C, Montero, D, Madurga, M, Palop, R and De Abajo, F J (1996) 'Hypnotic drug use in Spain: a cross–sectional study based on a network of community pharmacies', *Annals of Pharmacotherapy*, vol 30, no 10, pp 1092–1100
127   Matinez-Cano, H, Vela-Bueno, A, De Iceta, M, Pomalima, R, Matinez-Gras, I and Sobrino, M P (1996) 'Benzodiazepine types in high versus therapeutic dose dependence', *Addiction*, vol 91, no 8, pp 1179–1186
128   Kales et al, op cit Note 119, p 18
129   Kales et al, op cit Note 119, p 15. Matinez-Cano, H, Vela-Bueno, A, De Iceta, M, Pomalima, R and Matinez-Gras, I (1995) 'Benzodiazepine withdrawal syndrome seizures', *Pharmacopsychiatry*, vol 28, no 6, pp 257–262
130   Institute of Medicine, op cit Note 119, p 2
131   Ibid p 2
132   Ibid p 1
133   Rush, C R, Madakasira, S, Hayes, C A, Johnson, C A, Goldman, N H and Pazzaglia, P J (1997) 'Trazodone and triazolam: acute subject-rated and performance impairing effects in healthy volunteers', *Psychopharmacology*, vol 131, no 1, pp 9–18
134   Neutel, C I, Hirdes, J P, Maxwell, C J and Patten, S B (1996) 'New evidence on benzodiazepine use and falls: the time factor', *Age & Ageing*, vol 25, no 4, pp 273–278
135   Robin,D W, Hasan, S S, Edeki, T, Lichtenstein, M J, Shiavi, R G and Wood, A J (1996) 'Increased baseline sway contributes to increased losses of balance in older people following triazolam', *Journal of the American Geriatric Society*, vol 44, no 3, pp 300–304
136   Institute of Medicine, op cit Note 119, pp 22–29, 34–39
137   Ibid pp 32–33
138   Ibid pp 39–42
139   Ibid p 42
140   Ibid p 43
141   Ibid p 43
142   Ibid p 46
143   Ibid p 46
144   Ibid p 63
145   Ibid p 73
146   Ibid p 82
147   Ibid p 94
148   Quoted in Ault, A (1997) 'FDA advisers find no major Halcion danger', *Lancet*, vol 350, 13 December, p 1760

Chapter 7

1   Anon (1993) 'Stop Press', *Scrip*, no 1833, 29 June, p 24
2   Anon (1996) 'European Union revolution in the making', *Scrip*, no 2129, 17 May, p 4
3   Anon (1997) 'UK Halcion decision goes to European Court of Justice', *Scrip*, no 2234, 23 May, p 4

4   Anon (1999) 'European Court of Justice decision in Halcion case', *Scrip*, no 2407, 29 January, p 2
5   Anon (1996) 'Costs cut Pharmacia and Upjohn's 1995 profits', *Scrip*, no 2107, 1 March, p 5
6   Anon (1995) 'First-half results for Pharmacia and Upjohn', *Scrip*, no 2055, 29 August, p 7
7   Psychopharmacological Drugs Advisory Committee (PDAC) (1992) transcript of Psychopharmacological Drugs Advisory Committee Meeting, FDA Headquarters, 18 May, p 17
8   Ibid pp 152, 169, 338
9   Dukes, M N G (1991) letter from WHO regional office for Europe to S Wolfe, Public Citizen, 31 October, submitted to 1992 PDAC hearing at FDA by Public Citizen
10 Jones, K (1992) letter from director and chief executive, MCA, to Lee, finance director and secretary, Upjohn, 17 July, p 5
11 Interview with Professor Michael Rawlins, former Chairman of the UK Committee on Safety of Medicines, University of Newcastle, 14 November 1994, p 9
12 Interview with Professor Sir William Asscher, St George's Hospital Medical School, University of London, 6 October 1994, pp 9–10
13 Interview with former member of the CSM, London, 12 October 1994
14 Interview with Professor Michael Rawlins, op cit Note 11, p 19
15 UK Department of Health (1993) letter in 'Current Problems', 9 June, p 2
16 Interview with former member of special UK panel of appointed persons, England, 24 October 1994
17 Mackenzie, D (1981) *Statistics in Britain 1865–1930: the Social Construction of Scientific Knowledge*, Edinburgh University Press, Edinburgh, p 220
18 Interview with former member of the CSM, London, 12 October 1994
19 Quoted in M Day (1996) 'US drug safety regime "flawed"', *New Scientist*, 9 November
20 Interview with former member of special UK panel of appointed persons, op cit Note 16

Methodological Appendix

1   Jasanoff, S (1990) *The Fifth Branch: Science Advisers as Policymakers*, Harvard University Press, Cambridge, Massachussetts. Brickman, R, Jasanoff, S and Ilgen, T (1985) *Controlling Chemicals: the Politics of Regulation in Europe and the United States*, Cornell University Press, Ithaca, NY
2   Mackenzie, D (1981) *Statistics in Britain 1865–1930: the Social Construction of Scientific Knowledge*, Edinburgh University Press, Edinburgh. Richards, E (1991) *Vitamin C and Cancer: Medicine or Politics?*, Macmillan, London. Abraham, J (1995) *Science, Politics and the Pharmaceutical Industry: Controversy and Bias in Drug Regulation*, UCL/St Martins Press, London/New York. Walker, M J (1993) *Dirty Medicine: Science, Big Business and the Assault on Natural Health Care*, Slingshot Publications, London
3   Collins, H M (1981) 'Stages in the Empirical Programme of Relativism', *Social Studies of Science*, vol 11, pp 3–10. Nelkin, D (ed) (1992) *Controversies: Politics of Technical Decisions*, 3rd edition, Sage, Newbury Park, California

Glossary of Tranquillizers

Barbiturates

Butisol	sodium butabarbital
Veronal	barbitone

Benzodiazepines

Activan	lorazepam
Dalmane	flurazepam
Dormonoct	loprazolam
Halcion	triazolam
Librium	chlordiazepoxide
Mogadon	nitrazepam
Restoril	temazepam
Serenid-D	oxazepam
Valium	diazepam
Xanax	alprazolam
Loramet	lormetazepam

Index

For Product Safety Concerns and Information please contact our EU
representative GPSR@taylorandfrancis.com
Taylor & Francis Verlag GmbH, Kaufingerstraße 24, 80331 München, Germany

www.ingramcontent.com/pod-product-compliance
Lightning Source LLC
Chambersburg PA
CBHW070426270326
41926CB00014B/2960

9 781853 836503